I0100403

Southeast Asian Studies in China

The **Institute of Southeast Asian Studies (ISEAS)** was established as an autonomous organization in 1968. It is a regional centre dedicated to the study of socio-political, security and economic trends and developments in Southeast Asia and its wider geostrategic and economic environment.

The Institute's research programmes are the Regional Economic Studies (RES, including ASEAN and APEC), Regional Strategic and Political Studies (RSPS), and Regional Social and Cultural Studies (RSCS).

ISEAS Publishing, an established academic press, has issued almost 2,000 books and journals. It is the largest scholarly publisher of research about Southeast Asia from within the region. ISEAS Publishing works with many other academic and trade publishers and distributors to disseminate important research and analyses from and about Southeast Asia to the rest of the world.

Southeast Asian Studies in China

EDITED BY

Saw Swee-Hock and John Wong

ISEAS
Institute of Southeast Asian Studies
Singapore

EAI
East Asian Institute
National University of Singapore

First published in Singapore in 2007 by ISEAS Publishing
Institute of Southeast Asian Studies
30 Heng Mui Keng Terrace
Pasir Panjang
Singapore 119614

E-mail: publish@iseas.edu.sg
Website: <http://bookshop.iseas.edu.sg>

First published in Singapore in 2007 by EAI
East Asian Institute
AS5 Level 4, 7 Arts Link,
National University of Singapore
Singapore 117571

This book is published under the ASEAN-China Study Programme funded by Professor Saw Swee-Hock.

ISEAS Library Cataloguing-in-Publication Data

Southeast Asian studies in China / edited by Saw Swee-Hock and John Wong.
1. Southeast Asia—Study and teaching—China.
2. Southeast Asia—Study and teaching—Taiwan.
3. South China Sea—Study and teaching.
I. Saw, Swee-Hock, 1931–
II. Wong, John C. H., 1939–
DS524.8 C5S721 2007

ISBN-13: 978-981-230-404-9 (hard cover — 13 digit)
ISBN-10: 981-230-404-5 (hard cover — 10 digit)

Typeset by Superskill Graphics Pte Ltd
Printed in Singapore by Utopia Press Pte Ltd

Contents

The Contributors

HO Khai Leong is Associate Professor in the School of Humanities and Social Sciences, Nanyang Technological University, Singapore, and Associate Research Fellow at the Institute of Southeast Asian Studies (ISEAS), Singapore. He received his Ph.D. from Ohio State University. His research interests cover Malaysia and Singapore politics, ASEAN-China relations, corporate governance and administrative reforms. Among his major publications are *A New History of Malaysian Chinese* (co-editor); *Shared Responsibilities, Unshared Power: The Politics of Policy-making in Singapore; Performance and Crisis of Governance of Mahathir's Administration* (co-editor); *China and Southeast Asia: Global Changes and Regional Challenges* (co-editor); *Reforming Corporate Governance in Southeast Asia: Economics, Politics and Regulations* (editor); and *Ensuring Interests: Dynamics of China-Taiwan Relations and Southeast Asia* (co-editor).

KU, Samuel C.K. is Professor in the Institute of Interdisciplinary Studies for Social Sciences, National Sun Yat-sen University, Taiwan. He was formerly Director of the Institute and also the Centre for Southeast Asian Studies. He obtained his Ph.D. from Ohio State University. His main research interests are Southeast Asia's political development, Taiwan's relations with Southeast Asian countries, and China's relations with Southeast Asia. His publications include *Southeast Asia in the New Century: An Asian Perspective* (editor); *China and Southeast Asia: Global Changes and Regional Challenges* (co-editor); *Taiwan's Relations with Southeast Asia: Post-1997; Taiwan's Southward Policy and Its Changing Relations with Southeast Asia, 1990–1997.*

LAI Hongyi is Research Fellow in the East Asian Institute (EAI), National University of Singapore. He received his Ph.D. in political science from the

University of California at Los Angeles. His research covers China's political economy and external policies. His main publications are *Analysing China* (co-editor); *Hu-Wen Under Full Scrutiny* (*Hu Wen Quan Toushi*); *Reform and the Non-State Economy in China — The Political Economy of Liberalization Strategies*; and *China into the Hu-Wen Era* (co-editor).

LIU Hong is Chair of Chinese Studies and Professor of East Asian Studies, University of Manchester and Founding Director of the Centre for Chinese Studies. He has taught at the National University of Singapore and has held visiting appointments at Peking, Kyoto, Stockholm, and Harvard Universities. His research interests include the Chinese Diaspora and the linkages with China, China's relations with the Asian neighbours, Chinese social, business and knowledge networks, and socio-cultural changes. His main publications are *The Chinese Overseas* (editor); *Singapore Chinese Society in Transition: Business, Politics and Socio-Economic Change, 1945–1965* (co-author); *China and Southeast Asia: Changing Socio-Cultural Interactions* (co-editor); and *Sino-Southeast Asian Studies: Toward a New Analytical Paradigm.*

SAW Swee-Hock is Professorial Fellow and Advisor of the ASEAN-China Study Programme in the Institute of Southeast Asian Studies (ISEAS), Singapore. He was Founding Professor of Statistics in the University of Hong Kong and the National University of Singapore. He has held visiting positions in the London School of Economics, Cambridge University, Princeton University, and Stanford University. He received his Ph.D. in Statistics from the London School of Economics. He is a Member of the Board of Trustees of the National University of Singapore and a recipient of its Distinguished Alumni Service Award. His main research interests are statistics, demography, and investment. Among his major publications are *Economic Problems and Prospects in ASEAN Countries* (co-editor); *ASEAN Economy in Transition* (editor); *Growth and Direction of ASEAN Trade* (co-editor); *ASEAN-China Relations: Realities and Prospects* (co-editor); *ASEAN-China Economic Relations* (editor); *Malaysia: Recent Trends and Challenges* (co-editor); *Singapore-Malaysia Relations Under Abdullah Badawi* (co-author); *A Guide to Conducting Surveys; Securities Market in Singapore; Investment Management; The Population of Malaysia; The Population of Singapore;* and *Population Policies and Programmes in Singapore.*

SURYADINATA, Leo is Director of the Chinese Heritage Centre, Singapore, Adjunct Professor, Institute of International Defence and Strategic Studies, Nanyang Technological University, Singapore, and Visiting Senior Research

Fellow in the Institute of Southeast Asian Studies (ISEAS), Singapore. He was formerly a Senior Fellow at the Institute of Southeast Asian Studies and Professor of Political Science at the National University of Singapore. Currently, his main research interests are ethnic Chinese in Southeast Asia and ASEAN-China relations. His books include *China and the ASEAN States: The Ethnic Chinese Dimension; Pribumi Indonesians: The Chinese Minority and China: A Study of Perceptions and Policies; Ethnic Relations and Nation-Building in Southeast Asia: The Case of the Ethnic Chinese* (editor); *Southeast Asia's Chinese Businesses in an Era of Globalization: Coping with the Rise of China* (editor); *Chinese and Nation-Building in Southeast Asia; Ethnic Chinese as Southeast Asians* (editor); *Political Thinking of the Indonesian Chinese, 1900–1995; Southeast Asian Chinese and China: The Politico-Economic Dimension* (editor).

TANG Shiping is Senior Fellow in the Institute of Defence and Strategic Studies, Nanyang Technological University, Singapore. He was formerly Associate Research Fellow and Deputy Director in the Centre for Regional Security Studies, Chinese Academy of Social Sciences, Beijing, and also co-Director of the Sino-American Security Dialogue. He received his M.A. in Asian Studies from the University of California at Berkeley and Ph.D. in Molecular Biology from Wayne State University. He was accorded the Outstanding Young Investigator Award by CASS in 2004. His books include *Construct China's Ideal Security Environment* and *Living with China: The Evolution of Regional States' Post-Cold War China Policy* (co-editor).

WANG Shilu is Professor and Director of the Institute of Southeast Asian Studies, Yunnan Academy of Social Sciences, Kunming. Among his major publications are *Contemporary Vietnam; Contemporary Cambodia; Contemporary ASEAN; From ASEAN to Greater ASEAN: A Study of ASEAN at the 30th Anniversary; ASEAN and Asia-Pacific Towards the 21st Century: Outlook of ASEAN and Its Impacts on Asia-Pacific Region; Cambodia Economy Today; Southeast Asia: An Annual Report (2002–2005); Development of Science and Technology and External Cooperation in ASEAN.*

WONG, John is Research Director in the East Asian Institute (EAI), National University of Singapore. He was formerly Director of the Institute of East Asian Political Economy, Singapore, and Lecturer in Economics in the University of Hong Kong. He was Fullbright Visiting Professor at Florida State University and Chair of ASEAN Studies at the University of Toronto. He also held visiting appointments at Harvard's Fairbank Center, Yale's Economic Growth Center, and Oxford's St. Anthony College, and

Stanford University. He obtained his Ph.D. from the University of London. Among his major publications are *The Political Economy of China's Changing Relations with Southeast Asia; Understanding China's Socialist Market Economy; ASEAN Economy in Perspective: A Comparative Study of Indonesia, Malaysia and the Philippines; Regional Industrial Cooperation: Experience and Perspective of ASEAN and the Andean Pact; China's Economy into the New Century: Structural Issues and Problems* (co-author); *China's Political Economy* (co-editor); *China's Emerging New Economy: Growth of the Internet and Electronic Commerce* (co-author); *China-ASEAN Relations: Economic and Legal Dimensions* (co-editor).

ZHANG Jie is Research Fellow at the Institute of Asia-Pacific Studies, Chinese Academy of Social Sciences, Beijing. She is currently Visiting Scholar at the Monash Asia Institute, Monash University, Melbourne. She received her Ph.D. from Peking University. Among her main publications is *Living With China: The Evolution of Regional States' Post-Cold War China Policy* (co-editor).

ZHANG Xizhen is Professor of International Politics, Department of International Politics, Peking University. He was Visiting Professor in the University of Denver, the USA, Thammasat University and Ramkhamhaeng University, Thailand. He received his M.A. from Peking University. His books include *East Asia: Political Changes; Government and Politics in Southeast Asia; Norodom Sihanouk* and *Contemporary Southeast Asia Politics*; and *Southeast Asian Studies at the Turn of the New Century: Retrospect and Prospect* (co-editor).

ZOU Keyuan is Senior Research Fellow in the East Asian Institute (EAI), National University of Singapore. He had worked in the Department of Political Science at Dalhousie University, Law School of Peking University, and Institute of Geography at the University of Hannover. He was Academic Adviser to the China National Institute for South China Sea Studies in Hainan. He received his Ph.D. from Peking University. Among his main publications are *Law of the Sea in East Asia: Issues and Prospects; China's Marine Legal System and the Law of the Sea*, and *China-ASEAN Relations: Economic and Legal Dimensions* (co-editor). He is a member of the Editorial Board of the *International Journal of Marine and Coastal Law, Ocean Development and International Law* and *Journal of International Wildlife Law and Policy*. He is also Deputy Editor-in-Chief of the *Chinese Journal of International Law.*

Preface

Under the ASEAN-China Study Programme launched in 2003, the Institute of Southeast Asian Studies (ISEAS) organized the ASEAN-China Forum: Realities and Prospects on 23–24 June 2004. From this forum, a book entitled *ASEAN-China Relations: Realities and Prospects* edited by Saw Swee-Hock, Sheng Lijun and Chin Kin Wah was published by ISEAS in the following year to provide a more permanent source of valuable information for a wider audience.

Under the same Programme, the Institute of Southeast Asian Studies and the East Asian Institute (EAI) of the National University of Singapore organized the Conference on Southeast Asian Studies in China: Challenges and Prospects on 12–14 January 2006. The three-day conference was divided into two parts: the first was devoted to papers written and presented in English and the second to papers written in Chinese and presented in Mandarin. This was meant to facilitate the gathering of a larger group of Chinese scholars, including those conversant in Chinese but not English. The chapters incorporated in this book consist of those papers written in English and subsequently revised for publication in this book.

In recognition of the dominant political and economic presence of China in Southeast Asia, the conference was designed to promote a better understanding among the peoples of the two regions. Beyond superficial contacts through official visits, business and tours, people from both sides still have large gaps of knowledge about each other. Scholars and academics from both sides have an important role to play in terms of creating greater awareness of each other through research, workshops, and conferences. Whilst many universities and research institutes in the ASEAN region are conducting studies on various aspects of China, it is equally important to promote a better understanding of Southeast Asia among the people and the Government of China. The book traces the development of Southeast Asian Studies in China, discusses the current status of these studies, examines the problems encountered in the pursuit of these studies, and attempts to evaluate their prospects in the years ahead.

We would like to thank the chapter writers for their excellent cooperation, Professor Wang Gungwu, Chairman of EAI, and Mr K. Kesavapany, Director of ISEAS, for their encouragement in the organization of the conference and the publication of the book, and Mrs Triena Ong, Managing Editor at ISEAS, for overseeing the expeditious publication of the book.

Saw Swee-Hock and John Wong
August 2006

1

A Review of Southeast Asian Studies in China

Saw Swee-Hock

INTRODUCTION

With fast developing relations between China and ASEAN there is a growing need for both regions to better understand each other as their political and economic interests become increasingly interwoven. Of course, the rise of China has long attracted much academic interest in the country from all over the world, including Southeast Asia. However, the state of Southeast Asian Studies in China is a less well-explored terrain. Yet this is an important issue as growing Chinese engagement of Southeast Asia needs to be underpinned by sound academic research about the region. In order to better understand the changes and challenges facing Southeast Asian Studies in China, the East Asian Institute and the Institute of Southeast Asian Studies in Singapore jointly organized a Conference on Southeast Asian Studies in China: Challenges and Prospects, on 12–14 January 2006. The following is a brief overview of the key issues brought up during the conference.

HISTORY OF SOUTHEAST ASIAN STUDIES IN CHINA

The study of Southeast Asia has deep roots in China. Dating back to as early as the third century, the records of Southeast Asia composed of the memoirs and notes of China's envoys and their assistants, monks making pilgrimages to South and Southeast Asia as well as navigators and travellers. In particular, the famed Chinese explorer, eunuch Zheng He, greatly enhanced Chinese knowledge of the region through his seven voyages. Under the Qing dynasty, the waves of Chinese immigrants to Southeast Asia in search of livelihood also boosted China's understanding of, and ties with the region at the popular level.

Even though there exists rich ancient literature on Southeast Asia, modern academic research could be traced back to the early twentieth century when Jinan University was founded in 1906 and courses on overseas Chinese and Southeast Asian history were first taught. Since then, China's Southeast Asian Studies have undergone several phases of development which have been largely shaped by two factors — China's relations with Southeast Asia and the domestic political and academic environment in China.

China's relations with Southeast Asia would provide an external impetus for the development of the field, and condition public and scholarly attention to it. China's domestic environment, on the other hand, would directly impact upon the academic freedom, resources and even approaches for scholars in the field. Understandably, a restricted environment, few sanctioned research methods and theories, and scarce resources would impede the development of research on the region.

It was in the period from the 1950s to mid-1960s that China's Southeast Asian Studies were established as a field in the country, due in part to cordial ties between China and Southeast Asia. As China was also following Soviet-style development, there was also leeway for academic research, albeit restricted to the Soviet academic paradigm and Marxist orthodoxy. This period saw several important developments, including the setting up of four regional research centres as well as a few national policy-related research units. The former included two institutes in Guangzhou and one each in Xiamen and Kunming. They later become leading regional centres on Southeast Asian Studies in China. The policy-related research units were associated with the Beijing central government and the Shanghai Academy of Social Sciences. Meanwhile, university courses were also taught on the history, anti-colonial movements and languages of Southeast Asia. And academic research focused on overseas Chinese, Southeast Asian history, and the politics and external relations of the region.

These fledgling research activities were, however, paralysed by the Cultural Revolution from 1966 to 1976 when China was awash with chaos and intellectual activities were viewed with suspicion. The country's relations with Southeast Asia also dropped to a low point because of Cold War tensions between China and most Southeast Asian countries, China's export of communist revolution to the region, and Indonesia's suppression of the China-backed Communist Party as well as persecution of local ethnic Chinese.

It was only during the reform era under the leadership of Deng Xiaoping that Southeast Asian Studies started to be revived in China in the late 1970s to 1980s. Chinese politics also lost its radical tinge and more leeway opened up for academic research. Improved Chinese ties with the region generated a demand in China for better understanding of Southeast Asia and the relevant political and language experts as well. Southeast Asian languages were taught at several universities including Beida, Beijing and Guangzhou Foreign Language Colleges, and Guangxi Nationality College.

Not only were the previous regional centres revived, new ones also emerged. By the end of the 1980s, the research institutes on Southeast Asia grew from four prior to the Cultural Revolution, to twelve. The scholarly centres included Xiamen, Jinan, Zhongshan, Beijing, and Zhengzhou Universities as well as the Chinese, Yunnan, Guangxi and Shanghai Academies of Social Sciences. Governmental research units included those at the China Institute for Contemporary International Relations (CICIR) under the Ministry of State Security, the China Institute of International Studies (CIIS) under the Ministry of Foreign Affairs, Shanghai Institute for International Studies (SIIS), and the Institute for International Trade Studies under the Ministry of External Trade (and later Ministry of External Trade and Economic Work). All these activities paved the way for a recovery of the Southeast Asian Studies field in China.

The field received a further boost in the 1990s and 2000s as China's relations with Southeast Asia improved and gained significance, especially with closer political exchanges and economic relations. Meanwhile, research methods in the field were also updated and more disciplines were introduced as China's social scientists became more exposed and receptive to Western academic methods and theories. A growing number of discipline-based scholars were also devoting attention to Southeast Asia, thus leading to the diversification and professionalization of the field.

As policy-makers frequently seek advice from scholars, Southeast Asian specialists have greater opportunities for policy-related research and consultancy. This can be seen in, for example, the production of reports specifically for the central and local governments, the direct involvement of scholars in policy-related issues and the role of academic publications in influencing policy thinking. A specific example of such influence on policy was the participation of Chinese scholars in the ASEAN-China FTA study group where their recommendations were generally accepted by the leaders.

Given the vastness of China, it is important to note the role of local studies on policy-making, particularly in terms of local policy orientation toward Southeast Asia, and the policy recommendations made by provinces to the central government on this issue. For instance, Southeast Asian Studies in Yunnan and later in Guangxi have had a significant impact on China's relations with Southeast Asia, especially to neighbouring countries. Given the deepening and growing complexity of ASEAN-China relations, detailed technical researches at the local level will be increasingly important in terms of providing micro-level policy recommendation to help develop the relationship.

CURRENT STATUS

As of now, the major research centres on Southeast Asian Studies in China are primarily located in Beijing, Xiamen, Guangzhou, Shanghai, Nanning and Kunming. They have division of labour along the geographic dimension as well as the high-low politics dimension. First, central research centres, such as the CICIR, CIIS, SIIS, CASS and Beijing University, tend to focus on region-wide issues. In contrast, regional research centres tend to focus on sub-regional affairs and individual countries. Second, research centres in Beijing and Shanghai tend to study high political issues, namely, international relations, security, politics, military, regionalism and macro economy. Regional research centres in Fujian, Guangdong, Guangxi and Yunnan tend to focus on low political issues, including the economy, history, overseas Chinese, culture, ethnicities, religion, and other social issues.

Over the years, the focus of Southeast Asian research in China has also changed. A study of the two leading journals in Southeast Asian Studies in China from 1992 to 2004 by John Wong and Lai Hongyi provided us with a glimpse of that. It was found that the share of its articles on ASEAN and Southeast Asia, greater China's ties with Southeast Asia, overseas Chinese, and Southeast Asian Studies had increased noticeably. On the other hand, those on individual Southeast Asian countries declined significantly. While this is so, some countries are covered more frequently than others, with Indonesia covered the most. This is followed by a second group which includes Vietnam, Singapore and Malaysia, and then a third group comprising the Philippines and Thailand.

In terms of disciplines, China's Southeast Asian research was mainly focused on the economy in the 1990s when economic performance was impressive and Southeast Asia's mode of development seemed to offer lessons for China. In the 2000s, however, politics overtook economy as the primary focus. Greater attention was also paid to history and society that included overseas Chinese. All in all, the changes in research focus suggest that in recent times, China's scholars are more interested in the domestic and external politics, society and culture of Southeast Asian countries and the region.

PROBLEMS AND PROSPECTS

Despite the progress made in China's Southeast Asian Studies in recent years, the field still faces many challenges that are hampering its development. Overall, the current scale of Southeast Asian teaching programmes and curriculum development is not consonant with the present state of China-Southeast Asian relations. With the signing of the ASEAN-China Free Trade Agreement, economic ties are likely to become closer, thus increasing the need for more experts in Southeast Asian affairs and languages in China. An observation raised during the conference was that while large China companies have expressed interest in doing business in Southeast Asia, many do not have much information about the social, cultural, political and economic systems in the identified countries.

China therefore needs to make greater efforts to promote Southeast Asian teaching programmes and academic research to meet such demand. As a field, Southeast Asian Studies in China needs to enhance its resources, funding, pool of talents, language skills and academic rigour. However, the field now faces serious challenges in each of these capabilities.

First, with regard to information resources, timely, accurate and systemic information is critical for sound academic research, particularly for area studies. However, China is still lagging behind its counterparts in this respect. The Southeast Asian collections in Chinese libraries remain scanty. For example, even the largest collection on Southeast Asia in China, that is, the Centre for Southeast Asian Studies at Xiamen University (CSASXU), appears small compared to the library at the Institute of Southeast Asian Studies (ISEAS) in Singapore. The former has only 52,000 items (including books and theses), about a tenth of the ISEAS collection.

Second, the lack of funding for Southeast Asian research in China exacerbates this resource problem. It also prevents the relevant institutes from funding more overseas trips and holding more academic exchanges with scholars in the region, thus limiting their local knowledge of the region.

Third, the lack of talent continues to hobble Southeast Asian research in China. Students of international relations still tend to gravitate toward the great powers such as the United States, Europe and Japan in their research focus. This is especially so since the prestige, opportunities for academic advancement, and overseas travel and research are still more abundant for researchers delving into these regions. Not surprisingly then, fewer talents are attracted to Southeast Asian Studies. Indeed, up to now, many first-class Chinese universities such as Tsinghua, Fudan, Nanjing and Wuhan have still not set up Southeast Asian teaching programmes or offered regional courses.

Fourth, poor language abilities among researchers pose another problem for the progress of Southeast Asian Studies in China. Only a small number of researchers are conversant in Southeast Asian native languages. The most frequently cited foreign language is English. Hence most researchers on Southeast Asia in China are better equipped to study ASEAN, Singapore and the Philippines where the working language is English. Their knowledge about other countries in the region continues to be hindered by their failure to master local languages, which impedes their ability to use local materials.

All the above problems contribute to the lack of academic rigour in Southeast Asian research in China. As it is, the field still needs to increase its theoretical depth and empirical width. The situation has not improved much from the past when a study of articles published by four Southeast Asian journals in China from 1987 to 1991 found that most of them displayed academic efforts at lower levels. This included analyses of context, nature, process and implications of an issue or event as well as provisioning of information on an event or issue. While a few journal articles in recent times have attempted academic work at a higher level such as theoretical debates, empirical research and case studies, they still form a conspicuous minority.

Such poor rigour has been worsened by lax academic standards in research and publications. Compared with academic publications in the West, those in China in area studies in general follow a more lenient review process. There are usually no formal requirements for literature reviews, footnoting of sources, giving credit to cited arguments, rigorous development and demonstration of arguments and application of sound research methods and theories in the field. These tend to undermine the quality of research output.

Despite these problems, one should be cautiously optimistic about the future of Southeast Asian Studies in China. To be sure, a growing number of young Chinese are becoming more interested in Southeast Asia, thanks to fast-developing bilateral relations between China and ASEAN. More young Chinese have also been exposed and attracted to Southeast Asian cultures through travel or further studies. For instance, a growing number of young Chinese have been flocking to countries like Thailand to teach Chinese due to a lack of qualified local teachers. This may help stimulate more interest in Southeast Asian Studies. The evolving geo-political context may also help raise the profile of Southeast Asian Studies in China. Given China's rise and its professed foreign policy goal of becoming a responsible regional and world power, the government has paid more attention to academic research on neighbouring countries, especially Southeast Asia.

To enhance the status and quality of Southeast Asian Studies in China, some proposals were put forward. One is for the Chinese Education Ministry, as the most important player in controlling education, to place more importance on Southeast Asian teaching programmes and to promote its development. Much more financial support should also be provided to faculty so that they have more opportunities to do field research and attend international conferences abroad. There is also room for collaboration in terms of educational exchanges and cooperation between China and ASEAN. A relevant suggestion is for Southeast Asian governments to set up study centres promoting the region throughout China, following the examples of Australia and Japan.

2

Changing Academic Challenges of the Southeast Asian Studies Field in China

John Wong and Lai Hongyi

INTRODUCTION

This chapter reviews the development of China's Southeast Asian Studies since the 1950s, especially after the late 1970s. It also examines profiles of major Southeast Asian research centres in China and identifies their changing research focus. In doing so, we attempt to capture the changes in the field of Southeast Asian Studies and challenges faced by this specific academic circle in China.

Since the founding of the People's Republic of China (PRC) in 1949, China's Southeast Asian Studies have undergone the following stages of development — initial development from the 1950s to the mid-1960s, paralysis from the mid-1960s to the late 1970s because of the Cultural Revolution, rebuilding of the programme in the 1980s after economic reform, expansion in the 1990s, and diversification and rapid development in the 2000s. We argue that at each stage, China's Southeast Asian Studies have been influenced profoundly by both China-ASEAN relations and China's domestic political environment for academic research.

This chapter begins with a brief review of the history of Southeast Asian Studies in China, from the 1950s to the present. The next part analyses the contents of articles on Southeast Asia in China and identifies this changing research focus and interests. The following part suggests a number of remaining academic challenges for China's Southeast Asian scholars. Our studies draw on reviews on the field by China's and Singapore's scholars presented at the Conference on "Southeast Asian Studies in China: Challenges and Prospects" held on 12–14 January 2006 in Singapore. Data for our paper also come from our interviews with regional research institutes in China (administered by Tok Sow Keat), information provided by these research institutes or by their websites or publications, and our analysis of contents of leading publications. Our study also benefits from earlier and brief surveys of China's Southeast Asian programmes, including those by Wang (1985) and Curley and Liu (2002) especially by Liu Yong Zhuo (1994),[1] Chen Qiaozhi and others (1992), Zhang Liang and Yang (2002), and Liu Hong (2003). The former two systemic overviews of Southeast Asian Studies were published in 1992 and 1994 respectively, and its information appeared to be rather dated. Liu Hong provides a comprehensive and useful, as well as the most recent, study of Southeast Asian programmes in China.

DEVELOPMENT OF SOUTHEAST ASIAN STUDIES IN CHINA

The development of China's Southeast Asian Studies has been shaped by two factors — China's relations with Southeast Asia, the domestic political and academic environment in China. China's relations with Southeast Asia provide an external impetus for the development of the field and condition public and scholarly attention to it as well. Arguably, the relations create the governmental, public and scholarly "demand" for research on the region. China's domestic environment, on the other hand, directly affects the academic freedom, resources availability and even acceptable approaches for scholars in the field. Understandably, scarce resources, a very restricted environment, together with officially sanctioned research methods and theories would hinder development of research on the region.[2]

Overall, China's Southeast Asian Studies have undergone several phases of development. Propelled by China's normalization of relations with the region especially Indonesia and a relaxed domestic environment, the field experienced initial development from the 1950 to the mid-1960s. However, the field also bore strong imprints of Soviet-styled Marxist overtone and methodology. From the mid-1960s to late 1970s the field was largely paralysed by China's traumatic Cultural Revolution and harmed by its deteriorated relations with the region. In the 1980s and the early 1990s Southeast Asian Studies in China were rebuilt. Since the 1990s, the field has rapidly developed. It has been aided by China's improved and increasingly significant ties with the region, a more relaxed environment for research and improved methodology. Scholars have also aimed to catch up with the rapidly changing Southeast Asian economies and improve the quality of their research especially for theoretical, regional and comprehensive studies. In the 1990s, research heavily focused on the economy of the region that had been very dynamic and could offer illuminating lessons for China. In the 2000s a number of new factors facilitate the expansion of the programme. They include China's very close relations with the region, public attention to the region, a much relaxed academic environment, more diversified methodologies, and more funding. As a result, research is being diversified, covering politics, history, and society. However, China's scholars have much room for improving the quality of their research.

INITIAL PHASE: 1950s TO MID-1960s

During this period, Southeast Asian Studies were established as a field in China. The formation and initial development of the field was fanned by developments in China-Southeast Asia ties. In particular, China's ties with Indonesia, the most populous country in Southeast Asia, were forged and remained warmed until 1965. The bilateral relations were facilitated by China's successful diplomacy at the Bandung Conference and its signing of Dual Nationality Treaty with Indonesia in 1955, as well as Indonesian President Sukaro's state visit to Beijing in 1956.[3] This external environment called for closer studies of Southeast Asia in China.

In addition, China's domestic political and academic environment also shaped Southeast Asian Studies. China was an ally of the Soviet Union between 1950 and 1960. China followed the Soviet-styled industrialization and development. China's economic recovery and construction in turn was conducive to the building of academic programmes. Due to these two developments, Chinese scholars enjoyed a certain leeway in research while having to submit to the Soviet academic paradigm.[4]

China's Southeast Asian Studies were formed as a field during this period. A number of pioneering scholars were born in mainland China and graduated from the university in China before 1949. These home-grown specialists tended to be historians and people who understood Southeast Asian languages and culture. Some of them lived and even did field work in Southeast Asia for years. Other early scholars were originally overseas Chinese intellectuals and journalists who returned to China after 1949.[5] Many of these scholars were from Indonesia. These two groups of researchers specialized primarily in history, and secondarily in anthropology, culture, and ethnicities.

The nascent field witnessed several marked developments. First, four regional research centres as well as a few national policy-related research units were established. The former included two institutes in Guangzhou, one institute in Xiamen and one in Kunming. They later became the leading regional centres on Southeast Asia in China. The policy-related research units were associated with the central government in Beijing and the Shanghai Academy of Social Sciences. Second, courses on history, anti-colonial movements and languages of Southeast Asia were taught at universities.[6] Third, the research focused on overseas Chinese, history of Southeast Asia, and politics and external relations of the region. Considerable efforts were made to collect information on returned overseas Chinese through interviews and fieldwork. Fourth, the materials researchers relied on were Chinese historical records, interviews with overseas Chinese, and translated Western works on Southeast Asia. As stated, research methodology was largely detached from that in the Western world and followed closely to the Soviet style. Thus, studies emphasized Marxist historical materialism, class struggle, political struggle, people's liberation movements, and anti-colonialism.[7]

PARALYSIS IN CULTURAL REVOLUTION: MID-1960s TO MID-1970s

During this period, domestic politics and China's deteriorated ties with Southeast Asia dealt a double blow to the field. First, the Cultural Revolution of 1965–76 paralysed research on the region, as it did to various academic disciplines. Scholars were condemned as the "stinking ninth class" and were relegated to the bottom of society. They had to undergo *xiafang,* namely, political education through taking up manual jobs. The populace, including students and intellectuals, was mobilized to engage in political campaigns and studies as well as shun academic research. Second, China's relations with Southeast Asia also descended to a low point due to three following factors — hostility and suspicion between most Southeast Asia countries and China in the Cold-War context; Indonesia's suppression of the China-backed communist party and persecution of ethnic Chinese; and China's radical Maoism and promotion of revolution in Southeast Asia.[8] In this period very little substantial research on the region was done in China. Even part of the collections on the region was lost.[9]

REBUILDING OF THE PROGRAMME: LATE 1970s AND THE 1980s

With the ouster of Maoist leadership and the emergence of Deng's pragmatic leadership, Chinese politics was moderated, leaving increasingly large leeway for research. Necessitated by China's repair and normalization of its ties with Southeast Asian nations, rebuilding of Southeast Asian Studies started in the late 1970s. After China-U.S. relations thawed in the early 1970s, Malaysia, the Philippines and Thailand recognized China in the mid 1970s. In the late 1970s, Deng Xiao-ping and Premier Zhao Ziyang paid official visits to Thailand, Malaysia, and Singapore.[10] China's improved ties with the region generated a demand in China for better understanding of the region as well as political and language experts on the region. This provided an impetus for the recovery of the programme.

The rebuilding of the programme was led by old scholars who came back from *xiafang*. Gradually, scholars born in China joined research. From 1979 to 1990 the Chinese Academy of Social Sciences (CASS) produced over fifty M.A. programme graduates on the region who later became key researchers on the region.[11] In the 1980s, Southeast Asian history was taught at a few universities, including Zhongshan, Xiamen and Beijing Universities. In 1989 a new course on politics, economy and diplomacy of Southeast Asia was also taught at Beijing University (*Beida*). Southeast Asian languages were taught at several universities including Beida, Beijing and Guangzhou Foreign Language Colleges, and Guangxi Nationality College.[12]

Four major regional centres in Guangzhou, Xiamen, and Yunnan, as well as policy research units in Beijing and Shanghai were revived. New centres (like the one in Guangxi Academy of Social Sciences) emerged. Research institutes on Southeast Asia grew from four prior to the Cultural Revolution to twelve by the end of the 1980s. The scholarly centres included Xiamen, Jinan, Zhongshan, Beijing, and Zhengzhou Universities, as well as the Chinese, Yunnan, Guangxi and Shanghai Academies of Social Sciences. Government research units included those at the China Institute for Contemporary International Relations (CICIR) under the Ministry of State Security, the China Institute of International Studies (CIIS) under the Ministry of Foreign Affairs, Shanghai Institute for International Studies (SIIS), and the Institute for International Trade Studies under the Ministry of External Trade (and later Ministry of External Trade and Economic Work). The membership of the China Society for Southeast Asian Studies (*Zhongguo Dongnanya Yanjiuhui*) exceeded 500 in the early 1990s. Courses on Southeast Asia were resumed at the universities. Research efforts included providing the government background information on the region sifting and publishing collections of historical records, field reports as well as past monographs.[13]

Research in this period witnessed both continuity and change from the previous decades. Most of the studies still covered politics of countries in the region as well as traditionally overseas Chinese and history of Southeast Asia. However, research had also expanded and covered China-Southeast Asia relations, military in Southeast Asian countries, and from the second half of the 1980s, the economy of the region. Researchers relied heavily on Chinese historical records and limited foreign documents. Articles on politics and international regions of the region largely toed the official line of the Chinese Government and had very limited scholarly value.[14]

EXPANSION AND RAPID DEVELOPMENT IN THE 1990s

Southeast Asian Studies in China received a strong boost in the 1990s, as China's relations with the region improved and attained greater political significance. In the wake of the Tiananmen crackdown, the Western countries imposed sanctions on China in the early 1990s. However, Southeast Asian nations reacted differently, maintained and even improved their ties with China. In 1990, China normalized its ties with Indonesia, Singapore, Laos, and Vietnam. In 1992, China became a negotiation partner of ASEAN. In 1996, China upgraded its status to become an ASEAN dialogue partner. Informal meetings of ASEAN+3 and ASEAN+1 were launched in 1997. China-ASEAN economic ties also deepened. ASEAN's exports to mainland China and Hong Kong increased from US$4.53 billion in 1993 to US$7.47 billion in 1996 and US$26.5 billion in 1999; ASEAN's imports from mainland China and Hong Kong increased from US$4.34 billion in 1993 to US$9.22 billion in 1996 and US$19.41 billion in 1999.[15] The trade volume thus grew by over five-fold from 1993 to 1999. More importantly, China became an increasingly important export market for ASEAN nations and the latter ran a growing trade surplus with China. Increasingly, China's scholars viewed ASEAN as a legitimate and effective organization, and held a positive view on ASEAN enlargement, its role, as well as China's closer bond with the organization.[16] Intensified political and economic bonds and perceived significance of Southeast Asia by Chinese scholars served to stimulate rapid expansion of studies of the region.

Meanwhile, research methods in Southeast Asian Studies were updated and more disciplines were introduced. These developments were possible thanks to a more relaxed and open political atmosphere for academic research in China as well as Chinese scholars' receptiveness to Western academic methods and theories. The field shook off the shackles of the former Soviet research methodology and Marxist orthodoxy.

The programme rapidly expanded in the 1990s. Most of the leading scholars overseeing the development received their basic university education in China. Many of them obtained higher degrees and had been visiting scholars overseas. Many researched on overseas Chinese, but a decent number of them were discipline specialists in international relations, history, and economics. Over the years they had chances to visit Southeast Asia, including Singapore and the Philippines.[17]

China's Southeast Asianists paid increasingly greater attention to current issues. A study suggested that in the late 1990s an overwhelming majority (60 per cent) of articles on the region published in various Chinese journals related to the economy, followed by politics, culture, and history.[18] This was driven by deepening China-ASEAN economic and political ties as well as by researchers' diversified disciplinary training. In addition, a number of non-Southeast Asian specialists in individual disciplines applied their discipline-based knowledge to various issues on the region. They generated a wealth of monographs or books on various issues in Southeast Asia that had not been explored adequately in the field. These issues included literature, religion, law, education, origins of ethnicities, culture, Chinese media, as well as political systems, values and path of developments of individual countries (especially Singapore and Thailand).[19] Furthermore, dictionaries and long encyclopedia on overseas Chinese in the region were being published.[20]

Meanwhile, undergraduate and graduate courses covered more disciplines, and they were offered at more universities. Teaching curriculum on Southeast Asia spanned a number of disciplines, including history, politics, economy, international relations, society, nationality, and culture; it covered both regional and country-specific issues. Undergraduate, M.A., and Ph.D. programmes on the region were set up at a number of universities. In addition, training programmes on multiple or single indigenous languages in the region were offered at a dozen colleges.[21] Many new scholars with disciplinary knowledge but limited experience with field work and living in the region were being groomed.

PROFESSIONALIZATION AND DIVERSIFICATION IN THE 2000s

Into the 2000s, Southeast Asian Studies in China enjoy unprecedented opportunities and resources. Building on the momentum in the 1990s, China-ASEAN relations were moving to a higher level. In late 2002, the historical China-ASEAN Free Trade Agreement (CAFTA) was reached, under which China and ASEAN agreed to set up a free-trade zone by 2010. In that year, China and ASEAN also signed a Declaration on the Code of Conduct to avoid conflict in South China Sea. In 2003, after their relations were briefly strained by the SARS crisis, China and ASEAN cooperated over SARS management and their relations regained momentum. In the same year China joined the ASEAN Treaty of Friendship and Amity, China and ASEAN declared to build a strategic partnership toward peace and prosperity.[22] China-ASEAN economic ties continued to deepen. Their trade volume more than doubled that in 1999, and reached US$106 billion in 2004, placing ASEAN as the fourth largest trade partner for China.[23] In addition, bilateral tourists also increased. In 2000, 1.7 million people from ASEAN nations visited China, up by 55 per cent from 1.1 million in 1995. Chinese tourists to ASEAN nations amounted to 1.9 million in 2000, more than doubling the 0.8 million in 1995.[24]

As a result of intensified political, economic and social exchanges, Chinese leaders, business community and society are developing a strong interest in Southeast Asia. An increasingly commercialized media reinforces this interest. Studies on international relations and economy of Southeast Asia have become very popular in China. More resources and funding have become available to research centres on Southeast Asia. There are more opportunities for scholars to do fieldwork overseas as well.

Meanwhile, social sciences in China have become more internationalized and modernized. China-educated Southeast Asianists lead the field. They have more opportunities to exchange with scholars from the West and Southeast Asia, or to do fieldwork overseas including in Southeast Asia. They are more exposed to studies on the region abroad. In addition, more young scholars on Southeast Asia have obtained their degrees in a variety of disciplines overseas, and adopt Western and contemporary research methods. This reinforces the diversification of Southeast Asian Studies that started in the 1990s. In addition, an increasing number of discipline-based scholars devote their time to Southeast Asian research and teaching. They receive a considerable amount of funding for their research as well. The field is thus becoming professionalized. There is also growing interaction among scholars and between officials and scholars. Scholars in local research centres also have frequent exchanges with those at research units for the central government.[25] Moreover, policy-makers frequently seek advice from scholars including those in the universities. Southeast Asianists now have greater opportunities for policy-related research and consultancy. Books and journal articles on the region are also growing in number, covering a great variety of disciplines and countries.

Major research institutes are primarily located in Beijing, Xiamen, Guangzhou, Shanghai, Nanning and Kunming. There is division of labour along the geographic dimension as well as the high-low politics dimension (Table 2.1). First, central research centres, such as the CICIR, CIIS, SIIS, CASS and Beijing University, tend to focus on region-wide issues. In contrast, regional research centres tend to focus on sub-regional affairs and individual countries. The Institute for Southeast Asian Studies (ISEAS) at Xiamen University, as well as Jinan University and Zhongshan University in Guangzhou, tend to focus on maritime Southeast Asia including Indonesia, Malaysia, Singapore and the Philippines. The ISEAS at Guangxi and Yunnan Academy of Social Sciences (GASS and YASS) and the Centre for Southeast Asian Studies at Guangxi University tend to focus on mainland Southeast Asia, especially countries adjacent to Guangxi and Yunnan. These countries are firstly Vietnam, Burma, and Thailand and secondly Cambodia and Laos. Second, research centres in Beijing and Shanghai tend to study high political issues, namely, international relations, security, politics, military, and regionalism, as well as macro economics. Regional research centres in Fujian, Guangdong, Guangxi and Yunnan tend to focus on low political issues, including the economy, history, overseas Chinese, culture, ethnicities, religion, and other social issues.

Table 2.1
China's Research Centres on Southeast Asia in the 2000s

Research Centres	Regional Focus	Topical Focus
Beijing (CASS, CICIR, Beijing University); Shanghai (SIIA)	Southeast Asia as a region	International relations (IR), security, politics, economy, military, and regionalism
Xiamen (Xiamen University), Guangzhou (Jinan University; Zhongshan University)	Maritime Southeast Asia; South China Sea; individual countries	History, economy, and society (ethnicity, religion, and culture); recently politics and IR; overseas Chinese
Nanning (GASS; Guangxi University); Kunming (YASS)	Mainland Southeast Asia (country adjacent to the host province)	History, society (ethnicity; religion), and economy

CHANGING RESEARCH FOCUSES IN THE 1990s AND THE 2000s

After its revival in the 1980s, China's Southeast Asian research expanded considerably in the 1990s. Since the 1990s, the research focuses of the field have assumed academic significance. This section examines the changing research focus of China's Southeast Asian Studies in the 1990s and 2000s. This examination is based on analyses of the contents of leading academic journals on Southeast Asian Studies in China. Due to limited time and manpower, we will be able to analyse only two leading Chinese journals — *Southeast Asian Studies* and *Southeast Asian Affairs* from 1992 to 2004. This by no means implies that other specialized journals publishing articles on Southeast Asia are unimportant. The year of 1995 is left out as the issues of *Southeast Asian Affairs* are not available at our library. This, however, should not affect the overall pattern of our findings.

Two-thirds of the articles published in the two journals related to Southeast Asia. The share, however, fluctuated during 1992–2004. Overall, it grew modestly from 63 per cent in 1992 to 69 per cent in 2004. It peaked in 1998, registering nearly 77 per cent, reflected possibly a strong interest in the region in the wake of the Asian financial crisis. This share, however, declined to the lowest point at 58 per cent in 2003. In 2004, it recovered to 69 per cent.

A detailed examination of articles relating only to Southeast Asia suggests that from 1992 to 2004, the two journals published 1,070 articles related to Southeast Asia. The total number of articles on Southeast Asia or individual countries declined steadily from 114 in 1992 to only 64 in 2003. It bounced back to 97 in 2004. Overall, over half of the articles dealt with individual Southeast Asian nations. The next three issues or areas that were often covered included ASEAN and Southeast Asia, accounting for 22.7 per cent of the articles, the relations between mainland China, Taiwan and Hong Kong with the region 18.3 per cent and overseas Chinese in the region 18 per cent. One of the least covered major categories was Southeast Asian Studies (including works and research on the region), accounting for 2.7 per cent of the articles.

Over the years, the distribution of Southeast Asia-related articles among the aforementioned areas has changed. The share of individual Southeast Asian countries in articles declined significantly from 61 per cent in 1992 to only 34 per cent in 2004. On the other hand, the shares of other areas have increased. That of ASEAN and Southeast Asia, which referred to multi-country studies or issues related to ASEAN or Southeast Asia, grew from 23.7 per cent in 1992 to 30 per cent in 2004; that of the ties of greater China with Southeast Asia from 8 per cent to a whopping 21.6 per cent; that of overseas Chinese from 12.3 per cent to 19.6 per cent; and that of Southeast Asian Studies from a negligible 0.9 to a noticeable 6.2 per cent (Table 2.2 and Figure 2.1).

While individual countries on the whole take up an increasingly smaller share of the articles, some countries are covered more frequently than others.

Table 2.2
Distribution of Articles on Southeast Asia in Southeast Asian Studies and Southeast Asian Affairs by Areas (%)

Country	1992	1993	1994	1996	1997	1998	1999	2000	2001	2002	2003	2004	1992–2004 (average share)
Total Number of Articles	114	114	77	96	92	100	77	79	83	77	64	97	Total: 1070
1. ASEAN and Southeast Asia	**23.7**	**17.5**	**15.6**	**18.8**	**25.0**	**28.0**	**27.3**	**21.5**	**22.9**	**16.9**	**25.0**	**29.9**	**22.7**
2. Southeast Asian Countries	**61.4**	**68.4**	**61.0**	**54.2**	**52.2**	**57.0**	**45.5**	**40.5**	**50.6**	**44.2**	**34.4**	**34.0**	**50.3**
Indonesia	13.2	13.2	10.4	4.2	3.3	6.0	7.8	10.8	9.6	7.8	6.3	7.2	8.3
Malaysia	2.6	6.1	10.4	7.3	5.4	13.3	6.5	7.0	6.0	11.7	6.3	6.7	7.4
Singapore	8.8	8.8	11.7	7.3	4.3	10.0	9.1	7.6	6.0	3.9	6.3	6.2	7.5
Thailand	9.2	9.2	5.2	5.2	9.8	7.0	7.1	5.1	8.4	3.9	4.7	2.1	6.4
Vietnam	8.8	14.5	13.0	14.6	9.8	9.3	2.6	2.5	9.6	2.6	1.6	2.1	7.6
Philippines	8.8	7.9	2.6	8.3	8.7	9.3	9.1	6.3	4.8	5.2	4.7	4.6	6.7
Myanmar	5.7	1.3	6.5	2.1	4.3	1.0	3.2	1.3	6.0	9.1	4.7	4.1	4.1
Cambodia	0.9	3.9	1.3	3.1	4.3	0.0	0.0	0.0	0.0	0.0	0.0	0.0	1.1
Laos	2.6	3.5	0.0	2.1	2.2	1.0	0.0	0.0	0.0	0.0	0.0	0.0	0.9
Brunei	0.9	0.0	0.0	1.0	1.1	0.0	0.0	0.0	0.0	2.6	0.0	1.0	0.6
Indochina	0.0	0.0	0.0	0.0	0.0	0.0	0.0	0.0	0.0	0.0	0.0	0.0	0.0
3. Overseas Chinese in Southeast Asia	**12.3**	**10.5**	**18.2**	**21.9**	**13.0**	**15.0**	**19.5**	**24.1**	**18.1**	**18.2**	**25.0**	**19.6**	**17.9**
4. Greater China-SE Asia/ASEAN	**7.9**	**14.0**	**18.2**	**14.6**	**21.7**	**9.0**	**16.9**	**27.8**	**16.9**	**27.3**	**23.4**	**21.6**	**18.3**
5. Southeast Asian Studies	**0.9**	**1.8**	**1.3**	**5.2**	**0.0**	**3.0**	**1.3**	**0.0**	**1.2**	**3.9**	**7.8**	**6.2**	**2.7**

Figure 2.1
Southeast Asia-related Articles in *Southeast Asian Studies* and *Southeast Asian Affairs*

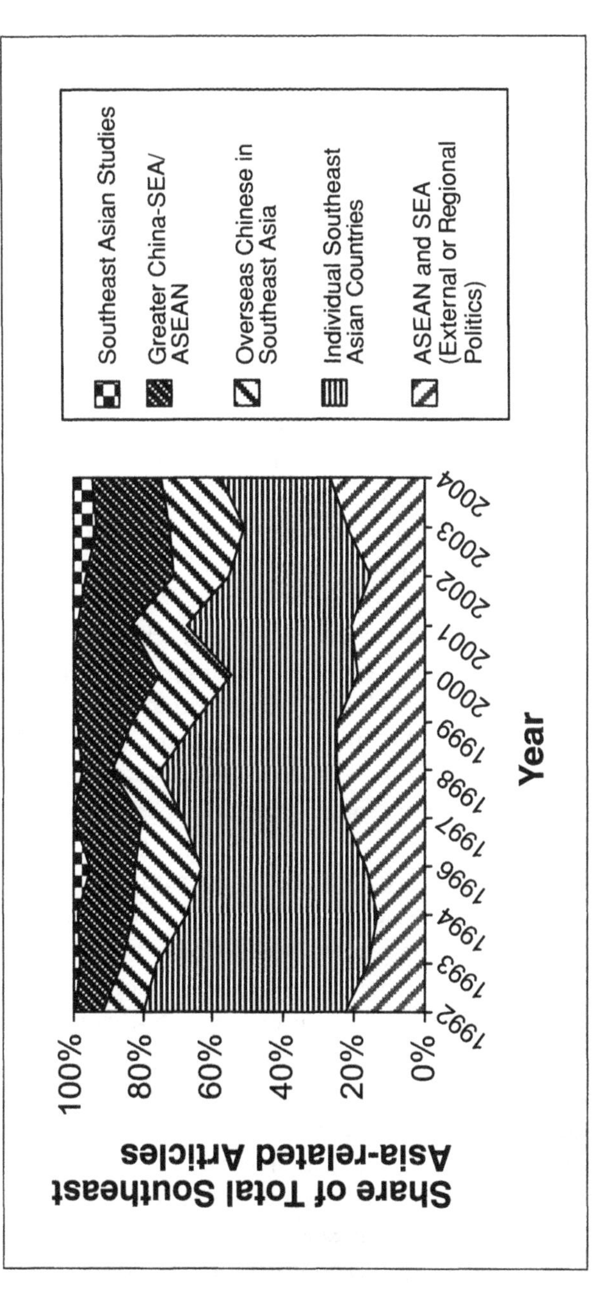

A comprehensive study on various economic articles on Southeast Asia provides a useful clue. Among Southeast Asian countries, Indonesia was covered the most frequently, taking up an average 8.3 per cent of the articles related to the region from 1992 to 2004. The second group of frequently-covered countries included Vietnam, Singapore, and Malaysia, each accounting for 7.4 per cent–7.6 per cent of the articles. The third tier of countries, each accounting for 6.4 per cent–6.7 per cent of the articles, was the Philippines and Thailand. At a greater distance behind was Myanmar, accounting for 4 per cent of the articles. The other countries, including Cambodia, Laos and Brunei, were discussed very infrequently. Over the years, articles on Indonesia, Thailand, and Vietnam declined significantly, those on the Philippines and especially Singapore dropped moderately.[26]

When we examine the distribution of articles in these two journals by disciplines in three selected years of the period of 1992–2004, that is, 1992, 1998, and 2004, a clear pattern emerges. While over half of the articles published in 1992 and 1998 related to the economy, this share fell drastically to only 16 per cent in 2004. Similarly, fewer articles dealt with the military over the years, as their share declined from 2.6 per cent in 1992 to 0.6 per cent in 2004. In contrast, articles in other major disciplines, including politics, society, history, overseas Chinese, and other disciplines have gone up, despite fluctuations in some of these disciplines. In particular, the share of articles in politics was a modest 11 per cent in 1992 and more than doubled to 25 per cent in 1998. By 2004, a largest plurality of articles (45 per cent) was concerned with politics. The share of articles on overseas Chinese grew consistently from 11.6 per cent in 1992, to 13 per cent in 1998 and to 17 per cent in 2004 (Figure 2.2).

As we see from the articles in two front-running journals on the region, China's Southeast Asian research in the 1990s predominantly focused on the economy. The underlying reason are as follows: The economy in the region had been very dynamic and witnessed drastic change including the financial crisis; the economic experience of the region, such as its advantaged agriculture, its attraction of FDI, and its mode of development, has useful implications for China; China had been developing its economic ties with the region in the decade. In terms of issues and areas articles on the region was overwhelmingly concerned with individual Southeast Asian countries. The issues of a secondary priority included ASEAN and the region, overseas Chinese in the region, and greater China's relations with the region. This pattern reflected the traditional approach of the field — a traditional emphasis on individual countries and overseas Chinese.

Figure 2.2
Distribution of Articles in *Southeast Asian Studies* and *Southeast Asian Affairs* by Disciplines

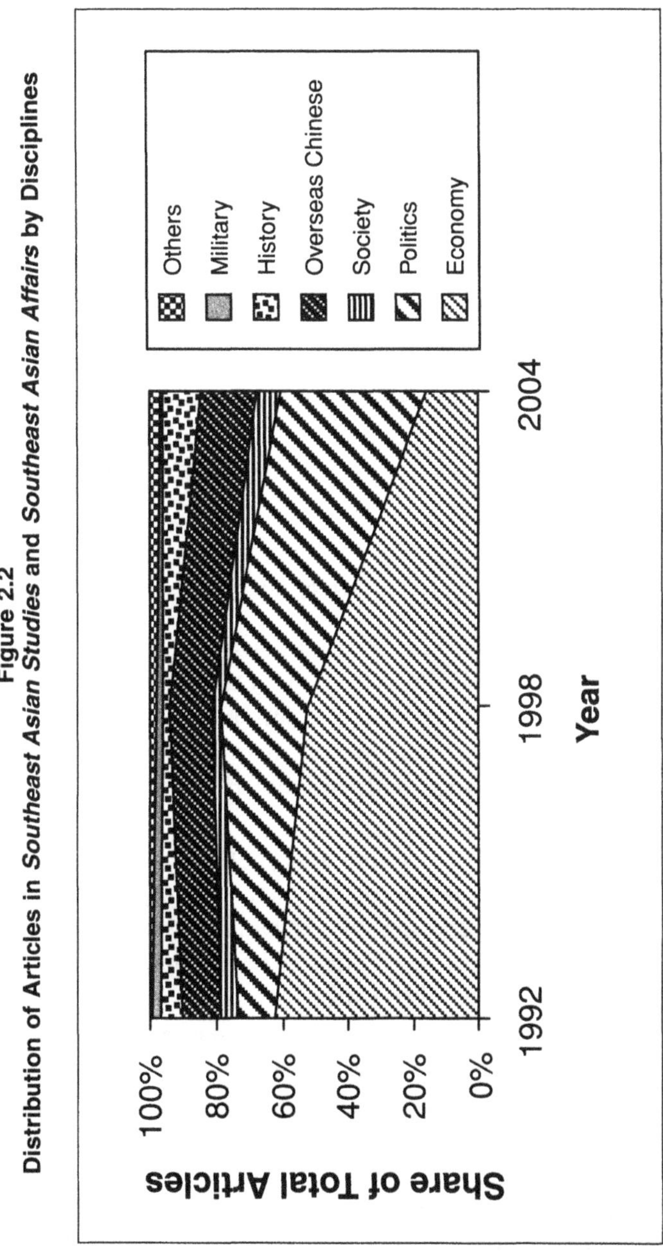

In the 2000s, however, the research focus has undergone changes. A growing body of publications shifted away from a heavy focus on individual countries and on economic issues to become more diversified. Politics has overtaken economics as the primary focus. Greater attention is being paid to history and society that includes overseas Chinese. Research focuses on major issues or areas have also changed. Attention to individual countries has decreased, and ASEAN and Southeast Asia as a whole is fast becoming an important focus. Next to these two issues, greater China's ties with the region and overseas Chinese in the region have become secondary focuses in publications. This change in research focus suggests that in the 2000s, China's scholars are also paying heavy attention to domestic and external politics, society and culture of Southeast Asian countries and the region. As China's ties with ASEAN and the region deepen, China's scholars are more interested in the region and ASEAN as well as their relations with greater China. In addition, as China's trade with the region is fast growing, the economic role of overseas Chinese in the region and in this trade tie is also receiving greater attention.

REMAINING CHALLENGES FOR RESEARCHERS IN CHINA

Nevertheless, China's Southeast Asian scholars still face a task of increasing the theoretical depth and empirical width of their research. They have yet to develop sophisticated studies of the region as well as individual countries. Meeting the tasks would require improvement in library collections, research funding, frequent exchange with overseas research community, language skills, and academic rigour.

China's Southeast Asian Studies have yet to mature as a field in terms of information resources, funding, talent pool, language skills, and academic rigour. In this section, drawing on our tentative observations and reports from the Chinese scholars, we will discuss briefly the outstanding challenges for China's scholars on Southeast Asia.

First, information resources. Information is the basis for academic research. In the recent years, China's researchers may well be able to access articles published in leading journals on social sciences through Internet subscription of their universities or institutes. However, area studies also demand timely, accurate, and systemic data on the countries or the region under study. In this regard, China still lags far behind their overseas counterparts.

The library of the Institute of Southeast Asian Studies (ISEAS) in Singapore operates as a centre for studies on Southeast Asia for the region. Its collections on Southeast Asia are among the best and most comprehensive in the world. The ISEAS Library has more than 522,000 multi-lingual and multi-format items. The collection consists mainly of current and contemporary information resources in the applied social sciences on Southeast Asia. It also comprises a large archival collection on the region. The collection falls into the following categories — general collection, reference, statistics, documents, biography files, newspaper clippings, special collection, current periodicals, rare books, private papers, audio-visual, maps, microforms, newspapers and library office collection. The library receives about 2,000 periodicals in English and in the vernacular languages. It has one of the largest collections of statistical yearbooks on countries in the region. It constitutes an invaluable source for quantitative and systemic research on the region and individual countries in major disciplines.

In comparison, the largest collection on Southeast Asia in China, that is, the Centre for Southeast Asian Studies at Xiamen University (CSASXU), appears small. This is so despite the fact that the centre has made considerable effort to build up its collection. Indeed, it has accumulated a large collection of newspapers from Southeast Asia published in the previous decades; it has also compiled an index on research papers on Southeast Asia, economic statistics on the region, and a data base of important documents on the region. The library, however, has only 52,000 items (including books and theses), about one tenth of that of the ISEAS collection. The CSASXU subscribes to 1,630 periodicals, 18.5 per cent less than the ISEAS. In addition, it is questionable whether the centre has as complete and thorough a statistical collection as the ISEAS which covers all the nations in the region for years, and most nations for decades. In the early 1990s, a researcher of the CSASXU complained about a shortage in funds for procuring books, research materials, copy machines for the library and about a lack of qualified librarians.[27] While the conditions may have improved in recent years, it is likely that funds for purchases of books in the vernacular languages are still limited. Scholars may need to take leave to use the library at the ISEAS in Singapore in order to overcome this inadequacy. Apparently, scholars at a few leading institutes have the funding to finance their trip and their research at the ISEAS. But this option is costly and inconvenient, nor is this option available to the majority of Southeast Asianists in China.

Other research centres may have a more serious problem with their library collections. The collection that comes close to Xiamen's is the institute in Jinan University which has a collection of 40,000 copies of books and materials, including 253 journals and 103 newspapers in Chinese, European, and Southeast Asian languages. Other institutes have smaller collections. The institute at Zhongshan University has only 12,000 books (half of which are in English) and 400 journals. The library at Guangxi Academy of Social Sciences (the academy and the institute combined) has 16,000 Chinese books, 3,000 books in foreign languages, and 60 periodicals in foreign languages. Both collections are less than half of that at Xiamen. The problem with research materials at these institutes may be more serious.

Second, funding. The ISEAS receives about US$5 million for research and operation a year. The CSASXU, on the other hand, receives about 3.4 million yuan for its research and operation out of governmental, institutional and private sources, equivalent to US$425,000, or about one-tenth that of the ISEAS.[28] Understandably, the more generous research funding has allowed the ISEAS to build up a larger book collection, hold more academic exchanges with scholars in the region, and fund more overseas trips for its researchers.[29] Institutes in Guangzhou, Nanning, and Kunming may well have less funding than that in Xiamen and may encounter a more severe shortage in funds.

Third, the pool of talent. China's research on other countries has started to recover and develop in the reform era. However, the United States has the strongest appeal to China's researchers in country and area studies, attracting China's best talents in international studies. Next to the United States may be Europe and Japan. While this situation may have improved somewhat, it may not have been completely reversed. Prestige, opportunities for academic advancement and overseas travels and research are still higher for researchers on the United States, Europe and Japan. The positive side is that China's interests in Southeast Asia have grown considerably and receive a boost from the China-ASEAN free trade agreement (CAFTA) in recent years. These developments will attract the best talents to China's Southeast Asian Studies.

Fourth, language skills for researchers. An earlier survey conducted in 1991 among scholars in Southeast Asian Studies found that 50 per cent of 192 respondents used English, and only 21 per cent of the respondents used Southeast Asian native languages, primarily Indonesian, Thai, Vietnamese, and Burmese.[30] Fourteen years have passed since this survey. The situation has improved modestly. A sampling of articles from *Southeast Asian Studies* in 2004 indicates that some authors are able to use Southeast Asian languages in their writing. The primary languages are Thai and Indonesian. However, they remain a clear and small minority of the authors. The most-frequently cited foreign language is English. Thus Chinese experts on Southeast Asia who can speak a foreign language tend to speak English alone. They are able to study ASEAN, Singapore, and the Philippines whose official working language is English. Their knowledge about other countries in the region may continue to be hindered by their inability to master the local languages. Among the major research institutes, Xiamen appears to be the first and likely the only one in offering extensive training in Southeast Asian native languages. While this is a good start, it may take years before it bears fruit in research.

Fifth, academic rigour. According to the findings of a study by Liu Yong Zhuo of articles published by the four major Southeast Asian journals in China from 1987 to 1991, 80–91 per cent of the articles contained academic efforts at lower levels, including analyses of the context, nature, process and implications of an issue or event as well as the provision of information on an event or an issue. About 1–11 per cent of the articles made the least academic efforts by providing merely basic information on an issue or event. For three journals, only 5–10 per cent of the articles contained higher academic "added value", such as unearthing new and substantial evidence in research, theoretical discussion and empirical verification on major issues, and thorough demonstration of new viewpoints.[31] A quick glimpse of articles in *Southeast Asian Studies* in 2004 indicates that this pattern has remained basically the same. The only encouraging sign is that there were a few articles that attempted to join the ongoing theoretical debates (such as democracy and development, developmental models, and international relations theories), apply existing theories to a new issue, or undertaking empirical research and case studies.

In a more recent discussion on the status of China's Southeast Asian Studies in 2002, professors from the CSASXU and Beijing University suggested that theoretical, comprehensive, or empirical (including case study) research on Southeast Asia in China lagged behind that in the United States, Australia, Japan, and Singapore. One key indicator was that Chinese scholars had yet to produce theoretically-based monographs on individual Southeast Asian countries and on the history of the region. They argued that these problems resulted from inadequate academic exchange with overseas scholars and among Chinese scholars, difficulties in publishing books in the field, a lack of funding, as well as limited theoretical qualification, language skills, overseas travel and field work.[32]

Compared with the academic publications in the English-speaking world, those in China in area studies in general probably follow a much more lenient review process. In addition, there are usually no formal requirements for literature reviews, footnoting of sources, giving credits to cited arguments, rigorous development and demonstration of arguments, and application of sound research methods and theories in the field. These leniencies actually discourage improvement in the quality of publications.

The under-development of theoretical and comprehensive studies of the region is further hindered by ambiguous division of labour among the leading regional centres on Southeast Asia, as noted above. There are clear overlaps among the research interests of the centres in Xianmen, Jinan and Zhongshan

Universities, as they all research on the broad aspects of Southeast Asia as a whole, including domestic politics, international relations (including its ties with China), the economy, and increasingly, culture and the society. While there is some sort of division of labour between three southwestern centres on Southeast Asia as described above, the line of division is not clear cut. A clearer and sounder division of labour among these centres can save valuable resources while fostering helpful but not excessive competition.

CONCLUDING REMARKS

In the past half a century, China's Southeast Asian Studies have experienced a lot of ups and downs. These periods of development include formation and initial development from the 1950s to the mid-1960s, destruction from the mid-1960s to the late 1970s, rebuilding of the programme in the 1980s, expansion in the 1990s, and diversification and professionalization in the 2000s. The forces that help shape China's Southeast Asian Studies have been China's changing relations with Southeast Asia, as well as China's domestic academic environment. The latter is related to China's overall relaxation of political control of research and the rising standard for academic research. Over the decades, accordingly, the field has developed to become more professionalized and has attracted more talents and resources.

Research focus has undergone changes as well. From the 1950s to the 1980s, Southeast Asian Studies in China focused primarily on history, languages, anti-colonialism and anti-imperialism, and overseas Chinese studies. Since the 1990s, the field has started to move away from this focus and towards social sciences-based contemporary issues. In most of the 1990s, articles on major Southeast Asian journals focused on individual countries and on economic issues. In recent years, increasingly, articles are being more evenly distributed among several outstanding areas pertinent to the region — ASEAN and Southeast Asia, individual countries, greater China's ties with the region, overseas Chinese and the Asia-Pacific. They also cover major social disciplines, including politics, economics, overseas Chinese, history, and to a lesser extent, society. Authors have increased their usage of materials in foreign languages, especially English. Some of them also take on theoretical issues and undertake careful empirical studies.

During the past twenty-seven years, China's centres on Southeast Asia have been revived and have expanded considerably. Regional centres include those in Xiamen, Jinan and Zhongshan Universities and at the Yunnan and Guangxi Academy of Social Sciences, as well as a relatively new centre in Guangxi University. There are also research centres that work for the central government and taken on a national profile. They include CASS, CICIR, CIIS, and SIIS. Finally, Beijing University has also set up its programme on the region. These research centres divide their research roughly along the regional-maritime-mainland Southeast Asia and along high-low politics dimensions.

China's scholars on Southeast Asia, however, have yet to develop rigorous theoretical approach to research, expand their case studies, and form comprehensive overviews of countries and the region. To do so, they need to polish their language skills, especially major native languages in Southeast Asia such as Malay and Thai, make use of theories and research abroad, and improve their analytical rigour. In order to make this happen, improvements are needed in library collections, research funding, as well as opportunities for overseas field work, conferences, and academic visits. Furthermore, requirements in research methods and the publication review process can be made more rigorous. While the field of Southeast Asian Studies in China faces daunting challenges, opportunities for improvement also abound.

NOTES

1. Liu Yong Zhuo, *Zhongguo Dongnanya Yanjiu de Huigu yu Qianzhan [A Review and Future Prospects for Southeast Asian Studies in China]* Guangzhou: Guangzhou People's Press, 1994; Chen Qiaozhi, Huang Zishang, and Chen Senhai, *Zhongguo de Dongnanya Yanjiu [China's Southeast Asian Studies: Status and Prospects]* Guangzhou: Jinan University Press, 1992; Liang Zhiming, Zhang Xizhen, and Yang Baoyun, "China's Southeast Asian Studies Facing the New Century: Retrospect and Prospects" [Mianxiang xin shiji de Zhongguo Dongnanyaxue yanjiu], *Nanyang Yanjiu [Southeast Asian Affairs]*, March 2002, No. 1 (General No. 109): 86–93; Liu Hong, "Southeast Asian Studies in Greater China", *Kyoto Review of Southeast Asia* 3 (March 2003). For other existing literature, refer to Wang Gungwu, "South China Perspectives on Overseas Chinese", *Australian Journal of Chinese Affairs* 13 (January 1985): 69–84; Melissa Curley and Liu Hong, "Introduction" in *China and Southeast Asia: Changing Socio-cultural Interactions*, edited by Curley and Liu. Hong Kong: Centre of Asian Studies, University of Hong Kong, 2002, pp. 1–10.
2. Tang and Zhang argued that institutional setting of China's scholarly community and the society profoundly influenced the pursuit of knowledge, including Southeast Asian Studies in China. Refer to Tang Shiping and Zhang Jie, "The State of Southeast Asian Studies in China: An Institutional Interpretation", paper presented at Conference on "Southeast Asian Studies in China: Challenges and Prospects", 12–14 January 2006, Singapore.
3. John Wong, *The Political Economy of China's Changing Relations with Southeast Asia,* London: MacMillan Press, 1984, p. 5.

4. Yuan Ding, "Zhongguo de Dongnanya Yanjiu zhi Yuanbian" [Evolution of China's Southeast Asian Studies], paper presented at Conference on "Southeast Asian Studies in China: Challenges and Prospects", 12–14 January 2006, Singapore; Liu Yong Zhuo, *Zhongguo Dongnanya Yanjiu de Huigu yu Qianzhan*, p. 38.
5. Leo Suryadinata, "Southeast Asianists in China in the Last Three Decades", paper presented at Conference on "Southeast Asian Studies in China: Challenges and Prospects", 12–14 January 2006, Singapore.
6. Liu, *Zhongguo Dongnanya Yanjiu de Huigu yu Qianzhan*, p. 37; Zhang Xizhen, "Overview of Teaching Programs and Curriculum Development on Southeast Asia in China", paper presented at Conference on "Southeast Asian Studies in China: Challenges and Prospects", 12–14 January 2006, Singapore.
7. Yuan, "Zhongguo de Dongnanya Yanjiu zhi Yuanbian"; Liu, *Zhongguo Dongnanya Yanjiu de Huigu yu Qianzhan*, pp. 35–39.
8. See Wong, *The Political Economy of China's Changing Relations with Southeast Asia*, p. 5.
9. Liu, *Zhongguo Dongnanya Yanjiu de Huigu yu Qianzhan*, p. 39.
10. Zhao also visited the Philippines. See Wong, *The Political Economy of China's Changing Relations with Southeast Asia*, p. 5.
11. Liu, *Zhongguo Dongnanya Yanjiu de Huigu yu Qianzhan*, p. 41; Leo Suryadinata, "Southeast Asianists in China in the Last Three Decades", pp. 4–6; Zhang Xizhen, "Overview of Teaching Programs and Curriculum Development on Southeast Asia in China".
12. Zhang, "Overview of Teaching Programs and Curriculum Development on Southeast Asia in China", p. 4.
13. Liu, *Zhongguo Dongnanya Yanjiu de Huigu yu Qianzhan*, pp. 35–39; Yuan, "Zhongguo de Dongnanya Yanjiu zhi Yuanbian", pp. 3–4.
14. Ibid.
15. Statistics posted at <http://www.aseansec.org>. Cited in Cao Yunhua and Tang Chong, *Xin Zhongguo-Dongmeng Guanxi Lun [New China-ASEAN Relations]*. Beijing: Shijie Zhishi Chubanshe, 2005, pp. 17–18.
16. Zhang Yunling, "China-ASEAN Relations — Role of Research in Shaping China's Policy Making", paper presented at Conference on "Southeast Asian Studies in China: Challenges and Prospects", 12–14 January 2006, Singapore.
17. Suryadinata, "Southeast Asianists in China in the Last Three Decades", pp. 6–8.
18. The study was done by Zhao Heman. Cited in Yuan Ding, "Zhongguo de Dongnanya Yanjiu zhi Yuanbian", pp. 7–8.
19. Yuan, "Zhongguo de Dongnanya Yanjiu zhi Yuanbian", pp. 5–7.
20. Suryadinata, "Southeast Asianists in China in the Last Three Decades", pp. 4, 15–16.
21. Zhang, "Overview of Teaching Programs and Curriculum Development on Southeast Asia in China", pp. 5–6.

22. Cao Yunhua and Tang Chong, *Xin Zhongguo-Dongmeng Guanxi Lun [New China-ASEAN Relations]*. Beijing: Shijie Zhishi Chubanshe, 2005, pp. 333–43.
23. "ASEAN Becomes China's Fourth Largest Partner: Official", posted <http://www.aseansec.org/afp/132p.htm>, accessed on 6 February 2006.
24. Cao and Tang, *Xin Zhongguo-Dongmeng Guanxi Lun [New China-ASEAN Relations]*, p. 17.
25. Zhang Yunling, "China-ASEAN Relations — Role of Research in Shaping China's Policy Making", pp. 4–5; Suryadinata, "Southeast Asianists in China in the Last Three Decades", pp. 6–8; Tang and Zhang, "The State of Southeast Asian Studies in China: An Institutional Interpretation".
26. Yang Yuhua, "Recent Distribution and Features of China's Studies on Southeast Asian Economies" [Jinnian guonei Dongnanya jingji yanjiu de fenbu yu tedian], *Nanyang Yanjiu (Southeast Asian Affairs)*, no. 3 (General no. 111) (September 2002): 96–100.
27. Wang Muheng, "Trend and Problems in Studies on Economic Issues by the Institute of Southeast Asian Studies at Xiamen University", in Chen Qiaozhi, Huang Zishang, and Chen Senhai, *Zhongguo de Dongnanya Yanjiu*, pp. 79–82.
28. Estimates based on interviews with informative scholars.
29. For information on collection at the library and funding for the ISEAS, refer to information on the library at <http://www.iseas.edu.sg/collection.htm>, as well as the annual report of the library of the ISEAS and the annual report of the ISEAS, 2004–2005, at <http://www.iseas.edu.sg/annreprt.html>.
30. Liu, *Zhongguo dongnanya yanjiu de huigu yu Qianzhan*, pp. 2–8.
31. Ibid., pp. 156–61. For critical assessments and discussion on the status of China's Southeast Asian Studies in the 1990s, refer to Chen, Huang and Chen, *Zhongguo de Dongnanya Yanjiu*, 1992.
32. Liang Zhiming, Zhang Xizhen, and Yang Baoyun, "China's Southeast Asian Studies Facing the New Century: Retrospect and Prospects" (Mianxiang xin shiji de Zhongguo Dongnanyaxue yanjiu), *Nanyang Yanjiu (Southeast Asian Affairs)* no. 1 (General no. 109) (March 2002): 86–93.

3

Southeast Asianists in China in the Last Three Decades: A Preliminary Survey

Leo Suryadinata

FEW STUDIES ON THE SUBJECT MATTER

Although the history of Southeast Asian Studies in China started prior to World War II, it began to develop only after the war. During the initial period, there was not much progress as the People's Republic of China (PRC) had just been established and ideological issues were still dominant then. It was soon followed by the Cultural Revolution and its ten-year disastrous aftermath where only academic studies of relative significance were published by PRC Southeast Asianists. It was only after the re-emergence of Deng Xiaoping in 1977/78, did Southeast Asian Studies in China obtain an opportunity to develop. Not surprisingly, Southeast Asian research institutions as well as books, journals, and articles came into being during the post-Mao period.

However, books and articles which address the situation of the Southeast Asian Studies in China (*Zhongguo Dongnanya Xue* 中国东南亚学) are still limited. To my knowledge, the first survey on the topic was done by the Australian National University (ANU) group led by Professor Wang Gungwu

(1981). Mainland Chinese scholars themselves have also published monographs and articles. The earliest one was, perhaps, Professor Yao Nan's Research on Southeast Asian Historical studies in China (article in Chinese 1984), followed by Hong Kong's Frances Lai's edited book (in English, 1987) in which a few PRC scholars wrote articles on their research institutes. A book-length study was done by Liu Yong Zhuo (in Chinese, 1994), and a review article by Liu Hong (in English, 2003). But two review articles, one by Professor Zhao Heman (in Chinese, 2000), and the other (in Chinese, 2002) jointly written by three professors: Liang Zhiming, Zhang Xizhen and Yang Baojun deserve special attention.

The Wang report was done soon after the re-emergence of Deng and therefore the picture painted was rather gloomy. However, the last two articles mentioned were written twenty years later and were produced by PRC scholars and presented a slightly brighter picture but remained critical of the shortcomings of PRC Southeast Asian Studies. One common characteristic in those PRC scholar writings, including those two articles, is that they talk about Southeast Asian Studies and their institutions in the PRC without referring to any individual PRC Southeast Asianists.

There are two possible reasons, one of which is that the Southeast Asian Studies (with the exception of historical studies based on Chinese sources) has been under-developed, and perhaps they feel that there are not enough leading Southeast Asianists to be highlighted. Indeed, many PRC books on Southeast Asia have been "edited books" or "joint-products", rather than individual works. It is also possible that in the PRC, during a particular period, "individualism" was discouraged. Everything was supposed to be done collectively and the name of the institutes rather than the work of their scholars should be highlighted. However, I noticed that this practice has been abandoned and most of the books published since 1990s have highlighted the name of the author/authors rather than the committee or institutes.

There is another possible reason for PRC reviewers not to highlight China's Southeast Asianists because they feel it is difficult to define what a Southeast Asianist is. In my view, there are at least two definitions of Southeast Asianists. One is a broad definition: Those whose works are on Southeast Asia, including scholars, researchers in various institutions, including government ministries/agencies, consultants, journalists, regardless of their publications and training. As long as their work is on Southeast Asian matters and they are "experts" in the region, they are Southeast Asianists. The other definition is a narrow one: Those researchers and scholars who have engaged in academic pursuits and published works regarding Southeast Asian Studies are Southeast Asianists. For the purpose of this chapter, I have taken the second narrow definition. They include linguists, literary critics, historians, political scientists, economists, anthropologists and sociologists.

WHO ARE PRC SOUTHEAST ASIANISTS?

By definition, Southeast Asianists should be area-based rather than discipline-based. A scholar who is known in a particular discipline and happened to edit a book on Southeast Asia is not considered to be a Southeast Asianist. For instance, Zheng Xueyi (1997), an economist who has published several books on China's economics and marketing, but has edited a book on Southeast Asian Chinese businesses is not included as a Southeast Asianist here. However, an economist, political scientist or international relations specialist who authored a book on Southeast Asia is classified as a Southeast Asianist. Therefore when speaking of Southeast Asianists, both area specialists and social scientists who have written and published their work on Southeast Asia are included in this chapter.

To deal with PRC Southeast Asianists is not an easy task. Due to time constraints, I have only selected Southeast Asianists who have published single-authored or joint-authored books (or both books and articles). Those who have written only articles published in Southeast Asia's journals in the PRC, but not published a single or joint-authored book, will not be included. This is of course a shortcoming of this chapter. They may have written good and major articles but due to time constraints, I am unable to evaluate them. Nevertheless, I have noticed that many scholars who have published articles in journals or as chapters in books eventually put their articles together and published them as books. In fact, many books published by PRC Southeast Asianists included in this chapter are "collected essays" rather than freshly written books. In addition, only Southeast Asianists who have been active in the past thirty years or so will be discussed. Old "Southeast Asianists" will only be included if they have new publications within this period discussed. Professor Chen Xujing, for instance, is not included in my discussion as his works on ancient Southeast Asian history were published informally in Hong Kong between mid-1955 and early 1960s and circulated among the limited scholars (Zhuang Guotu, 2006).

In their recent articles, Prof. Zhao Heman (2000, p. 529) and Prof. Liang Zhiming et. al., (2002, p. 87) maintain that there are more than 600 Southeast Asianists in the PRC. They did not give details of these Southeast Asianists except that they have done research on Southeast Asia in various institutions in the PRC. Perhaps they constitute the members of China's Southeast Asian Studies Association (中国东南亚研究会) regardless whether they have published academic books or not. Since my definition of Southeast Asianist is narrow, and only include those who have published self-authored or jointly authored books in the last thirty years or so, I could only identify forty-five Southeast Asianists. Of course, this list is only partial as I do not have a complete list of books published by PRC Southeast Asianists. Therefore, this chapter should be regarded as a preliminary survey.

To make my presentation clearer, I have divided them (see Appendix I), into three groups: the first generation (pioneers, born between the 1910s and 1920s), the second generation (born between the 1930s and 1940s) and the third generation (born between the 1950s and 1960s).

FIRST GENERATION SOUTHEAST ASIANISTS

The first generation completed their university training prior to the establishment of the PRC. Originally they were not specialists on subjects related to Southeast Asia but they later moved to study the Southeast Asian region. They are the pioneers of Southeast Asian Studies in the PRC. I have only selected four of them as these are the scholars who were still active in the period that this chapter covers: Professors Yao Nan, Zhu Jieqin, Han Zhenhua, and Tien Ju-kang (Tian Rukang). The first three passed away in the 1990s. Examining the background, training and publications of these three scholars, one immediate impression is that all of them were born in mainland China and received their basic university education in pre-Mao China.

Yao was in Singapore for seven years after graduation and was one of the founders of China's Nanyang Society in Singapore (1940), but he returned to China before the Japanese Occupation. He taught at various universities (including Fudan), promoting Southeast Asian Studies. In the 1980s, he was still active in translating English books on Southeast Asian history into Chinese and published two collections of his essays in 1984 and 1995. Zhu and Han did not have a chance to go overseas for further studies. They were mainly dealing with Chinese historical records and were interested in China's historical relations with Southeast Asia and beyond. Zhu Jieqin taught the history of the overseas Chinese and in 1992 published a book on the topic, while Han published China's foreign relations with Southeast Asia (1992).

Only Tien Ju-kang who was born in Yunnan and graduated at a Chinese university soon after the end of World War II, obtained the opportunity to go to London University. He received a doctoral degree with a dissertation on the social structure of the Shan states between Yunnan and Burma. But his most memorable work is the social structure of the Chinese in Sarawak (1953), which has become a classic. Nevertheless, Tien continued his research on the indigenous minorities in Southeast Asia in the 1980s but not on Southeast Asian Chinese anymore. Tien is also one of the few leading anthropologists in China.

In fact, apart from the four scholars, Prof. Liang Liji and Prof. Xu Younian, who were born in the 1920s, should also be included in this category. However, as they were "returned overseas Chinese" and only "returned" to the motherland after the establishment of the PRC, I have classified them under the second generation.

SECOND GENERATION SOUTHEAST ASIANISTS

There are about 21 Southeast Asianists. In addition to the abovementioned two (that is, Liang Liji and Xu Younian), there are Zhou Nanjing, Liang Yingming, Liang Zhiming, Zhang Yu'an, Wu Lehua, Zhang Xizhen, Huang Kunzhang, Kong Yuanzhi, Lin Jinzhi, Liao Shaolian, Li Guoliang, Cai Renlong, Wen Guangyi, Wen Beiyan, Zhao Heman Chen Qiaozhi, Wu Fengbin, Yu Dingbang and He Shengda. All of them completed their university training after the establishment of the PRC. They came from both northern and southern institutions.

Looking at their background, 10 are "returned overseas Chinese" (*guiqiao* 归侨), mainly from Indonesia and 11 are local-born. With the exception of Chen Qiaozhi who was an economist and Zhang Xizhen, a international relations scholar, all are either history graduates or oriental languages majors. During their days, other social science disciplines were not yet popular (introduced) to Chinese universities. Nevertheless, these scholars did not confine their research and writings to their original disciplines. In addition, they have a common characteristic: they were the products of local Chinese universities.

There is no doubt that Peking University is one of the centres of Southeast Asian Studies in China. Scholars, many of whom were originally from Indonesia, came to study and later became the core of this group. Liang Liji, Zhou Nanjing, and Liang Yingming, were joined by Liang Zhiming and Kong Yuanzhi and others to form the core group. Liang Yingming, Liang Zhiming and Zhou Nanjing jointly wrote a text book on contemporary history of Southeast Asia, published in 1994. Each of them has a specialized area, publishing books individually.

Zhou, a professor at the Peking University, has been active and prolific. His most important achievement, in my view, is perhaps his major projects: *Dictionary* (one volume, 1993) and *Encyclopedia of Overseas Chinese* (1993–2002, twelve volumes). He served as the editor-in-chief of the above-mentioned dictionary and encyclopedia. The project on the encyclopedia is particularly impressive. Of course his colleagues such as Liang Yingming, Liang Zhiming and He Fangquan, together with twenty-three other scholars on "overseas Chinese", were instrumental in completing the gigantic project. Zhou has also edited a number of important source books: Materials on Assimilation Problems in Indonesia (1996); Materials on Anti-Chinese Movements in Indonesia (1998), and Citizenship Problems of Chinese Overseas (2005). His own research works focused on Indonesia and the Philippines and he has published three collections of his articles (1993, 1995 and 2004).

Liang Zhiming is currently known as the most outstanding Chinese historian on Vietnam. He had stayed and studied in Hanoi as a post-graduate student. Nevertheless, his interest has been the study of colonialism in Southeast Asia. He led a team of young scholars and published a book on the subject in 1999.

Liang Liji was one of the founders of the Indonesian language section and has trained many Indonesianists at the Peking University. His major contribution has been in the teaching of the Indonesian language and literature and was the editor-in-chief of the large Indonesian-Chinese dictionary (1989). He was later invited to the UKM and produced a publication on the Ming dynasty relations and Melaka in Malay (1996). Kong Yuanzi, a Shanghainese who also studied at Peking University, probably under Liang, also emerged as a major figure in the field. Kong, who studied about a year at the University of Indonesia, has translated many Indonesian and Malay novels and short stories, took part in the dictionary project and published a large number of essays on the Indonesian language, culture and overseas Chinese. Later these essays were collected in book form (1992, 1999). One of the articles on Indonesian Chinese loan words received a prize from Peking University. He published two books in Malay and Indonesian on Zheng He (Cheng Ho). His colleague, Zhang Yu'an, a Chinese Northerner and a graduate of the Indonesian studies at Peking University, is a specialist on Indonesian folklore and has published several books on the topic (1999, 2003).

Zhang Xizhen, a native of Honan, was also a graduate of the Department of International Relations, Peking University. He pursued his post-graduate studies at Illinois University, is now a professor at his alma mater and has since published two books: One on Southeast Asian politics (1992) and the other on Southeast Asian governments and politics (1999).

In the southern universities and research institutions, there are also many *guiqiao* Southeast Asianists. Many are centred in four higher institutions: Xiamen University, Jinan University, Sun Yat-sen University and Guangxi University.

Zhu Jieqin (mentioned earlier among the first generation Southeast Asianists) was based in Jinan. He helped to develop overseas Chinese studies in the university and served as the series editor of books on overseas Chinese history. But the second generation Southeast Asianists mentioned here — Chen Qiaozhi, Li Xueming, Huang Kunzhang, Wen Beiyan and Pan Yatun — were not his students. Chen majored in economics and has been interested in Singapore (1992). He gradually expanded his field to include ASEAN countries. He has also published a book on the economies of overseas Chinese (1998). Li Xueming, a returned overseas Chinese from Indonesia, published a book on Indonesian Chinese history (1987; 2005) together with Huang Kunzhang. Li also translated two Indonesian Chinese history books. Huang Kunzhang, his colleague, focused his study initially on Indonesian Chinese, then moved on to cover overseas Chinese in Australia (1998) and Canada (2001), but his largest number of works has been on the Chinese in Indonesia. He authored a book on contemporary Indonesian Chinese history (2005) and numerous articles, which were later published as books (2000). Huang's contemporary, Wen Beiyan, published a book on Indonesian education and another on the Indonesian economy and society (1989 and 1997). Pan Yatun, a China-born, has been active in researching on overseas Chinese literature, with special reference to Southeast Asia (1995, 1996 and 2002). He has also edited several volumes of literary works of Southeast Asian Chinese writers.

Xiamen University has a strong centre but initially did not have many second generation scholars. Han Zhenhua (mentioned among the first generation) was from Xiamen University. Again, a few Southeast Asianists that I have selected — Li Guoliang, Wu Fengbin, Cai Renlong and Lin Jinzhi — are not Han's students. Li, a graduate in History from Wuhan University, published on the economic history of the Chinese Overseas (1998). Wu Fengbin jointly wrote a general history of the overseas Chinese in Southeast Asia (1994). He was also a co-editor of the first volume of *Gong An Bu*, the Minutes of the Board Meetings of the Chinese Council in Batavia (Indonesia) around the eighteenth century, together with Leonard Blusse of Leiden University (2002). The publication was based on a joint project between Leiden University and Xiamen University, and so far five volumes have been published since 2002 and it involved many Xiamen University graduates, especially those who were in the Netherlands. *Gong An Bu* is an important primary source for the writing of Chinese history in Java.

Cai Renlong, originally from Indonesia, graduated in Indonesian studies at the Peking University and co-authored a book on Indonesian history with

Wen Guangyi (1985). He later published a single-authored book on Indonesian Chinese society (2000). Lin Jinzhi was born in Malaya and graduated in history from Xiamen University. He later specialized in overseas Chinese investment and businesses in China (1983, 1988).

Sun Yat-sen University also has a Southeast Asian programme but only Wen Guangyi and Yi Dingbang are discussed in this chapter. Wen originally came from Jakarta and was educated in China where he jointly wrote a book on the history of Indonesian Chinese in 1985 with Cai Renlong. Yu, on the other hand, was born in China and graduated in history from Xiamen University but stayed to teach in his alma mater. He specializes in China-Myanmar relations (2000) and published a Modern History of Southeast Asia (1996, 2003 revised edition).

In Guangxi and Yunnan, Zhao Heman and He Shengda are two leading figures. The former focused on the history of the Indochinese states but also worked on contemporary Cambodia (1985) and Vietnam (1995). He Shengda focused on Myanmar (1992) and the Indochinese states, and has also produced a general history of Southeast Asian society and culture (1996) and contemporary Southeast Asia (1998).

THIRD GENERATION SOUTHEAST ASIANISTS

As the second generation Southeast Asianists are either retired or retiring, those in the third generation have come to assume their leadership positions. Unlike those in the second generation, all of the third generation scholars were born in China. Their basic university education was in China but many have been overseas for research or further studies. Some of their works are oriented towards the disciplines but many are still linked to overseas Chinese. Nevertheless, works on contemporary Southeast Asian affairs by them are appearing.

Of these third generation Southeast Asianists, twenty have been selected based on their publications. These are: Liang Minhe, Wu Xiao'an, Wei Min, Zhuang Guotu, Li Minghuan, Yuan Bingling, Zeng Ling, Chen Yande, Shen Hongfang, Wang Qin, Liu Hong, Tang Lizhi, Cao Yunhua, Wang Xinsheng, Yuan Ding, Zhang Yinglong, Zhou Yu'e, Gu Xiaosong, Wang Shilu and Wang Zhengyi.

Let us start from the north. At Peking University, the Southeast Asianists consists of those in traditional disciplines of language and history as well as in political science and law. Wei Min, a Ph.D. in International Politics from Peking University, is teaching at the same university. He recently published a book on nationalism and regionalism in ASEAN (2005).

Liang Minhe, who is a graduate from the Indonesian studies at Peking University, jointly published a general book with Kong Yuanzhi on Indonesian culture and society. Amsterdam-trained Wu Xiaoan published his impressive dissertation on Chinese business in the making of the Malay States (2003). He was originally a graduate from Xiamen University and received a scholarship to study in the Netherlands.

In the south at Xiamen University, which appears to be the strongest in Southeast Asian Studies in the PRC at the moment, has a larger number of Southeast Asianists. Zhuang Guotu is most prolific. Zhuang, who was a local university product, has also been to Leiden University as a visiting scholar in the Department of History for about two years. He published his first book in 1989 on China's policy towards the overseas Chinese during the feudal era (in Chinese). Since then he has authored, translated and edited about fifteen books, mainly on the Chinese overseas. His latest joint-authored book is on the changing position of the Southeast Asian Chinese (2003).

Li Minghuan also graduated from Xiamen University but she went for post-graduate studies at Amsterdam University and obtained a doctorate degree. She studied Southeast Asian Chinese migrant communities in Europe and published a book on the subject (in English). Besides she also wrote in Chinese and published a book on overseas Chinese organizations with special reference to Southeast Asia (1995). Another Chinese graduate from Xiamen University who did a Ph.D. in Leiden is Yuan Bingling. Her well-researched dissertation on the Chinese *kongsi* in Kalimantan, has also been published and favourably reviewed (2000). Both Yuan and Li Minghuan were involved in the *Gong An Bu* project, an important source book mentioned earlier.

Xiamen graduates such as Zeng Ling (Ph.D.) and Chen Yande (M.A.) have also published their works. The former has lived in Singapore for many years and published a few books on Singapore Chinese culture and history (2003), while the latter has stayed in the Philippines and published two books on the Philippine Chinese (1998, 2002) and one book on nationalism in Southeast Asia (2004). Shen Hongfang, who holds an M.A. degree in Economics, has also taught at Xiamen University. She is a specialist in the Philippines and has published at least two books, one on the Philippines (1985) and the other on East Asian economic development models (2002). Wang Qin is also a Xiamen University alumnus. He obtained both his B.A. and M.A. in Economics from the same university. He has published a book on Singapore's economy (1995) and edited a few books, mainly on Southeast Asian economies.

Liu Hong, a native of Fujian, who is teaching at the National University of Singapore (NUS) is also a Xiamen graduate. He is included in this study because he still has close links with Xiamen University. He received a Ph.D. in History from Ohio University, wrote a dissertation on Indonesian history and has published a few books. Two of his books are on Southeast Asia: One is a collection of his essays on various aspects of Southeast Asian Studies (2000) and the other is a case study on Singapore (2003). He has also jointly authored a book (in English) on Singapore with a colleague (2004). Tang Lizhi, the youngest selected in this study, obtained a Ph.D. in Economics from Xiamen University, and has recently published his dissertation on overseas Chinese FDI in China (2003), which is a new subject.

In Jinan, Cao Yunhua, Zhang Yinglong, and Zhou Yu'e may be considered as "new blood". Cao wrote many books on Singapore (1992, 1997), ASEAN (1995), and the ethnic Chinese (2001). Zhang Yinglong co-authored the book on Singapore and Malaysia but his specialty was on Malaysia (1991), while Zhou Yu'e specialized in Chinese education in Southeast Asia (1996).

In Sun Yat-sen University, Wang Xinsheng and Yuan Ding are most prominent. Wang published a single-authored book on modern politics and diplomacy of Southeast Asia (1998) and a few other jointly authored books, while Yuan Ding authored two books on contemporary China's policy towards overseas Chinese (1994, 2002).

In Guangxi, Gu Xiaosong specializes in Vietnam. He has published two books: Vietnamese economic reform (1992) and Vietnamese socialism (1998). In Yunnan, Wang Shilu studies contemporary Cambodia and has published two books on the country (1998, 1999). He has also co-authored two books on ASEAN (1998, 1999).

Last but not least, I would like to mention Wang Zhengyi, a Ph.D. in Economics from Nankai University. He went to New York University and France for his post-doctoral research and has published a book on geo-politics with special reference to Southeast Asian development. (1997). Unlike the previous scholars who are affiliated with universities strong in Southeast Asian Studies, Wang first taught at his alma mater which is not known for its area studies. He has now moved to teach at Peking University.

CONCLUDING REMARKS

Academic research is closely linked to political and economic developments. The development of Southeast Asian Studies in China is no exception. Without a freer environment and substantial research funding, it is bound to be hindered and slow. Only when Deng Xiaoping introduced the Four Modernization Programmes was Southeast Asian Studies in China able to enjoy a faster growth.

As mentioned, PRC Southeast Asianists can be divided into three generations. It was only during the second generation that the returned overseas Chinese from Southeast Asia began to play a major role in this scholarship. Nevertheless, they were joined by the China-born scholars in developing the studies. But by the third generation, Southeast Asian Studies have come under the purview of the China-born scholars.

It is worth noting that the four first generation scholars mentioned above, with the exception of Tien Jukang, were mainly well versed in Chinese; while half of the number of the second generation scholars are well-versed in both Chinese and one Southeast Asian language (e.g. Indonesian) as they were *guiqiao* from Indonesia. Nevertheless, there were also two China-born scholars who majored in Indonesian. The third generation scholars have varying degrees in their command of English but none are able to use any Southeast Asian language in their works.

During the first two generations, the focus of their research was mainly historical and related to overseas Chinese in Southeast Asia. The study of so-called "Southeast Asian Studies proper" was limited (e.g. Tien Jukang's dissertation). Generally, the academic credentials of these Southeast Asianists were limited to basic degrees from Chinese universities, and very few of them were able to conduct fieldwork in the Southeast Asian region prior to 1980. Even during the 1980s, due to limited resources — both financial and research materials — PRC Southeast Asianists were still unable to do much fieldwork and had limited opportunities to learn from their counterparts overseas.

As a result, many relied on secondary sources and second-hand knowledge. Their publications have often reflected these shortcomings. Nevertheless, many second generation PRC Southeast Asianists organized themselves and produced some impressive collective works (such as an encyclopedia and general history of the overseas Chinese). It seems that the strongest works of PRC second generation Southeast Asianists are still those based on Chinese sources rather than original Southeast Asian or Western sources. In addition, their strength is still more on overseas Chinese studies rather than non-Chinese Southeast Asian Studies.

Although the third generation PRC Southeast Asianists still received their first academic training from Chinese universities, quite a few have nevertheless also gone overseas, either as research students or visiting scholars. A few even obtained their Ph.D.s from the West. These Southeast Asianists not only received Western social science training, but also had better command of Western languages (including English). Some have published high quality works, comparable to the works of their counterparts overseas.

Nevertheless, the majority of PRC Southeast Asianists' works are in Chinese, and hence these are not read by non-Chinese speakers. Southeast Asianists in this region and in the West are not familiar with the Chinese works, therefore, it is important for China's Southeast Asianists to publish works in English, or at least, have some good works translated into English.

My observations are quite similar to those made by a few Chinese professors such as Zhao Heman and Liang Zhiming, et al. There is no doubt that the PRC has made some achievements in the field of Southeast Asian Studies, however the studies still suffer from a number of shortcomings such as low academic quality, poor coordination leading to duplication of work already done by others, and weak basic, as well as applied, research.

Liang Zhiming, et al. concluded in their article: "Compared with the advanced international standards...the present stage of China's Southeast Asian Studies still has a considerably big gap in theory, methodology and organization."

Nevertheless, like mainland Chinese scholars, I am also quite optimistic regarding the future of Southeast Asian Studies in the PRC. With the rise of China as an economic power and the importance of Southeast Asia for China, more attention will be given to the studies of this area. With the continuing liberalization, Chinese scholars will also be able to venture into various fields and produce more Southeast Asianists with their excellent works.

REFERENCES

Cai Renlong (蔡仁龙).《东南亚著名华侨华人传》[The Biographies of the Overseas Chinese in Southeast Asia]. 北京：海洋出版社, 1986.

———.《印尼华侨与华人概论》[A General Overview of the Overseas Chinese and Ethnic Chinese of Indonesia]. 香港：南岛出版社, 2000.

———.《印度尼西亚华人企业集团研究》[A Study of Indonesian Chinese Business Groups]. 香港：香港社会科学出版社有限公司, 2004.

Cao Yunhua (曹云华),《新加坡的精神文明》[The Spiritual Civilization of Singapore]. 广州：广东人民出版社, 1992.

———.《东南亚的区域合作》[Regional Co-operation in Southeast Asia]. 广州：华南理工大学, 1995.

———.《新加坡启示录》[The Inspirations Gained from Singapore]. 北京：中国对外经济贸易出版社, 1997.

———.《变异与保持: 东南亚华人的文化适应》[Change and Continuity: The Cultural Adaptation of Southeast Asian Chinese]. 北京：中国华侨出版社, 2001.

Chen Qiaozhi (陈乔之) and Cao Yunhua (曹云华).《新加坡的宏观经济管理》[The Macro Economic Management of Singapore]. 广州：广东人民出版社, 1992.

Chen Qiaozhi (陈乔之) 等著.《冷战后东盟国家对华政策研究》 [Post-Cold War ASEAN Policies towards Ethnic Chinese]. 北京：中国社会科学院, 2001.

Chen Qiaozhi (陈乔之).《华侨华人社会经济研究》 [The Study of the Overseas Chinese Society and Economy]. 香港：地平线出版社, 1998.

Chen Yande (陈衍德).《现代中的传统 — 菲律宾华人社会研究》 [Tradition in Modernity: A Study of Philipine Chinese Society]. 厦门：厦门大学出版社, 1998.

———.《集聚与弘扬 — 海外的福建人社团》 [Fukienese Associations Overseas]. 长沙：湖南人民出版社, 2002.

Fang Xiongpu (方雄普).《朱波散记 — 缅甸华人社会掠影》 [Profiles of Burmese Chinese Society]. 香港：南岛出版社, 2000.

Gong An Bu《公案簿：吧城华人公馆（吧国公堂）档案》 [Minutes of the Board Meetings of the Chinese Council of Batavia]，1–3 册. 厦门：厦门大学出版社, 2002–2005.

Gu Xiaosong (古小松).《越南的经济改革》 [Economic Reforms in Vietnam]. 南宁：广西人民出版社, 1992.

———.《越南的社会主义》 [Vietnamese Socialism]. 南宁：广西人民出版社, 1998.

Guo Liang (郭梁，即李国梁).《东南亚华侨华人经济简史》 [A Short History of Southeast Asian Chinese]. 北京：经济科学出版社, 1998.

He Shengda (贺圣达).《缅甸史》 [History of Burma]. 人民出版社, 1992.

———.《东南亚文化发展史》 [History of Southeast Asian Cultural Developments]. 云南：云南人民出版社, 1996.

He Shengda (贺圣达), Ma Yong (马勇) and Wang Shilu (王士录).《走向21世纪的东南亚与中国》 [Southeast Asia and China towards the Twenty-first Century]. 昆明：云南大学出版社, 1998.

Huang Kunzhang (黄昆章).《风雨沧桑五十年 — 第二次世界大战后印尼华侨华人社会的变化》 [Changes in Indonesian Chinese Society after World War II]. 香港：丹青出版社, 2000.

———.《印尼华侨史（1950至今)》 [Indonesia's Overseas Chinese History]. 广州：广东高等教育出版社, 2005.

Han Zhenhua (韩振华).《中国与东南亚关系史研究》 [A Study of Historical Relations between China and Southeast Asia]. 南宁：广西人民出版社, 1992.

———.《南海诸岛史地研究》 [A Geographical and Historical Study of South Seas Islands]. 北京：社会科学文献出版社, 1996.

Kong Yuanzhi (孔远志).《印度尼西亚语发展史》 [Historical Development of the Indonesian Language]. 北京：北京大学出版社, 1992.

———.《印度尼西亚文体学》 [Styles of the Indonesian Language]. 北京：北京大学出版社, 1993.

———. *Sam Po Kong dan Indonesia* [Cheng Ho and Indonesia]. Jakarta: Haji Masagung, 1993.

________. 《中国与印度尼西亚文化交流》 [Cultural Interactions between China and Southeast Asia]. 北京： 北京大学出版社, 1999.

________. 《印度尼西亚马来西亚文化探析》 (An analysis of Indonesian and Malaysian cultures). 香港： 南岛出版社, 2000.

________. *Pelayaran Zheng He dan Alam Melayu* [Cheng Ho's Voyages and the Malay World]. Bangi: Universiti Kebangsaan Malaysia, 2000.

Lai Bojiang (赖伯疆). 《海外华文文学概观》 [A General View of Overseas Chinese Literature in China]. 广州： 花城出版社, 1991.

________. 《东南亚华文戏剧概观》 [A General View of Chinese Drama in Southeast Asia]. 北京： 中国戏剧出版社, 1993.

Lai, Frances. *State of East and Southeast Asian Studies Since 1979 in China, Hong Kong and Singapore.* Hong Kong: Lingnan College, 1987.

Li Guoliang (李国梁, 即郭梁) 合著. 《华侨华人与中国革命建设》 [Overseas Chinese and China Revolutionary Construction]. 福州： 福建人民出版社, 1993.

Li Minghuan (李明欢). 《当代海外华人社团研究》 [A Study of Contemporary Overseas Chinese Associations]. 厦门： 厦门大学出版社, 1995.

________. *We Need Two Worlds: Chinese Immigration Associations in a Western Society.* Amsterdam: Amsterdam University Press, 1999.

Li Xuemin (李学民) and Huang Kunzhang (黄昆章) 合著. 《印尼华侨史(古代至 1949 年)》 [Indonesia Overseas Chinese History: From Ancient Times to 1949]. 广州： 广东高等教育出版社, 2005.

Liang Liji (梁立基) 主编. 《新印度尼西亚语汉语词典》 [Kamus Baru Bahasa Indonesia-Tionghoa]. 北京： 商务印书馆, 1989.

________. *Hubungan Empayar Melaka-Dinasti Ming Abad Ke-15* [Relations between Malacca Empire and Ming China]. Bangi: Penerbit Universiti Kebangsaan Malaysia, 1996.

________. 《印度尼西亚文学史》 [History of Chinese Literature]. 上下册, 北京: 昆仑出版社, 2003.

Liang Minhe (梁敏和) and Kong Yanzhi (孔远志). 《印度尼西亚文化与社会》 [Indonesia Society and Culture]. 北京： 北京大学出版社, 2002.

Liang Yingming (梁英明). 《融合与发展: 东南亚华人研究论文集》 [Integration and Development: Collected Essays on Southeast Asian Chinese]. 香港： 南岛出版社, 1999.

________. 《战后东南亚华人社会变化研究》 [A Study of Post-war Chinese Society in Southeast Asia]. 北京： 昆仑出版社, 2001.

Liang Yingming (梁英明) and Liang Zhiming (梁志明)等著. 《近现代东南亚(1511–1992)》 [Modern Southeast Asia 1511–1992]. 北京： 北京大学出版社, 1994.

Liang Zhiming (梁志明) 等著. 称 《殖民主义史： 东南亚卷》 [History of Colonialism: Southeast Asia]. 北京： 北京大学出版社, 1999.

________. 张锡镇、杨保筠, 《面向新世纪的中国东南亚研究回顾与展望 [China's Southeast Asian Studies towards a New Century: Retrospect and Prospect]

《南洋问题研究》 [Research on Southeast Asian Problems], 2002(1): 86–93.

———. 《东南亚历史文化与现代化：学术论文集》 [Historical Culture and Modernization in Southeast Asia]. 香港：香港社会科学出版社, 2003.

Liao Shaolian (廖少廉). 《东盟国家经济发展动态》 [ASEAN Economic Development]. 北京：社会科学文献出版社, 1990.

Lin Jinzhi (林金枝). 《近代华侨投资国内企业史研究》 [A Study of Overseas Chinese Investments History in China Domestic Industry]. 福州：福建人民出版社, 1983.

———. 《近代华侨投资国内企业概论》 [A General Introduction to Overseas Chinese Investments in China Industry in Recent History]. 厦门：厦门大学出版社, 1988.

Liu Hong (刘宏). 《中国 — 东南亚学：理论架构，互动模式，个案分析》 [Sino-Southeast Asian Studies]. 北京：中国社会科学院出版社, 2000.

———. 《战后新加坡华人社会的嬗变：本土关怀，区域网络，全球视野》 [Change of Post-war Singapore Chinese Society]. 厦门：厦门大学出版社, 2003.

——— and Wong Sin-Kiong. *Singapore Chinese Society in Transition: Business, Politics, & Socio-economic Change, 1945–1965*. New York: Peter Lang, 2004.

———. "Southeast Asian Studies in Greater China", *Kyoto Review of Southeast Asia* (March 2003), 7 pages, <http://kyotoreview.cseas.kyoto-u.ac.jp/issue/issue2/article_p.232_p.html> 10/28/2005.

Liu Yongzuo (刘永焯). 《中国东南亚研究的回顾与前瞻》 [China Southeast Asian Studies: Retrospect and Prospects]. 广州：广东人民出版社, 1994.

Pan Yatun (潘亚暾). 《海外华文文学现状》 [Present Situation of Overseas Chinese Literature in Chinese]. 北京：人民文学出版社, 1996.

———. 《儒商列传》 [Biographies of Confucian Businessmen]. 广州：暨南大学出版社, 1995.

———. 《新加坡作家作品评论集》 [Reviews of Singapore Chinese Writers and Their Works]. 新加坡：新加坡文艺协会, 2002.

Shen Hongfang (沈红芳), 著. 《菲律宾》 [The Philippines]. 上海：上海辞书出版社, 1985.

———. 《东亚经济发展比较模式研究》 (Comparative Studies of East Asian Economic Development Models), 厦门：厦门大学出版社, 2002.

Sun Fusheng (孙福生). 《印度尼西亚现代政治史纲》 [Modern Political History of Indonesia: An Outline]. 厦门：厦门大学出版社, 1989.

Tang Lizhi (唐礼智). 《东南亚华人企团对外直接投资研究》 [Southeast Asian Business Groups and Foreign Direct Investments]. 厦门：厦门大学出版社, 2004.

Tien Ju-kang (Tian Rukang, 田汝康). *The Chinese of Sarawak: A Study of Social Structure*. London School of Economic and Political Science, Department of Anthropology, 1953.

Tien Ju-kang and Barbara E. Ward. *The Early History of the Chinese in Sarawak*. London, n.p., 1956.

Tien Jukang, *Religious Cults of the Pai-I along the Burma-Yunnan Border*. Ithaca: N.Y.: Southeast Asian Program, Cornell University, 1986.

Wang Gungwu et al., *Southeast Asian Studies in China: A Report*. Canberra: Research School of Pacific Studies, Australian National University, 1981.

Wang Qin (王勤). 《新加坡经济发展研究》 [A Study of Singapore's Economy]. 厦门：厦门大学出版社, 1995.

Wang Qin and others (王勤) 等著.《当代新加坡》 [Contemporary Singapore]. 成都：四川人民出版社, 1995.

Wang Shilu (王士录). 《当代柬埔寨》 [Contemporary Cambodia]. 成都：四川人民出版社, 1994.

———. 《当代柬埔寨经济》 [Contemporary Cambodian Economy]. 昆明：云南大学出版社, 1999.

Wang Shilu (王士录) and Wang Guoping (王国平). 《从东盟到大东盟：东盟30年发展研究》 [From ASEAN to Great Alliance]. 北京：世界知识, 1998.

———. 《走向21世纪的东盟与亚太：东盟的发展趋势及其对亚太的影响》 [ASEAN and Asia-Pacific towards the 21st Century]. 北京：当代世界出版社, 1999.

Wang Xinsheng （汪新生）. 《现代东南亚政治与外交》 [Modern Southeast Asian Politics and Diplomacy]. 南宁：广西人民出版社, 1998.

Wang Zhengyi (王正毅). 《地缘地带发展论：世界体系与东南亚的发展》 [World System and the Development of Southeast Asia]. 上海：上海人民出版社, 1997.

Wei Min (韦民). 《民族主义与地区主义的互动：东盟研究新视角 [Interactions between Nationalism and Regionalism: A Study of ASEAN from a New Perspective]. 北京：北京大学出版社, 2005.

Wen Beiyan (温北炎)等, 《印度教育》 [Indonesian Education). 广州：广东高等教育出版社, 1989.

———. 《印度尼西亚社会与经济》 [Indonesian Society and Economy]. 广州：暨南大学出版社, 1997.

Wen Guangyi （温广益）等著. 《印度尼西亚华侨史》 [History of Indonesian Chinese]. 香港：海洋出版社, 1985.

Wu Fengbin (吴凤斌) 等著. 《东南亚华侨通史》 [A General History of Southeast Asian Overseas Chinese]. 福州：福建人民出版社, 1994.

Wu Lehua （巫乐华）. 《南洋华侨史话》 [A Popular History of Nanyang Chinese]. 天津：天津教育出版社, 1991.

Wu Xiaoan (吴小安). *Chinese Business in the Making of Malay State 1882–1941*. London and New York: Routledge, 2003.

Xu Younian (许友年). 《印尼华人马来语文学》 [Indonesian Chinese Literature in Malay]. 广州：华城出版社, 1992.

Xu Younian (许友年). 《论马来民歌》 [On Malay Pantun]. 福州: 福建人民出版社, 1984.

———. 《马来民歌研究》 [A Study of Malay Pantun]. 香港: 南岛出版社, 2000.

Yao Nan (姚楠). 《中国对东南亚史的研究》 [Chinese Studies on Southeast Asia], 載于姚楠, 《星云椰雨集》. 新加坡: 新加坡新闻与出版社有限公司, 1984, pp. 218–40.

———. 《南天余墨》 [Writings while Staying in the South]. 沈阳: 辽宁大学出版社, 1995.

Yu Dingbang (余定邦). 《中缅关系史》 [Historical Relations of China-Burma]. 北京: 光明日报, 2000.

———. 《东南亚近代史》 [Modern History of Southeast Asia]. 贵州: 贵州人民出版社, 1996 (2003 第二版).

Yuan Bingling (袁冰凌). *Chinese Democracies: A Study of Kongsis of West Borneo (1776–1884)*, Leiden: Universiteit Leiden, 2000.

Yuan Ding (袁丁). 《晚清侨务与中外交涉》 [Overseas Chinese Affairs during the Late Qing Dynasty]. 西安: 西北大学出版社, 1994.

———. 《近代侨政研究》 [A Study of Recent Overseas Chinese Affairs]. 香港: 天马图书有限公司, 2002.

Zeng Ling (曾玲). 《越洋再建家园: 新加坡华人社会文化研究》 [A Study of Singapore Chinese Society and Culture]. 南昌: 江西高校出版社, 2003.

Zhang Xizhen (张锡镇). 《东南亚政府与政治》 [Government and Politics of Southeast Asia]. 台北: 扬智文化事业有限公司, 1999.

———. 《当代东南亚政治》 [Contemporary Southeast Asian Politics]. 南宁: 广西人民出版社, 1994 (1995 第二版).

———. 《西哈努克家族》 [The Sihanouk Family]. 北京: 社会科学文献出版社, 1996.

Zhang Yinglong (张应龙) 合著. 《新加坡马来西亚华侨史》 [Singapore and Malaysia Overseas Chinese Histories]. 广州: 广东高等教育出版社, 1991.

Zhang Yu'an (张玉安) 主编. 《东南亚古代神话传说》 [Ancient Fairy Tales and Legends of Southeast Asia]. (东方神话传说, 第 6–7 卷) 上下册. 北京: 北京大学出版社, 1999.

Zhang Yu'an (张玉安), Pei Xiaorui (裴晓睿) 合著. 《印度的罗摩故事与东南亚文学》 [The Indian Ramayana and Southeast Asian Literature]. 北京: 昆仑出版社, 2005.

Zhang Yu'an (张玉安), Chen Shulong (陈树龙) 主编. 《东方民间文学比较》 [Comparison Oriental Folktales]. 北京: 北京大学出版社, 2003.

Zhao Heman (赵和曼). 《迈向 21 世纪的中国东南亚研究》 [China Southeast Asian Studies towards the 21st Century]. 載于陈乔之(主编), 《面向 21 世纪的东南亚: 改革与发展》. 广州: 暨南大学出版社, 2000, pp. 529–36.

———. 《柬埔寨》 [Cambodia]. 南宁: 广西人民出版社, 1985.

———. 《越南经济的发展》 [Economic Development of Vietnam]. 北京：中国华侨出版社, 1995.

———. 《东南亚手册》 [Handbook of Southeast Asia]. 南宁：广西人民出版社, 1998.

———. 《少数民族华侨华人研究》 [A Study of China Minorities and Overseas Chinese]. 北京：中国华侨出版社, 2004.

Zheng Xueyi (郑学益) 主编. 《商战之魂》 [Soul of Business War]. 北京：北京大学出版社, 1997.

Zhou Nanjing (周南京). 《风雨同舟: 东南亚与华人问题》 [Problems of Southeast Asian Chinese]. 北京：中国华侨出版社, 1995.

Zhou Nanjing (周南京) 主编. 《世界华侨华人辞典》 [Dictionary of Overseas Chinese]. 北京：北京大学出版社, 1993.

———. 《菲律宾与华人》 [The Philippines and Ethnic Chinese]. 马尼拉：菲律宾华裔青年联合会, 1993.

Zhou Nanjing (周南京) 主编. 《华侨华人百科全书》 [Encyclopedia of Overseas Chinese]. （12 卷），北京：中国华侨出版社， 1998–2003.

———. 《风云变幻看世界 — 海外华人问题及其他》 [Overseas Chinese Problems and Others]. 香港：南岛出版社, 2001.

———. 《华侨华人问题概论》 [A General View on Overseas Chinese Problems]. 香港：香港社会科学出版有限公司, 2003.

Zhou Yu (周聿娥). 《东南亚华文教育》 [Chinese Language Education in Southeast Asia]. 广州：暨南大学出版社, 1996.

Zhu Jieqin (朱杰勤). 《东南亚华侨简史》 [A Short History of Southeast Asian Chinese]. 北京：高等教育出版社, 1990.

Zhuang Guotu (庄国土). 《中国封建政府的华侨政策》 [China Feudal Government Policies toward Overseas Chinese]. 厦门：厦门大学出版社, 1989.

———. 《华侨华人与中国的关系》 [Relations between Overseas Chinese and China]. 广州：广东高等教育出版社, 2001.

Zhuang Guotu (庄国土) 等著. 《二战以后东南亚华族社会地位的变化》 [Post-war Changes in the Social Position of the Chinese in Southeast Asia]. 厦门：厦门大学出版社, 2003.

Zhuang Guotu (庄国土). "Southeast Asian Research in China: A Historical Review" (Paper presented at the International Conference hina and Malaysia in the Era of Globalization: Country, Regional and International Perspectives jointly organized by the Institute of China Studies, University of Malaya, and the Institute of Malaysian Studies, Xiamen University, at the Mines Beach Resort and Spa, Seri Kembangan, Selangor, 21–22 March 2006).

Appendix: PRC Southeast Asianists — Basic Information

First Generation (1910s–1920s)

Name	Birthplace and year	University education	Specialization (Area)	Academic affiliation
Yao Na 姚楠	1912–1997 (China)	B.A. (1929–33) Jinan University	Historian, Chinese foreign relations, translator	Various Chinese universities, including Fudan
Zhu jieqin 朱杰勤	1917–1990 (China)	Post-graduate degree (1936) Zhongshan univ.	Overseas Chinese history	Jinan Univ.
Tien Ju-kang 田汝康	1916 (China)	B.A. from Kunming (B.A. 1940); Ph.D. in Anthropology, London Univ.	Shan in Burma and Chinese in Sarawak	Fudan Univ., Shanghai
Han Zhenhua 韩振华	1921–1993 (China)	B.A. (1946) Xiehe Univ., M.A. (1948) Sun Yat-sen Univ.	Historical relations between China and Southeast Asia	Xiamen Univ.

Second Generation (1930s–1940s)

Name	Birthplace and year	University education	Specialization (Area)	Academic affiliation
Zhang Yu'an 张玉安	1945 (Jilin, China)	B.A. (1969) in Indonesian language, Peking Univ.	Indonesian language and folklores	Peking Univ.
Zhang Xizhen 张锡镇	1947 (China)	B.A. (1976) and M.A. (1983) in International Politics, Peking Univ. Studied at Illinois Univ.	Contemporary Southeast Asian politics, Cambodia	Peking Univ.
Liang Yinming 梁英明	1931 (Indonesia)	B.A. (1960) in World History, Peking Univ.	Chinese in Indonesia, Southeast Asia	Peking Univ.
Liang Zhiming 梁志明	1935 (Changsha, China)	B.A. (1959) in History, Peking Univ. Studied in Hanoi, 1963–66.	Vietnam history, Southeast Asian history	Peking Univ.

Name	Birthplace and year	University education	Specialization (Area)	Academic affiliation
Zhou Nanjing 周南京	1933 (Indonesia)	B.A. (1958) in World History, Peking Univ.	History of Indonesia and Philippines, ethnic Chinese in Indonesia and the Philippines, ASEAN	Peking Univ.
Kong Yuanzhi 孔远志	1937 (Shanghai)	B.A. (1961) in Oriental Languages (Indonesian), studied in Jakarta for a year	Indonesian and Malay language and culture, Zheng He in Indonesia and Malacca	Peking Univ.
Liang Liji* 梁立基	1927 (Indonesia)	B.A. in Oriental Languages from Peking Univ.	Indonesian literature, China-Malaya historical relations	Peking Univ.
Wu Lehua 巫乐华	1937 (born in Guangzhou but grew up in Indonesia)	B.A. (1961) in History in Sun Yat-sen Univ.	Southeast Asian Chinese history, China's policy towards overseas Chinese	Peking Overseas Chinese Council
Wu Fengbin 吴凤斌	1946 (China)	B.A., Sun Yat-sen Univ.	Overseas Chinese in Southeast Asia	Xiamen Univ.
Liao Shaolian 廖少廉	1944 (China)	B.A. (1967) in Economics, Sun Yat-sen Univ.	ASEAN economies in general	Xiamen Univ.
Li Guoliang 李国梁	1942 (Hubei, China)	B.A. (1965) in History, Wuhan Univ.	Southeast Asian economic history in general	Xiamen Univ.
Cai Renlong 蔡仁龙	1931 (Indonesia)	B.A. (1961) in Oriental Languages (Indonesian)	Indonesian Chinese businesses	Xiamen Univ.

Name	Birthplace and year	University education	Specialization (Area)	Academic affiliation
Lin Jinzhi 林金枝	1932 (Malaya)	B.A. (1956) in History, Xiamen Univ.	Overseas Chinese investments and remittances to China	Xiamen Univ.
Wen Guangyi 温广益	1934 Indonesia	B.A. (1960) Sun Yat-sen Univ.	Indonesian Chinese history	Sun Yat-sen Univ.
Yu Dingbang 余定邦	1938 (China)	Postgraduate degree in History, Sun Yat-sen Univ.	Modern history of Southeast Asia, Myanmar	Sun Yat-sen Univ.
Chen Qiaozhi 陈乔之	1942 (China)	B.A. (1966) in Political Economics, Jinan Univ.	Southeast Asian economics in general, Singapore	Jinan Univ.
Huang Kunzhang 黄昆章	1937 (Indonesia)	B.A. (1962) and post-graduate degree (1965) in World History, Kainan Univ.	Ethnic Chinese history in Indonesia, Australia and Canada	Jinan Univ.
Wen Beiyan 温北炎	1940 (Indonesia)	B.A. (1968) in Indonesian Language	Indonesia in general	Jinan Univ.
Zhao Heman 赵和曼	1939 (China)	B.A. in History (1959), Wuhan Univ.	Vietnam and Cambodian history	Guangxi Univ.
He Shengda 贺圣达	1948 (China)	B.A. (1982), M.A. (1985), Yunnan Univ.	Burma, Greater Mekong Region	Yunnan Academy of Social Science
Xu Younian* 许友年	1922 (Indonesia)	Secondary school education, self-taught (returned to China 1951)	Indonesian language and literature	Guangdong Foreign Language Academy

* Please see explanations in the text.

Third Generation (1950s–1960s)

Name	Birthplace and year	University education	Specialization (Area)	Academic affiliation
Liang Minhe 梁敏和	1952 (China)	M.A. (1974) in Indonesian Language, Peking Univ.	Indonesian language and culture	Peking Univ.
Wu Xiaoan 吴小安	1965 (China)	B.A. (1988) & M.A. in History, Xiamen Univ., Ph.D. (1999) in history, Amsterdam	History of the Chinese in Malaysia	Peking Univ.
Wang Zhengyi 王正毅	1965 (China)	B.A. (1986), Ph.D. (1993) in Econ., Nankai Univ. Post-Doc., New York Univ.	Geo-politics of Southeast Asia	Peking Univ.
Wei Min 韦民	1966 (China)	Ph.D. (2003) in law (International Relations)	Regionalism and nationalism in ASEAN	Peking Univ.
Wang Qin 王勤	1958 (China)	B.A. (1982) & M.A (1988) in Economics (Xiamen univ.)	Singapore, Indonesia	Xiamen Univ.
Zeng Ling 曾玲	1954 (Fujian)	Ph.D. in History, Xiamen Univ.	Singapore Chinese History and Folklore	Xiamen Univ.
Shen Hongfang 沈红芳	1953 (China)	M.A. in Economics, China	Philippines, ASEAN	Xiamen Univ.
Zhuang Guotu 庄国土	1952 (Xiamen)	Ph.D. (1989) in History, studied in Leiden.	China's policy towards SEA, overseas Chinese in general	Xiamen Univ.
Li Minghuan 李明欢	1953 (Swatow, China)	M.A. (1982) in History, Xiamen Univ.; Ph.D. (1998) in History, Amsterdam Univ.	Southeast Asian Chinese in general, *Qiaoxiang*, Chinese in Europe	Xiamen Univ.

Name	Birthplace and year	University education	Specialization (Area)	Academic affiliation
Yuan Bingling 袁冰凌	1962 (China)	B.A. in History Xiamen; Ph.D. in History, Amsterdam	Chinese in Indonesia (especially Kalimantan and Batavia)	Fuzhou Univ.
Liu Hong 刘宏	1962 (China)	B.A. (1982) Xiamen Univ., M.A. (1985), Fudan and Ph.D. (1995) in History, Ohio Univ.	History of overseas Chinese in Southeast Asia.	National University of Singapore/ Xiamen Univ.
Chen Yande 陈衍德	1950 (Xiamen, China)	B.A. (1982) and M.A. (1985) in History, Xiamen Univ.	Philippine Chinese	Xiamen Univ.
Wang Xinsheng 汪新生	1952 (China)	B.A. (1982) in History, Peking Univ.; M.A. (1985) Sun Yat-sen Univ.	International politics of Southeast Asia, ASEAN and Chinese overseas	Sun Yat-sen Univ.
Yuan Ding 袁丁	1957 (Guangzhou)	B.A. (1982) from Sun Yat-sen Univ. and Ph.D. (1985) in History from Jinan Univ.	China's policy towards overseas Chinese, Chinese migration	Sun Yat-sen Univ.
Cao Yunhua 曹云华	1956 (China)	B.A. (1982), M.A (1988) Teachers Training Univ., Ph.D (2002) Jinan Univ.	Singapore, Malaysia, ASEAN	Jinan Univ.
Zhang Yinlong 张应龙	1958 (China)	B.A. (1982) in History, and Ph.D. (1994) in History, Jinan Univ.	Chinese in Malaysia	Jinan Univ.
Zhou Yu 砖 周聿娥	1956 (Inner Mongolia)	M.A. (1982) in Contemporary China History and M.A. (1983) in History, Sun Yat-sen Univ.	Chinese education in Southeast Asia	Jinan Univ.

Name	Birthplace and year	University education	Specialization (Area)	Academic affiliation
Gu Xiaosong 古小松	1958 (Guangdong)	B.A. (1982) in Foreign Language, Ph.D. (Jinan)	Vietnam	Guangxi Academy of Social Science
Wang Shilu 王士录	1952 (Yunnan, China)	B.A. (1981) in History, Nankai Univ.	International relations of Southeast Asia; Cambodia	Yunnan Academy of Social Sciences
Tang Lizhi 唐礼智	1970 (China)	B.Sc. (Huadong Normal Univ.) Ph.D. (2002) in Applied Economics, Xiamen Univ.	Foreign Investment, MNC	unknown

Sources: Books cited; information obtained from various websites.

4

The State of Southeast Asian Studies in China: An Institutional Interpretation

Tang Shiping and Zhang Jie

INTRODUCTION

As a region that is historically deeply intertwined with China, Southeast Asia is a natural focus of the Chinese state and its scholarly community. Rather than a comprehensive historical survey of Southeast Asian Studies (hereafter SEAS) in China,[1] our survey will seek to advance an institutional interpretation of it.[2] By an institutional perspective, we mean that we view the pursuit of knowledge as being profoundly influenced by the institutional setting of a scholarly community and the society at large.

Thus, our survey does not intend to provide a comprehensive survey of the history and present status of SEAS in China. Rather, we are more interested in understanding how and why China's SEAS has been shaped by the overall institutional environment, and how its future will continue to be shaped by this institutional environment. More specifically, we seek to underscore that the evolution of Southeast Asian Studies in China has been profoundly shaped by three factors: The changing but steadily increasing demand of the Chinese state, the ever deepening inter-dependence between

China and Southeast Asia (which partly and indirectly influences SEAS in China through influencing the demand from the state), and the rise of the mass media.[3]

The chapter starts with a brief organizational overview of SEAS in China. Next, it briefly reviews the evolution of Southeast Asian Studies after the founding of the People's Republic of China, highlighting several important developments in its evolutionary path. It then connect these shifts with the three institutional factors. Finally, it explores the future of SEAS in China and what can be done to improve its prospect through institutional changes.

SEAS IN CHINA TODAY: THE ORGANIZATIONAL SETTING

The institutional setting of Southeast Asian Studies in China today can be first understood organizationally. It contains three explicit and implicit dimensions of division of labour. The first explicit division of labour is between institutions affiliated with universities and institutions affiliated with central or local Academy of Social Sciences (ASS) (for a brief introduction to these institutions, see Table 4.1). Institutions affiliated with universities have more responsibility for training new generations of scholars, and they usually maintain a graduate programme but also play a role in training undergraduates. In contrast, institutions affiliated with ASS are more-or-less fully dedicated think-tanks and have less responsibility for training new generations of scholars, and these institutions normally maintain only a small graduate programme. Consequently, for a very long time, the flow of graduates has largely been uni-directional from universities to research institutions, although more recently universities have begun to recruit more established scholars from think-tanks now that they can offer a more attractive employment package for scholars. This has been especially obvious in Beijing and Shanghai.

The first explicit division of labour also leads to a second implicit division of labour. Institutions affiliated with central or local ASS are more responsible for advancing policy proposals for central and local governments, while institutions affiliated with universities usually play only a supporting role in these activities. Despite the fact that scholars within institutions affiliated with central or local ASS will usually solicit inputs from scholars who are affiliated with universities when formulating major policy proposals, the final product is usually drafted by scholars from think-tanks.

The third explicit division of labour is between the institutions located at the centre of policy-making (Beijing and Shanghai) and those located in provinces. Those institutions at the centre of policy-making almost exclusively serve the central government, while those in provinces also exclusively serve

Table 4.1
Major Institutions of SEAS in China[4]

Institution	Founding	Number of Regular Staff	Research Journals
Xiamen University SEA Research Institute (Xiamen)[5]	1956/ 2000	20	*Nanyang wenti yanjiu* [Southeast Asian Affairs], quarterly *Nanyang wenti yicong* [Southeast Asian Studies], quarterly
Fujian CAS Institute of Oversea Chinese Studies (IOCS/Fuzhou)	1983	7	*Huaqiao huaren yu qiaowu*, quarterly
Jinan University ISEAS (Guangzhou)	1960	25	*Dongnanya yanjiu* [Southeast Asian Studies], bi-monthly
Jinan University IOCS (Guangzhou)	1981	9	
Zhongsan University ISEAS (Guangzhou)	1959	27	
Guanxi CAS ISEAS (Nanning)[6]	1979/ 1989	21	*Dongnanya zongheng* [Around SEA], (formerly Indochina), monthly
Yunan CAS ISEAS (Kunming)	1981	16	*Dongnanya* [Southeast Asia], quarterly
Zhenzhou University, Inst. of Viet. Studies (Zhenzhou)	N. A.	N. A.	None
Peking University, Centre for SEAS (Beijing)[7]	2002	N. A.	*Beida yatai yanjiu* (Asian Studies in Peking University)[8]
CASS, Inst. Asia-Pacific Studies (IAPS), Beijing	1988	12 (out of 45)	*Dangdai Yatai* [Contemporary Asia-Pacific Studies], monthly
CICIR-Dept. of SEA and Pacific Studies (Beijing)	2002	N. A.	*Xiandai guoji guanxi* [Contemporary International Relations], monthly
Shanghai ASS IAPS (Shanghai)	1990	(N.A.) out of 12	None

the local government. Such a division of labour gives those institutions at the centre better access to national policy-making. Meanwhile, institutions in different provinces are responsible for advancing possible policy recommendations for local governments,[9] although an equally, if not more, important role of regional research institutions is to serve as a sort of lobbying group for the local government.

The division of labour between those institutions at the centre and those at local levels also helps forge a strange relationship between the two sets of institutions. While there is no officially hierarchical relationship between those research institutions at the centre and those at local provinces, there seems to have been an implicit understanding between the two: The latter will pay due respect to the former, if only to make sure that the former will at least not stand in the way when the latter lobbies for a project or an initiative at the centre. These three dimensions of division-of-labour should be kept in mind when trying to understand the institutional aspects of SEAS in China.

THE EVOLUTION OF SEAS IN CHINA: THREE INSTITUTIONAL FACTORS

Three sets of development have largely shaped the evolution of China's SEAS (and its area studies in general). They are: the changing yet steadily increasing demand from the state since the founding of the People's Republic, the rapidly expanding inter-dependence between Southeast Asia and China after the open reform policy, and the rise of the mass media since the 1990s.

A. The Changing Yet Steadily Increasing Demand From the State

The most critical institutional factor that has shaped SEAS (and its international/area studies in general) in China has been the changing yet steadily increasing demand from the state, especially for making its foreign policy. At the beginning of the People's Republic, the decision-making process in foreign policy was tightly controlled and highly concentrated in the Mao-centred Politburo. Within this context, the scholarly community (including think-tanks) had very little input to the foreign policy decision-making process. During this time, the responsibility of understanding Southeast Asian countries (and other countries) was mostly taken by governmental bureaucracies (for example, the foreign ministry, the military, and the intelligence agencies).

Therefore, while some research institutions dedicated to SEAS were established in the later 1950s to early 1960s, and the state did understand that it had to divide the outside world into different areas of studies, the primary task of these institutions was to train students. In other words, these institutions received very little direct demand from the state itself. Partly due to the lack of direct demand from the state during this phase, the first generation of SEAS scholars in China was able to concentrate on their own scholarly interests without having to answer to the demand from the state. As a result, research output published during this time was primarily in two sub-areas: Overseas Chinese studies and historical-cultural studies of Southeast Asia. During this phase, SEAS had yet to blossom fully into an independent discipline of scholarly interest.

The launching of China's open-and-reform policy symbolized not only the end of the era in which ideology dominated foreign policy, but also the gradual decentralization of decision-making in China on at least two fronts. First, the style of the decision-making process in China has become increasingly similar to that of a modern state: In order to formulate effective policies, the state self-consciously solicits inputs from various communities, including governmental agencies, the scholarly community and think-tanks, and retired senior officials. This is due not only to a realization that the research community can contribute constructively to the decision-making process, but also a recognition (or admission) that the state bureaucracy alone cannot meet the increasing demand for understanding the outside world. As China interacts regularly, extensively, and deeply with almost every country of the world, China's growing interests has also gradually spread to every corner of the earth with new problems and issues emerging every day. Under these circumstances, it will be impossible for the state bureaucracy alone to handle the task of understanding such a diverse body of states: Certain jobs will have to be outsourced to the scholarly community (including the think-tanks). This development has facilitated the forging of a new relationship between the state and the scholarly community: While the state has the final say in policy-making and the power and prestige of the scholarly community ultimately depends on the state, the scholarly community has gained real voices in the decision-making process.

The second consequence of decentralization of the decision-making process has been that while major decisions on foreign policy remain tightly controlled by the central government, local governments (especially at the provincial level) will also have to study pressing issues of an ever-increasingly international flavour (for example, border trade, border control, human trafficking, and drug trafficking). As Ash convincingly demonstrated, different sub-regions in China have developed extensive and specialized (economic) connections with the outside world (Ash 2005), and some issues will inevitably arise from these growing connections. These important issues are of immediate concern to local governments, and thus demand their attention. Yet, most of these issues are unlikely to be given priority (and may not be taken care of at all) by the central government in the maze of bureaucracy in Beijing. Under these circumstances, with very limited knowledge and few instruments for understanding the outside world, local governments also need to outsource these tasks to somewhere else, and they naturally turn to local research institutions for help.

Thus, other than further institutionalizing the implicit division-of-labour between institutions at the centre and those at the provincial level, the diffusion of decision-making power from the centre to the local level has also greatly contributed to the overall development of SEAS in China. With greater demand from the local governments, scholars who are affiliated with regional institutions now receive not only far more financial and political support but also respect from local governments. Naturally, regional research institutions are also far busier than they used to be.

These two processes of decentralization of decision-making, coupled with China's ever increasing interaction with the outside world (including Southeast Asia), led to the present situation in which the state increasingly relies on the scholarly community for formulating viable policy proposals. This growing demand from the state, coupled with China's growing wealth, has been finally able to make SEAS (and area studies in general) an important discipline in China (Tang, Zhang, and Cao 2005).

B. The Ever Increasing Inter-dependence Between Southeast Asia and China

The overall political, economic, and social development of Southeast Asia as a region has also played an important role in shaping SEAS in China, primarily from the demand side. Since the open-and-reform policy was implemented, especially since the 1990s, China and ASEAN have developed an increasingly close relationship in economic, political (including traditional and non-traditional security), and cultural areas. As China interacts with Southeast Asian countries more extensively and deeply, there will be a growing demand from the Chinese state to understand Southeast Asian countries in all aspects. This growing demand has also undoubtedly played a critical role in propelling SEAS to its highly visible position in today's China.

These demands come from three primary fronts. The first is to learn the overall developmental experience of Southeast Asian states (mostly Singapore, Malaysia, Thailand, Indonesia, now more recently Vietnam).[10] More recently, the ever increasing economic inter-dependence between ASEAN and China and the launching of the ASEAN-China FTA has also stimulated a growing need to understand the current economic aspects of Southeast Asian countries.

The second is to learn the important lessons from Southeast Asian countries, especially in the area of domestic governance and financial management during the 1997 Asian financial crisis. SEAS scholars and other elites in China are determined that the country must maintain social order and stability in its long road towards a modern state, and they are determined to avoid the social turmoil experienced by some Southeast Asian countries (for example, the Philippines). In fact, the effort to understand political and social transitions in Southeast Asian countries has been part of a larger effort to grapple with the enormously daunting task of managing modernization while maintaining social and political stability.

The third is to learn the "ASEAN Way", and more generally, the foreign policy and security behaviour of ASEAN states. While China was initially very reluctant to join the ARF, China has now become an ardent supporter of the ASEAN Regional Forum (ARF) and the "ASEAN Way" in general after becoming a dialogue partner of the ARF in 1994. Along the way, the security-studying community in China has paid great attention to the constructing of a security community in ASEAN (Acharya 2001). Meanwhile, because China sees ASEAN as a hedging force against a rupture in the all-important U.S.-China relations,[11] China has paid special attention to the evolving security relations between the ASEAN states and the United States. In addition, the launching of initiatives such as ASEAN+3, ASEM, APEC, and now the East Asian Summit has further stimulated the growing demand from the state to understand the foreign policies of ASEAN countries.

C. The Rise of the Mass Media and Public Consumption

The launching of various research journals marked the time that Southeast Asian Studies became a discipline. With these journals, research output on Southeast Asian Studies, like other social science disciplines, also joined the public domain.[12]

At the same time, especially after the gradual opening of the media industry in the 1990s, there is a growing demand from the public for knowledge about the outside world. This is especially true for the general public with a certain degree of education and its elites: on average, the public and elite in China have paid perhaps far more attention to international affairs than those in other countries (Table 4.2).[13] As a result, the field of Southeast Asian Studies, just like area studies (and international studies) in general, has entered an era of serving the state, growing as a discipline, and satisfying public consumption, all at the same time.

While news on developed countries (especially the United States) and "hotspots (*redian*/热点)" has been featured regularly in newspapers, news about Southeast Asian countries also occupies an important place in daily coverage (Hey, we are so close!) . Moreover, in TV and radio programmes on international affairs, news coverage and commentaries on Southeast Asian affairs have also been regularly featured.

This phenomenal rise of the mass media and subsequently the growing demand for scholars' view on current affairs in the public media, we shall argue, has been a mixed blessing for SEAS (and more generally for international studies) in China. On the one hand, the rise of the media industry has certainly contributed to the growing visibility of SEAS (and more generally, international studies) and a better education of the public on international affairs. Moreover, the rise of the public media also provides more Chinese scholars, especially the younger generation, with more media exposure and opportunities to become public intellectuals.

On the other hand, however, the growing importance of the public media also means that serious scholarship is no longer the sole way of making a living and gaining fame. For some younger scholars, to be a media star is far easier and far more "profitable" than to first establish himself in the scholarly community: If you can earn fame and profit by simply appearing regularly on TV, why bother to do the lowly and hard work in a shabby office?[14] In this sense, the ethical foundation of the scholarly community has been gradually encroached upon by the increasing materialism of the overall society.

THE RESULT: THE STATE OF SEAS IN CHINA TODAY

The three fundamental institutional factors have profoundly shaped the evolution of SEAS as a discipline. On the one hand, they have propelled

Table 4.2
Volumes on SEA published in China 1958–2004[15]

Period	pre-1980	1980s	1990s	2000–04
Number of Volumes	11	24	115	43

Sources: Index of Books, China National Library.

Southeast Asia into a visible place in front of the state and the general public. On the other hand, however, they have also been responsible for the most glaring deficiencies associated with SEAS in China. Let us begin with the good story first.

A. The Growing Demand: The Positive Side

The first is that all three institutional factors have contributed to make Southeast Asia a very prosperous sub-field in the overall field of international studies in China. This is most evidently reflected in the number of volumes on Southeast Asia published in China (Table 4.3). In the 1990s, there was an explosion in published volumes on Southeast Asia (partly stimulated by the 1997 Asian financial crisis). In this phase, there have been more than 100 volumes published, more than the total published in the four decades before. And judging from the continuing interest in SEA, we see no sign of the trend receding: If we project the future based on the number of volumes published between 2000 and 2004, more than 120 volumes will be published by the first decade of the twenty-first century.

Second, the powerful demand from the state, together with a growing demand from the public, has also profoundly shaped the focus of SEAS in China today. While the first batch of work done by the first generation of SEAS scholars in China was mostly in historical and cultural studies with little relevance to policy-making, those fields and issues of immediate concern and interest to the state and the general mass media (most notably, economics and politics/security) have enjoyed the most growth after the open-and-reform policy and are now dominating the field. Considering that the foremost responsibility for China's SEAS now is to satisfy the growing demand from the state, such a development is hardly surprising.

This has been clearly reflected in the trend of published articles: in the backdrop of a growing demand stimulated by the growing importance of Southeast Asian countries to China, economic and political (security) studies of Southeast Asian countries have been dominating SEAS in China. As we

Table 4.3
Weight of Individual Southeast Asian Countries in SEAS in China (1994–2004)

State	Sin.	Viet.	Thai.	Mal.	Indo.	Phi.	Bur.	Cam.	Laos	Bru.
No. of Papers	740	561	211	198	174	153	140	76	45	22

Source: *Zhongguo qikan wang.*

examine the two leading journals on Southeast Asia in China (*Nanyang wenti yanjiu* and *Dongnanya yanjiu*), economic and political (security) studies of Southeast Asian countries make up about seventy per cent of the total papers published between 1994 and 2004 (Table 4.4). Further, judging from the consistency of the trend, we see no sign that this trend will change any time soon (Figures 4.1 and 4.2).

Indeed, such a trend is even evident in the field of overseas Chinese studies that had been traditionally dominated by historical and cultural studies: Historical studies of overseas Chinese have now declined to the ninth

Table 4.4
The Dominance of Economy and Politics in SEAS in China (1994–2004)

Percentage of the total	Economy	History	Politics and IR	Oversea Chinese	Society & Culture
NYWTYJ	44.9%	16.8%	13%	22.3%	2.9%
DNYYJ	33%	4.4%	41.3%	13.7%	7.4%
Total	37.8	9.4%	30%	17.2%	5.6%

Papers published by *Nanyang wenti yanjiu* (NYWTYJ) and *Dongnanya yanjiu* (DNYYJ).
Sources: *Zhongguo qikan wang.*

Figure 4.1
Papers Published by *Nanyang wenti yanjiu* (NYWTYJ), 1994–2004

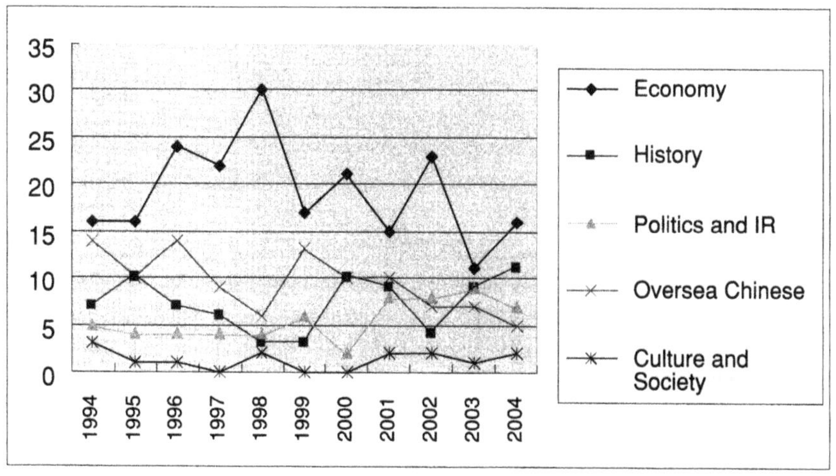

Figure 4.2
Papers Published by *Dongnanya Yanjiu* (DNYYJ), 1994–2004

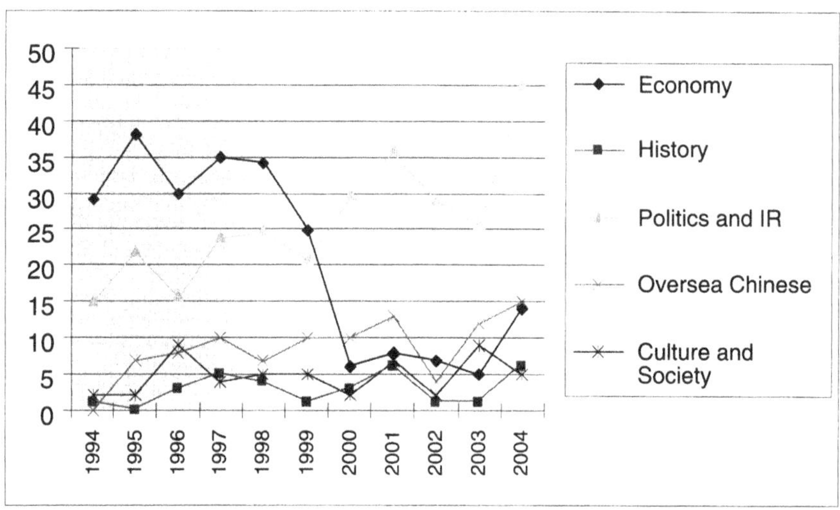

place in 1995–2003 from the second place in 1985–95, while studying the economic aspect of overseas Chinese remain number one (Xu 2005, Table 3 on p. 117).

B. The Growing Demand: The Negative Side

Previous explanations of the (often poor) state of international studies (of which area studies and Southeast Asian Studies are a part) tend to blame the scholarly community and scholars themselves ("scholarly culture/学术文化").[16] We contend that such a cultural explanation gravely misses the more important cause. Instead, we believe that the overall institutional environment is more decisive because institutions not only influence the pursuit of knowledge directly by providing direct demands but also indirectly by shaping individuals' perception of the value of different types of knowledge (North 1990, p. 70. See also Becker 1976, p. 11).[17] We shall elaborate on two pressing aspects briefly below.

(a) The Difficult Balancing Act between the State and Scholarship

The first dimension is the difficulty of maintaining a balance between scholarly contribution and the demands of the state. The open-and-reform era has undoubtedly given the scholarly community (including the community of SEAS) more freedom and more resources in pursuing knowledge that are deemed to be important by scholars themselves. It, however, also brought forth a profound dilemma: How can the scholarly community strike a balance between satisfying the state's demand and their scholarly interests?

For a long time and to a decisive degree, the primary task for China's SEAS community (and its international studies community) is to satisfy the demand from the state. As a result, scholars often have to grapple with a tough trade-off. This is so because while scholars may want to do more long-term and fundamental scholarly work, most of their prestige and power must necessarily come from the state. Unlike in the natural sciences where the scientists' scientific interest coincides with the state's more often, in disciplines such as SEAS (and international studies in general), the interest of the state and the interest of a scholar often diverge or even collide: The state is not interested in scholarly contribution, but in clearly laid out practical solutions to practical problems.

Under such an institutional system, it is inevitable for many scholars to choose to concentrate on satisfying the direct demand of the state, and some

Table 4.5
Media Outlets with a Heavy Emphasis on International Affairs

Newspapers with an exclusive focus on international affairs	Name	Estimated Circulation (per issue)
	Cankao Xiaoxi	>2 million
	Huanqing Shibao (Global Times)	>1 million
	Guoji Xianqu Daobao (International Leader Herald)	>200, 000
Magazines with an exclusive focus on international affairs	*Shijie Zhishi* (World Affairs) *Huanqiu* (Globe)	N. A. N. A.
TV Programme with an exclusive focus on international affairs	*Guoji Guancha* (Global Observer), programme in Chinese, CCTV-4	
	World Insight, programme in English, CCTV-9 (International)	
TV Programme with a large focus on international affairs	Dialogue, programme in English, CCTV-9 (International)	

research institutions now tend to emphasize policy relevance and de-emphasize in-depth research. Indeed, the situation has become so severe nowadays that there is almost no need to publish any scholarly work in some think-tanks, because a scholar's career is almost exclusively dependent upon the state's judgment on the policy recommendations advanced by him/her. Moreover, many so-called research articles look more like policy recommendations for the state, even though decision-making bodies of the state will only look at a tiny fraction of the research output, and most policy recommendations have no chance of being taken by the state.

There is, however, a grave danger here, and the danger is that the overwhelming demand from the state will create many blind spots within the discipline precisely because the scholarly community de-emphasizes scholarship in order to satisfy the demand of the state: Certain subjects or topics that are deemed unimportant by the state will receive little funding, and most scholars will be reluctant to purse such unrewarding research projects.[18]

If so, one must sometimes wonder whether some of the policy recommendations advanced by scholars without much background in in-depth research are sound policies precisely because the scholars behind those policies do not and cannot base their policy recommendations upon in-depth research. Fundamentally, a short-sighted focusing only on issues that are of immediate concern to the state will jeopardize the scholarly community's ability to supply sound policy recommendations to the state in the long run.[19]

(b) The Difficult Balancing Act between the Media and Scholarship

The second dimension is the difficulty of maintaining a balance between scholarly contribution and the demands of the public in the age of the mass media. In the age of the mass media, it is simply more profitable to write for newspapers and magazines or appear on TV programmes than to write for scholarly journals: The mass media pays far more than scholarly journals in real money.[20] Under such an environment, it would be rational for some scholars to write more for newspapers and magazines than for scholarly journals.

Such a trend is evident in almost all fields of international studies. For instance, in the field of overseas Chinese studies, the portion of scholarly work in the total publications has steadily decreased from 1995 to 2003, and non-scholarly work (mostly commentaries) now makes almost 40 per cent of the total published pieces in magazines and scholarly journals (Xu Yun 2005, p. 116).

Worse, with enticement from the media, many scholars (perhaps mostly from the younger generation) now write almost on everything.[21] The situation has become so bad that a prominent scholar, Professor Wang Jisi, lamented that: "for outsiders and regular folks, it is difficult to tell which book is for public assumption and for profit, and which book is scholarly contribution." (Wang Jisi 2003, p. 28. See also Zhang Ruizhuang 2003, p. 71).[22]

Another consequence of the rise of the media is that most of the research has concentrated on so-called "hot issues (*redian wenti*/热点问题)" because the media usually covers hot issues. As a result, many researchers tend to study what is hot, without sustaining and systematic interest in a specific area. Consequently, the time that scholars can devote to long-term and serious work is now greatly reduced.[23]

Moreover, because it is more profitable to study hot issues, scholars who are interested in more long-term and fundamental topics are gradually marginalized. As a result, more and more scholars are becoming "generalists": In some important research institutions, it is becoming increasingly difficult to find area specialists with a decent command of history, language, and culture of a single country. Not surprisingly, research outputs nowadays tend to be superficial, and there has been an outstanding lack of in-depth studies on Southeast Asia today.

Such an over-concentration of talent and resources to a few "host issues" is not only a wasting of talent and resources, but also fundamentally weakens the foundation of knowledge accumulation which is diversity. As a result, China's SEAS and its international studies in general may face a shortage of diverse and in-depth researches. In the end, this shortage may not even be able to meet the growing and diversifying demands of the state.

In this sense, the growing demand from the mass media is now becoming an obstacle towards solid scholarly work. The growing demand from the media has not only squeezed the time for scholarly work, but also reduced the diversity of research. If so, while scholars may now enjoy more media attention and better material life, their contribution to the enterprise of human knowledge and their general contribution to the society may nonetheless actually decrease.

C. Summary

Overall, in the age of heavy demand from the state and the mass media, the SEAS community (and the larger international studies community) in China are in danger of meeting short-term demand while jeopardizing its capability for meeting future demand. While the demand from the state and the public will inevitably increase and diversify as China becomes more integrated with the world, the scholarly community has become overly focused on a few hot issues.

HISTORICAL AND CULTURAL LEGACIES

Our argument that institutional factors have played a far more prominent role in shaping SEAS (and the overall pursuit of knowledge) in China does not equal to a denial that historical and cultural factors have also shaped SEAS in China. In fact, one can argue that institutional factors often interact with historical and cultural factors to shape the pursuit of knowledge. In this section, we shall briefly review some of the most important historical and cultural factors in shaping SEAS in China.

For a very long time, SEAS in China relied on the first generation of scholars who were mostly returnees of overseas Chinese and their students. These scholars laid the initial foundation of SEAS in China and made lasting contributions to the coming of SEAS as a respectable discipline. One of the most critical reasons behind their achievements has been that these scholars had long experience in living and studying in the countries they studied, and almost all of them had a command of the native languages of the countries they studied.

A period of relative isolation and then the disastrous Cultural Revolution, however, had largely wasted the prime time of the first generation of SEAS scholars. After the open-and-reform movement, China will have to train and rely on a new generation of dedicated scholars in order to sustain SEAS as a discipline.

The dominance of English as a language of science, however, has produced a powerful effect on the younger generation: while thousands are willing to pay for expensive training courses in English, Chinese universities are hard pressed to recruit students who are willing to study a minor language with very limited utility, and the native language of most Southeast Asian countries generally falls into this category. Moreover, because having a command of a native language of a Southeast Asian state will not be enough in today's English-dominated scholarly community and a scholar will have to have a decent command of English in order to prosper, this means that an aspiring student of Southeast Asia will have to face the very unattractive option of learning two foreign languages. If so, it should not be a surprise that most will choose to avoid such an option. Worse, because China for a very long time did not have the resources to provide students with intensive training in foreign languages in the respective foreign countries, few students had the chance to master one native Southeast Asian language even if they were willing to take on the difficult task.

As a result, nowadays, it is very hard to find Chinese scholars who have the command of a native Southeast Asian language and even more difficult to find scholars who are proficient in both a native Southeast Asian language and English. Consequently, today's new generation of Southeast Asian scholars have to rely largely on second-handed materials (that is, translated texts or English texts) for their research. In most Chinese SEAS publications, you see very few citations of original materials in Southeast Asian countries' native languages.

Moreover, because China did not have the resources for supporting in-depth research projects based on extensive field works (and scholarly work in general) for a very long time, there were virtually no opportunities for Chinese scholars to do field work in Southeast Asian countries without external support. Together with the deficiencies in native Southeast Asian languages, few Chinese scholars were able to gain long experiences of living and studying in the country of their interest.[24] As a result, even as the volumes on Southeast Asia keep piling up, there has been an outstanding lacking of work based on in-depth field work at the micro-level.

Finally, cultural factors have also profoundly shaped China's SEAS and China's social sciences in general. For a very long time, the only venerable social science in China has been history. Yet, as China increasingly came to embrace the "scientific spirit", merely doing history is no longer adequate. More and more, social sciences in China are also moving towards a positivism terrain: We want to know not only the historical facts, but also more importantly, what lie behind those historical facts.

The training of social scientists in China, however, has lagged far behind what is needed to move social sciences into a more "scientific" terrain. As a result, a large portion of the newly graduated Ph.D. and M.A. students have very limited training in doing social sciences; most of them have only the skills and mentality for doing history.

PROJECTING INTO THE FUTURE: OPTIMISM, DIFFICULTIES, AND REMEDIES

As China now actively and deeply engages ASEAN countries in almost every front and takes its strategy towards ASEAN as an integral part of China's overall regional strategy (Zhang and Tang 2005), one can only expect China's interest in ASEAN to remain steady, if it does not actually increase. Hence, overall, we can only see good times ahead for SEAS in China.

More specifically, we expect economics and politics (including security) to occupy the top echelon of SEAS in China, because of the heavy demand from the Chinese state. Meanwhile, history may continue to decline and it is highly unlikely for historical studies of Southeast Asia to return to its glorious past. Studying history has been becoming less "profitable". Similarly, we can also expect studies on the overseas Chinese community and its interaction with Southeast Asian countries to occupy a less prominent place.

Our optimism, however, is not unqualified. In fact, we expect the discipline to grow with pain, mostly because of the institutional settings highlighted above. If our argument that institutional arrangements hold a more prominent place in shaping the direction of the acquisition of knowledge and skills is correct, then we also need to think institutionally in order to rectify the deficiencies of SEAS in China.

First, although SEAS can and should be employed to manage the relationship between China and ASEAN countries, the SEAS community must try to find a fine balance between scholarship and meeting the immediate demands of the state.

Second, while English and attending an elite graduate programme in the West may be necessary for a younger scholar to be recognized in his home country, we must recognize that in order to understand our region, merely knowing English and doing research with second-hand materials will not be enough. If so, those scholars who took pains to study two foreign languages (English plus another) must be better recognized in their home country. Unless individuals expect decent return from their investment of time, resources, and talent in pursuing certain tasks, we cannot expect them to pursue those tasks. Otherwise, we can only expect the present trend to rely primarily on English materials for our research to continue, and it will deeply bias our research from an Anglo-Saxon perspective.

We therefore advocate two programmes. First, Southeast Asian countries and China should jointly set up a programme to support aspiring students in gaining the necessary language training and living experience in the countries in which they are interested. Money is important and we have to provide more East Asian money and other support for those students who are willing to take the effort and pain to learn a foreign language other than English in order to facilitate a better understanding of our region.

Second, Southeast Asian countries and China should jointly set up a programme that encourages and supports scholars from both sides to study each other based on fieldwork done with a decent period of time.[25]

Without such programmes, China and Southeast Asian countries may continue to rely on a third party for their intellectual exchanges, even though the two sides were able to communicate directly for centuries. On this front, money is not the issue, political will is.

NOTES

1. For good historical surveys of China's studies of Southeast Asian history, see He Shenda (2003). For a comparative survey, see Wang Gungwu (2004).
2. Understanding the pursuit of knowledge from an institutional perspective can also be understood as "sociology of knowledge" (Mannheim 1956; Scheler 1980). Unlike Mannheim and Scheler, we want to emphasize that there is universal and true knowledge even in social sciences because we concur with Popper that the accumulation of knowledge is a self-correcting process in the long run (Popper 1979).
3. We also implicitly assume that the evolution of the overall SEAS scholarly community itself has also been shaped by the three factors, although we touch upon this aspect only occasionally here.
4. All information is from institutions' websites. While there were explicit and implicit areas of specialization among the institutions at the beginning, almost all institution are moving toward more full-fledged and inter-disciplinary research institutions.
5. The centre, when it was founded in 1956, was known as Academy of Southeast Asian Studies, focusing mostly on oversea Chinese in Southeast Asia.
6. The centre, when it was founded in 1979, was known as Institute of Indochina Studies.
7. This centre is an inter-departmental programme of Peking University, mostly drawing resources from the Department of History, School of International Studies, and Department of Oriental Languages.
8. Formerly known as *Nanya dongnanya Ziliao* (South Asia and Southeast Asia), *Yafei yanjiu* (Asia and Africa Studies).
9. Of course, this is not to deny that some of these local policy initiatives may eventually gain national recognition and become national policy. A fine example of this has been the making of the Kunming Initiative. The Kunming Initiative was initially formulated by Yunan Institute of International Studies and Yunnan Academy of Social Sciences, but later received backing from the central government.
10. Among Southeast Asian countries, Singapore perhaps holds a unique place in SEAS in China. As the miracle story in Southeast Asia, a country with the ethnic Chinese population in the majority, the Singaporean experience provides both inspiration and aspiration for the Chinese elite and its intellectual community: If Singapore can do it, why can't we? This is prominently reflected in the number of papers focusing on Singapore: Singapore has been the No. 1 country of interest to SEAS scholars in China (Table 4.2).
11. Of course, Japan is not far away from the background too.
12. In Chinese, people often call both (research) journals (kanwu/刊物 or qikan/期刊) and (popular) magazines (zazhi/杂志) as "magazines(zazhi/杂志)", and the two terms are often deemed to be exchangeable. In contrast, in English, a journal is a "specialized periodical", and it is different from a regular magazine. To avoid

confusions, we have advocated that we call only "研究型期刊 / 刊物 (academic or research journal)" as journals, and they are for the specialized professional scholarly audience; while "zazhi/杂志 (magazines)" are for popular consumption. If so, then publications by scholars in magazines ("杂志") cannot be considered as research outputs, and only research articles published in "研究型期刊 / 刊物 (academic or research journal)" can be taken as research outputs. Quite sadly, such a standard is only gradually accepted in leading research institutions and universities.

13. This might have something to do with the centuries of humiliation. In any case, it is perhaps highly unlikely for a single country other than China to have three major newspapers focusing exclusively on international affairs. *Cankao Xiaoxi* (circulation more than two million per issue), *Huanqiu Shibao* (*Global Times*, circulation more than one million), and *Guoji Xianqu Daobao* (*International Leader Herald*, circulation about 200,000) all enjoyed steadily increasing or stable readership.
14. By "profitable" or "unprofitable", I am adopting Prof. Wang Gungwu's phraseology here. See Wang (1985).
15. By volumes, we mean single-authored, co-authored, and edited volumes. The first volume on Southeast Asia in China was published in 1958 by Higher Education Press, a translation of Kochetov's lecture notes, *Modern History of SEA and Far Eastern Countries*. Yu Dingbang and Huang Yunjing (2000), p. 9.
16. Numerous Chinese scholars have discussed the deficiencies of China's international studies from this angle. See, for example, Pang Zhongying (2000), Su Changhe (2001). To our knowledge, the only brief discussion with a flavour of institutional analysis is Zhang Ruizhuang (2003), p. 70.
17. Apparently, economists have better understanding about the impact of institutional structure upon the pursuit of knowledge.
18. Once again, such a development reflects that individuals will allocate their talent according to the expected return from their investment of time, resources, and talent. The theory of allocation of talent can actually be derived from the argument that institutions not only create direct demand for knowledge but also mandate what kinds of skills and knowledge will pay off for individuals and organizations. For the theory of allocation of talent, see Baumol (1990); Fershtman and Weiss (1993); Fershtman, Murphy, and Weiss (1996).
19. The situation may actually be much worse: Without in-depth scholarly work as its foundation, some of the policy recommendations advanced by some are merely justifying and lauding the state's policies.
20. In fact, scholarly journals are now beginning to eliminate payment to authors, moving towards conforming to international practices: Scholars must now write for scholarship, not for money.
21. For instance, a young scholar from CICIR who is supposed to study U.S.-China relationship even talked about whether the Olympic Games in Athens will make a profit or loss on CCTV.
22. Of course, the crucial difference between a scholar and a layman is that the

former only say things that he believes he has the knowledge on (Hayek 1960, pp. 25–26). Please note, however, that to be mindful of one's area of expertise is not the same as to be silent on issues.

23. Focusing overly on "hot issues" is related to the state's demand too: The state is normally more concerned with pressing hot issues, thus studying hot issues is also more conducive to gaining recognition form the state.
24. Hence, most research output on Southeast Asian economies have been at the macro level.
25. So far, the only programme that has done this job has been Asia Fellow (Studying Asia in Asia) initiated by the Ford Foundation.

REFERENCES

Acharya, Amitav. *Constructing a Security Community in Southeast Asia*. London: Routledge, 2001.

Ash, Robert S. "China's Regional Economies and the Asian Region: Building Interdependent Linkages", in *Power Shift: China and Asia's New Dynamics*, edited by David Shambaugh. Berkeley: University of California Press, 2005, pp. 96–131.

Baumol, William J. "Entrepreneurship: Productive, Unproductive, and Destructive", *Journal of Political Economy* 98, no. 5 (October 1990): 893–921.

Becker, Gary S. *The Economic Approach to Human Behavior*. Chicago: University of Chicago Press, 1976*b*.

Fershtman, Chaim and Yoram Weiss. "Social Status, Culture and Economic Performance", *Economic Journal* 103, no. 419 (July 1993): 946–59.

Fershtman, Chaim, Kevin M. Murphy, and Yoram Weiss. "Social Status, Education, and Growth", *Journal of Political Economy* 104, no. 1 (February 1996): 108–32.

Hayek, Friedrich A. *The Constitution of Liberty*. Chicago, Ill.: University of Chicago Press, 1960.

He, Shenda. "China's Studies of Southeast Asian History: Achievements and Prospects", *Shijie Lishi* [*World History*], no. 2 (2003): 102–12.

Mannheim, Karl. *Ideology and Utopia: An Introduction to the Sociology of Knowledge*. London: Routledge and Keegan Paul, 1956.

North, Douglass C. *Institutions, Institutional Change and Economic Performance*. Cambridge: Cambridge University Press, 1990.

Pan, Zhongying. "Three Major Problems of International Studies in China", *Ouzhou* [*European Studies*], no. 6 (2000): 36–41.

Popper, Karl. *Objective Knowledge: An Evolutionary Approach*, 2nd edition. London: Routledge and Keegan Paul, 1979.

Scheler, Max. *Problems of a Sociology of Knowledge*, translated by Manfred S. Frings. London: Routledge and Keegan Paul, 1980.

Su, Changhe. "International Relations in China: Problems and Directions", *Shijie Jingji yu Zhengzhi* [*World Economics and Politics*], no. 1 (2000): 72–75.

Tang, Shiping, Jie Zhang, and Xiaoyang Cao. "Area Studies in China: Achievements, Deficiencies, and Prospects", *Shijie Jingji yu Zhengzhi* [World Economics and Politics], no. 11 (2005): 8–17.

Wang Jisi. "International Relations Studies in China Today: Achievements, Trends and Conclusions", in *International Relations Studies in China*. Beijing: The Ford Foundation, 2003, pp. 19–40.

Wang, Gungwu. "Loving the Ancient in China", in *Who Rules the Past*, edited by Elizabeth McBrady. Melbourne: Oxford University, 1985, pp. 175–95.

Wang, Gungwu. "Singapore versus China: Two Approaches toward Southeast Asian Studies", *Nanyang Wenti Yanjiu* [*Southeast Asian Affairs*], no. 2 (2004): 1–15.

Xu, Yun. "Overseas Chinese Studies in China: A Quantitative Analysis", *Jinan Daxue Xuebao (renwen kexue and shehui kexue ban)* [Journal of Jinan University (Humanity and Social Sciences)], no. 1 (2005): 115–25.

Yu, Dingbang and Huang Yunjing. "SEA Studies in China: Past, Present, and Future", *Shehui Kexuejia* [*Social Scientists*] 15, no. 6 (November 2000): 8–10.

Zhang, Ruizhuang. "Problems of International Relations as a Discipline in China", *Shijie Jingji yu Zhengzhi* [*World Economics and Politics*], no. 5 (2003): 70.

Zhang, Yunling and Shiping Tang. "China's Regional Strategy", in *Power Shift: China and Asia's New Dynamics*, edited by David Shambaugh. Berkeley: University of California Press, 2005, pp. 48–68.

Zhang Ruizhuang. "Problems of International Studies in China", *Shijie Jingji yu Zhengzhi* [*World Economics and Politics*], no. 5 (2003): 70–75.

5

Overview of Teaching Programmes and Curriculum Development on Southeast Asia in China

Zhang Xizhen

This conference focusing on Southeast Asian Studies in China provides us with a very good opportunity to review the historical evolution and status of China's Southeast Asian Studies with many representatives from almost every institution in China concerned with Southeast Asian Studies. Talking about Southeast Asian Studies in Chinese teaching programmes and subject construction on Southeast Asian Studies are an important part of it. This chapter, therefore, recalls the development of the teaching programme and curriculum development on Southeast Asian Studies in China, summarizes the achievements and progress made in the past two decades, and meanwhile analyses the remaining problems and challenges we face.

To prepare for this chapter and gather detailed data and information, I organized a nationwide symposium at the School of International Studies, Peking University, from 3–4 December 2005. Twenty-five representatives from twelve universities, such as Peking University, Diplomacy University,

University of Foreign Studies, Xiamen University, Zhongshan University, Jinan University, Yunnan University, etc., reviewed the development of teaching programmes and curriculum development on Southeast Asian Studies, analysed its status and exchanged teaching experience. Most representatives thought that great progress has been made in teaching programmes during the last two decades, which was the "golden age" for Southeast Asian Studies in China. However, they argued that the current scale of Southeast Asia teaching programmes and curriculum development is unable to meet the development needs of Sino-Southeast Asia relations, and match the position of China's large nation status. China needs to make greater effort to promote its Southeast Asia teaching programmes and academic research and to nurture more Southeast Asia talents.

A BRIEF HISTORY OF CHINA's SOUTHEAST ASIAN TEACHING PROGRAMMES

Chinese are the earliest people beyond Southeast Asia who knew well this region. Since the Qin dynasty (221–205 B.C.), Chinese have been migrating to this area in search of their livelihood on the unacquainted land. During China's long ancient history, almost every dynasty sent its ambassadors to ancient kingdoms in Southeast Asia, and these ambassadors left various diaries, documents and other writings about the kingdoms where they stayed as legacy for studying this area. A second group of Chinese who made contributions to the understanding of this region were travellers who were usually intellectuals. When they came and stayed with their fathers or relatives who were usually merchants or diplomats abroad, they wrote some articles, diaries, travel notes and memoirs. A third group of Chinese who had experience in Southeast Asia were Buddhist monks who went to India through this area by sea, to study Buddhism. Some of them wrote a lot about what they saw when they stayed or spent some years there. Today these valuable records have become important sources for the present Southeast Asian Studies.

Although there is very rich ancient literature on Southeast Asia, it became real academic research very late in China. Modern academic studies on Southeast Asia can be traced back to the early twentieth century. In 1906, Jinan University was founded (first in Nanjing, then it moved to Shanghai, and finally to Guangzhou) mainly for the young generation of overseas Chinese in Southeast Asia. In the university, some courses on overseas Chinese were taught and the earliest books on the region were published. Professor Li Changfu (李长傅) who taught courses on Chinese settlement and histories of countries in Southeast Asia at the university published a book entitled

History of Chinese Settlement Abroad in 1937, then *Histories of Countries in Nan Yang* in 1938. the Bureau of Nan Yang Cultural Affairs (南洋文化事业部) was established at Jinan University in Shanghai and published scholarly journals on Southeast Asia: The *Nanyang Studies* and the *Nanyang Information.* In Peking University Professor Feng Chengjun（冯承均）who taught history of Sino-Nanyang communication, also published a book entitled *History of Sino-Nanyang Communication* in 1937.

Almost at the same time, a small group of overseas Chinese intellectuals in Singapore established the China Nanyang (South Seas) Society, which has continued to publish the *Journal of the Nanyang Society* and monographs until 1982.

During the Anti-Japan War, a group of overseas Chinese scholars returned to China and did research at the Institute of Nanyang Studies established by the government of the Republic of China in Chongqing, a contemporary capital of China during the war. However the first institute of Southeast Asian Studies owned by the government was disbanded a few years later due to the war although a few books had been published by Zhang Liqian（张礼千), Yaonan（姚楠), Xu Yenqiao（许云樵）and Zhu Jieqing（朱杰勤). All these scholars and others constituted the first generation of experts on Southeast Asia in China.

After the war, the government of the Kuomintang government founded a school called "National Oriental Language School" in Nanjing, then capital of China, for Southeast Asian language training. The first generation of Southeast Asia experts came to the school and became teachers there. After the People's Republic of China was founded, the school moved to Beijing and merged with Peking University in 1952, as part of the Department of Oriental Languages until now. Languages taught are Indonesian, Malay, Thai, and Vietnamese. The teaching of Southeast Asian languages produced many young scholars and laid the foundation for today's Southeast Asian teaching programmes and studies in China.

In the 1950s, China's new government paid great attention to Southeast Asian Studies and teaching programmes and the first group of academic institutions was set up in Southern China. The first institute of Southeast Asian Studies was set up in Xiamen University, Fujian Province in 1956. Originally called the Institute of Nanyang (South Sea) Studies, it is now called the Research School of Southeast Asian Studies. Three years later a section of Southeast Asian History at the Department of History of Zhongshan (Sun Yat-sen) University in 1959 later developed into the Institute of Studies of Southeast Asian History. In 1960, another section of Southeast Asian Studies was set up at Jinan University. Its predecessor was the Economic

Research Group of Hong Kong, Macao, Overseas Chinese and Southeast Asia established in 1958, which was attached to the Institute of Philosophical and Social Sciences Studies of Guangzhou, Chinese Academy of Sciences. Later the research section became the Institute of Southeast Asian Studies, Middle-South China Branch, Chinese Academy of Sciences. The fourth section of Southeast Asian Studies was founded in the Yunnan Institute of History in 1963, which later became the Institute of Southeast Asian Studies, Yunnan Academy of Social Sciences. The same year, the Association of Southeast Asian Studies in Fujian Province was set up as a local academic organization in Southeast Asian Studies.

In 1966 when the Cultural Revolution broke out, all academic researchers stopped their research jobs, including Southeast Asian teaching and studies, until the Cultural Revolution ended in 1976. With the opening and reform policy starting at the end of 1970s, China's government began to pay attention to Southeast Asian Studies. China's Southeast Asian teaching and studies thus began to enter into a new era of development. Very soon old institutes that were closed during the Cultural Revolution were re-opened, and furthermore some new institutions were founded. In 1979, the Institute of Indo-China's Studies was established in Guangxi Academy of Social Sciences based in Naning, capital of Guangxi Province. It was developed into the Institute of Southeast Asian Studies in 1989. In 1981, a section of Vietnamese studies was set up in the Department of History at Zhengzhou University, and was later developed into the Institute of Vietnamese Studies, the only such institute in China.

In addition to the above institutes specializing in Southeast Asian Studies, some other institutes related to Southeast Asian Studies were established. The most important are the following: first is the Institute of Asia-Pacific Studies, established in 1988 and based in Beijing, one of the research institutes in the Chinese Academy of Social Sciences (CASS). The institute has two functions: providing academic researches and acting as a think-tank for the government. Second is the China Institute of Contemporary International Relations established in 1980, which serves as a think-tank to the Department of National Security. One of its sections focuses on Southeast Asian Studies.

Southeast Asian teaching programmes are developing with the increase of institutions of Southeast Asian Studies at different levels. In all the universities' Southeast Asian institutes, there are usually Southeast Asian teaching programmes as well as Master's and Ph.D. programmes. In some institutes at provincial and central governments, there are also Master's and Ph.D. programmes available. Additionally, a few history departments of universities offer Southeast Asian history courses.

Before the 1980s, Southeast Asian teaching programmes and courses were concentrated in three fields: Southeast Asian languages, histories, and overseas Chinese.

STATUS OF AND NEW DEVELOPMENTS IN SOUTHEAST ASIAN TEACHING PROGRAMMES AND CURRICULUM CONSTRUCTION

After the end of the Cultural Revolution, China's government immediately began paying great attention to personnel training in this field. From September 1980 to July 1981, the National Commission of Education mandated the Institute of Southeast Asian History, Zhangshan University to organize a one-year-long training programme in Southeast Asian history in order to bring up a new generation of China's Southeast Asianists. The author, as a member from the Department of International Politics, Peking University, attended the programme with five other members sent by other universities.

In the 1980s, the course "Southeast Asian History" was taught at some universities such as Zhongshan University, Xiamen University, and Peking University. By 1989, a new course "Politics, Economy and Diplomacy in Southeast Asia" was first offered by the author in the Department of International Politics, Peking University. In the 1990s, more and more universities began offering courses on Southeast Asian history, economy, overseas Chinese, politics, culture and ethnology.

After entering the new century, great achievements and progress were made in Southeast Asian teaching programmes and the construction of specialities and courses. Today, many universities such as Xiamen University, Zhongshang University, Jinan University, Yunnan University are teaching these kinds of courses to undergraduate students. Furthermore, Master's and Ph.D. programmes had been established in some universities, such as Peking University, Xiamen University, Zhongshang University, Jinan Uninversity, and Yunnan University.

The greatest progress was made in Southeast Asian indigenous language specialities. Before the 1980s, there were only four universities in China with Southeast Asian language specialities, namely Peking University, Beijing Foreign Language College, Guangzhou Foreign Language College and Guangxi Nationality College. Today, there are ten major universities having indigenous language specialities.

As for indigenous language specialities, great progress has been made since the opening and reform policies were carried out at the end of the

1970s. A great number of young people graduated from the indigenous language programmes. Today, nationwide there are ten universities and colleges which have such language teaching programmes. Beijing Foreign Studies University is the largest, offering seven Southeast Asian languages teaching programmes, including Thai, Lao, Vietnamese, Malay, Khmer, Burmese, and Indonesian. Peking University offers Thai, Filipino, Burmese, Vietnamese and Malay; Shanghai Foreign Language University, Thai; Guangxi Nationality College, Vietnamese, Lao, Burmese, Thai and Khmer; Communication University of China, Malay, Filipino, and Vietnamese; Guangdong Foreign Language and Trade University, Indonesian, Thai, and Vietnamese; Yunnan Nationality University, Khmer, Lao, Burmese, Vietnamese; University of International Business and Economics, Vietnamese. In addition, there are two People's Liberation Army (PLA) colleges with this kind of language training programme. The PLA Nanjing International Relations College offers Thai, Vietnamese, and Burmese and PLA Luoyang Foreign Language College offers Burmese, Indonesian, Vietnamese, Khmer, Lao, and Malay language studies.

In some provinces close to Southeast Asian countries, development of indeginous language teaching programmes is much faster. Taking Guangxi as an example, besides Guangxi Nationality College, there are twelve other smaller colleges and schools that offer Vietnamese language courses because this language is more and more popular in Guangxi. It is estimated that there are 4,000–5,000 students learning Vietnamese.

These language teaching programmes contribute to the development of China's Southeast Asian Studies. Most graduates from such programmes, however, have not entered academic fields but governments and companies. Therefore, in general, around ninety per cent of researchers in Southeast Asian Studies still could not do their research by directly reading indigenous languages. English is still a major language medium for most of China's researchers.

As mentioned above, there were not many courses in non-indigenous language specialities before the 1980s, except on history and overseas Chinese. In the last twenty years, the number of Southeast Asian courses has been rapidly growing. They are classified as follows:

Southeast Asian history

东南亚史

东南亚古代史

东南亚近现代史

Southeast Asian comprehensive studies
东南亚研究
东南亚专题研究
东南亚综合研究
东南亚地区研究

Southeast Asian politics
东南亚政治与外交
东南亚各国政府与政治
东南亚国家政治
东南亚政治人物评论

Southeast Asian economy
东南亚经济
东南亚经济与金融
东南亚与港澳台金融
东南亚旅游

Southeast Asian international relations
东南亚国际关系
东南亚概况与对外关系
东南亚概况与对华关系
东南亚华人华侨与国际关系
中国与东南亚关系史
中国与东南亚关系
中国东南亚文化交流史
南海主权与国际海洋法
中国与东南亚经贸关系史
中国海外交通史

Southeast Asian overseas Chinese and ethnic Chinese
华侨华人研究
中外关系与中国海外移民
中国海外移民的历史与现状
华人华侨经济史
东南亚华人华侨史

Southeast Asian society, nationality and culture
东南亚宗教与文化
东南亚民族与民族问题
东南亚宗教概论
东南亚文化

东南亚宗教文化史
东南亚民族
东南亚社会与文化

Country study
泰国历史与现状
泰国文化研究
马来西亚研究
印尼专题研究

Other courses related to Southeast Asia
亚太国家关系
亚太政治与经济
亚太国际组织
亚太国际关系研究
东亚模式研究
亚太经济发展与区域经济合作
关于东南亚的中文史籍介绍
关于东南亚的外文史籍介绍

CHALLENGES AND PROBLEMS OF CHINA's TEACHING PROGRAMMES AND CURRICULUM ON SOUTHEAST ASIA

1. Development and construction of the Southeast Asia curriculum could not meet the demands of development in Sino-Southeast Asia relations, and there is great imbalance in the development of the subjects nationwide.

In the past decade, bilateral relations between China and ASEAN nations have become closer. Especially in the recent years, with the rapid pace of FTA between two sides, more and more of those who studied Southeast Asia affairs and learned the indigenous languages are needed. Many large Chinese companies are going to invest in and do business with Southeast Asian countries, but they do not have much information about the social, cultural, political and economic systems and investment environment in the identified countries. Therefore, Southeast Asia experts are always invited to give lectures to the companies.

As mentioned above, although many Southeast Asian specialities and courses on the area have been set up, they still lag behind the demand for two reasons. First, in the field of international studies, in terms of universities' and scholars' attention, great priority is still given to big powers such as the United States, Japan, Europe, and big powers' relations, thereby Southeast Asia is not given enough attention. Up to now, there are still many first class universities, such as Fudan, Nanjing, Wuhan, Qinghua, Nakai universities, etc., that have not set up Southeast Asian teaching programmes or offered courses on the region.

Second, the distribution of universities with Southeast Asian teaching programmes and courses is very unbalanced. Universities with Southeast Asian specialities, programmes and courses are concentrated in the southern coastal provinces, such as Fujian, Guangdong, Guangxi, Yunnan. In all other provinces, except a few universities like Peking University, there are almost no other universities that have Southeast Asian specialities and non-Southeast Asian language subjects.

2. The focus on current politics, economy and foreign relations is rising, while the focus on history is decreasing.

As mentioned above, before the 1980s, subjects on Southeast Asia in universities were concentrated on history. Later, however, with all Chinese policies becoming more and more pragmatic under reform circumstances, courses in universities also began adjusting to social demands. Therefore, more and more of the young generation of faculty began to offer new courses on Southeast Asia, such as economics, politics, international relations, and religion and culture. On the other hand, the number of old faculty members teaching Southeast Asian history is diminishing because more and more of them are retiring and some of them are switching their interests from history to *status quo* subjects.

Today the subject of Southeast Asian history is faced with serious difficulties in many universities. Firstly, there are no young successors to continue the history course when old professors teaching the course retire, so that this subject, which used to be well-known in some universities, has to be suspended. For example, the subject of Southeast Asian history which lasted for many decades in the History Department of Peking University has been suspended for a few years. Secondly, history courses are getting increasingly unpopular among students who are paying much attention to more useful courses. Thirdly, some school leavers also ignore the importance of the subject.

3. A lack of qualified textbooks in most subjects on Southeast Asian Studies.

It is very important that every subject or course should have a qualified textbook which can benefit many groups of students. So far, for history subjects, there are few books which can be used as textbooks. The best one among them, written by Professor Liang Yingming and Liang Zhiming, is *Modern and Contemporary History of Southeast Asia.* Even in the historical field there has not been a better textbook on the ancient history of Southeast Asia.

In the field of overseas Chinese studies, there are many books and some of them can be used as textbooks. But a comprehensive overseas Chinese textbook is still needed.

In politics, economics and international relations, no qualified textbooks have been published yet. Some scholars have appealed to senior professors to concentrate more on writing textbooks.

The most important reason for not paying so much attention to writing textbooks is that it is believed that textbooks cannot reflect the author's academic level and ability. As a basis for academic promotion, textbooks are usually not seen to be as persuasive as academic works.

4. The current model of talent development is unable to produce multi-ability talents who can meet the need of the society.

Based on the Education Ministry's regulation on specialities, a department of Southeast Asian languages can only have language specialities, instead of specialities in Southeast Asian Studies; meanwhile the speciality of Southeast Asian Studies is only set up in a department of international studies. These two departments organize teaching activities separately, therefore students learning languages could not take courses on Southeast Asian politics offered by the department of international studies, and *vice versa*. Thus graduates from the language department may gain a lot of information, but are unable to analyse it and do research, while graduates from the department of international studies are unable to do their research by directly reading materials in indigenous languages. Students are encouraged to take courses in other departments but there are usually few opportunities because of the overlapping of courses.

To resolve this problem, the Department of Oriental Languages, Peking University, enacted some reforms and set up a Speciality of Southeast Asian Culture and Master's/Ph.D. Programme in the department so as to produce graduates with abilities in both language and culture. But they have not been able to produce talents with multiple-abilities in language and politics or economics because of the limitations imposed by the faculty's specialties.

5. Quality of Teachers in the Field of Southeast Asian Studies needs to Improve.

The first generation of Southeast Asia professors are basically the repatriated overseas Chinese who were born in Southeast Asia and returned to China in the 1950s and 1960s, some attracted by the promise of a New China and some repelled by anti-Chinese riots, especially in Indonesia and Malaysia. Familiar with local cultures and languages and having first-hand experience in Southeast Asia, they nevertheless rarely had the opportunity to return for further fieldwork due to the circumstances of the Cold War. Hence they relied heavily on texts and published materials for their analyses. Many were trained in history; according to an early 1990s survey, 43 per cent of China's Southeast Asianists were trained in history, 14 per cent in economics, and 12 per cent in international relations/politics. The field in which most of them were interested was the overseas Chinese issue. By the end of the twentieth century, almost all of this generation had retired.

The second generation was trained in Chinese universities in the 1970s, 1980s and 1990s. They are more familiar with current theoretical debates in the humanities and social sciences, while some have had opportunities to do field research in Southeast Asia or library research in the West, but they lack the indigenous language capacity and intimate local knowledge possessed by their predecessors. English is still a major language medium for most Chinese researchers.

Limited by funding, most teachers have no opportunities to frequent Southeast Asia for field research for a long time, or attend international conferences. Most of them are unable to use first-hand materials to do research. Therefore, the general level of academic research of teachers still lags behind Western scholars, especially in the political and economic fields because of information limitations.

6. There are still some forbidden areas of research.

In the recent two decades, the academic atmosphere in China has become more liberated and open, but there are still some forbidden areas, such as the communist issues in Southeast Asia, Sino-Vietnam relations in the 1970s and 1980s, and the current political situation in Myanmar. Articles on these issues cannot be published although they can be discussed in classes.

CONCLUSION

Much progress has been made in Southeast Asian teaching programmes and curriculum development in China in the last two decades. This is reflected in the rapid development and expansion of Southeast Asian languages teaching programmes, a great number of non-language courses on Southeast Asia, and increasing numbers of students attending these courses.

However, we are still faced with many problems and difficulties in promoting Southeast Asian teaching programmes and curriculum development, such as not meeting the development needs of Sino-Southeast Asian relations; uneven subject development in area studies and fields of study; the lack of qualified textbooks in most courses of Southeast Asian Studies; the model of not nurturing multi-ability talents to meet the needs of the current society; quality of teachers to be improved; and some forbidden areas for research.

To resolve so many problems, the most crucial factor is the Ministry of Education, which can play the most important role. In China, higher education is still closely controlled by the central government. I hope, first, that the Ministry of Education will attach more importance to Southeast Asian teaching programmes and curriculum development, and promote their development more vigorously; second, that by easing regulations, much autonomy will be given to schools and universities to adjust the structure and relations among different specialities and subjects in order to produce multi-ability talents; third, that much more financial support should be provided to faculty so that they have more opportunities to do field research and attend international conferences abroad.

NOTES

Liu Hong on Southeast Asian Studies in Greater China <http://kyotoreview.cseas.kyoto-u.ac.jp/issue/issue2/article_232.html>.

Liang Zhiming (梁志明), Zhang Xizhen (张锡镇), and Yang Baoyun (杨保筠). "China's Southeast Asian Studies at the Turn of the New Century", in *China's Southeast Asian Studies at the Turn of the New Century: Retrospect and Prospect* (in Chinese), edited by Liang Zhiming, Zhang Xizhen, and Zhao Jing. Hong Kong: Hong Kong Press for Social Sciences, 2002, pp. 9–21.

Liu Yong Zhuo (刘永焯). *Southeast Asian Studies in China: Retrospect and Prospect* (in Chinese). Guangzhou: Guangdong Remin Chubanshe, 1994.

6

From "Sino-Centricity" to "Autonomous Narrative" in Southeast Asian Chinese Studies in China: A Sporadic Review

Ho Khai Leong

INTRODUCTION

More than two decades ago, a delegation of Australian historians and social scientists led by Professor Wang Gungwu visited universities, centres, and institutes in the People's Republic of China (PRC) to find out more about the state of Southeast Asian Studies in the country. The curiosity was generated by the fact that while academics knew much about the state of Southeast Asian Studies in North America, Europe and Japan, they were less cognizant as to the state of the art in China. Many of the important observations made by these scholars were that Southeast Asian Studies scholarship in China has had the unfortunate experience of neglect and discontinuities in the 1960s and 1970s;[1] and that PRC scholars doing Southeast Asian Studies were predominantly concerned with the problems of Chinese overseas[2] and "the Chinese influence in Southeast Asia".[3] One member of the delegation, David

Marr, made a salient observation that there seemed to be a lack of seriousness in Chinese Southeast Asian Studies scholarship in researching "the autonomous histories of Southeast Asian kingdoms".[4] His mere suggestion that PRC scholars needed to pay some attention to the subject raised the ire of the host and propelled him into a long, argumentative defence.

In the last twenty-five years, Southeast Asian Studies in China has experienced a sea-change. Since the early 1980s, Southeast Asian Studies in the country developed much more rapidly after the open-door economic reform policy initiated by Deng Xiaoping.[5] Institutes and centres on Southeast Asian Studies have been better financed by governments, staffed with young and energetic scholars trained in the various humanities and social sciences, and have produced many fine and pioneering works. A review of the state of literature in 1987 revealed various positive developments in this regard.[6] By early 2000, Southeast Asian Studies in China has gradually matured into a more coherent academic discipline supported by the state.[7] Much has been achieved and much remained to be done, however. Liao Shaolian, in his recent review of the state of Southeast Asian Studies scholarship in the PRC, listed four problems that need to be solved for the field to go forward. There were: 1. lack of training and knowledge for some researchers; 2. duplication of research; 3. lack of research materials, and 4. limited academic exchanges.[8]

While the domain of Southeast Asian Studies (especially the discipline of history, and its theories, methodologies and epistemologies) *home* scholars (a term used by Thongchai Winichakul)[9] in Southeast Asia in recent years have engaged in continuous critique and self-reflection, China's scholars on Southeast Asian Studies seemed to be less concerned about the substantive methodological and epistemological problems in their disciplines. They continue to be preoccupied with organizational and institutional matters, such as funding and networking with other institutions. An obvious factor motivating the emergence of Southeast Asian Studies towards the end of 1990s was the rise of China as a powerhouse in the Asia-Pacific region. In effect, Southeast Asian Studies emerged in response to China's problems, at a point in contemporary history when the PRC intends to be politically and economically relevant to the region. So far, there exist few remarks of self-examination of the state of the discipline by Chinese scholars. Among these few critical remarks, there is an observation that there is a certain kind of "China-centric" impulse in the scholarship, not unlike the Eurocentric perspective of Western social sciences in the 1950s and 1960s.[10] Zhang Ying Long of Jinan University (Guangzhou), for example, observed that as far as Overseas Chinese studies in China were concerned, there is a lack of Southeast Asian or world perspectives by PRC scholars.[11] While some of the studies on Chinese overseas by Chinese scholars may be theoretically sophisticated and ethnographically informed, the reference point is always China. Similarly, the scholarship on overseas Chinese by Chinese scholars were preoccupied by a China-dominant paradigm (中国本位论述), often using China as a reference in their narratives.[12]

D.G.E. Hall, in 1955, argued that Southeast Asian history "cannot be safely viewed from any other perspective until seen from its own".[13] The early realization of European, and later American, historians and social scientists in shifting the intellectual paradigm have enabled at least two generations of scholars, both home and foreign, to write consciously from the perspectives of local orientations. Autonomous histories, an increasingly dominant paradigm in the study of Southeast Asia history, find echoes in much of the works we encounter today. While it would probably be too demanding (and unfair) to situate the nascent Chinese Southeast Asian scholarship within this conceptual debate, I detect some changes, albeit subtle and embryonic, in the intellectual construction of China as a reference point in recent works produced by PRC scholars in their research on Chinese societies in Southeast Asia. Risking over-simplification, I have selected four books for sporadic review for this purpose.

FROM "CHINA-CENTRICITY"....

The four books chosen for review are: (1) 黄露夏编著：《马来西亚华侨华人编年史》 [*Malaysia. Chronological History of Overseas Chinese*, by Huang Luxia]; (2) 曾少聪著：《漂泊与根植：当代东南亚华人族群关系研究》 [*Studies in Contemporary Southeast Asian Chinese and Ethnic Relations* by Zeng Shaocong]; (3) 邱格屏著：《世外无桃源：东南亚华人秘密会党》 [*Southeast Asian Chinese Secret Societies* by Qiu Gebing]; and (4) Wu Xiao An, *Chinese Business in A Malay State, 1882–1941*. The first three books are written in Chinese, and the fourth in English. These publications are chosen for this review based on the following criteria: The books are focused on issues pertinent to the Southeast Asian Chinese; the authors are in their forties and early fifties, representing a new generation of Chinese scholars on Southeast Asian Studies; the publications are recent additions to the literature and published by reputable publishers in the PRC and elsewhere.

These scholarly monographs offer insightful analysis on the role of such factors as cultural community, guilds and associations, secret societies, business organizations in the conduct of ethnic relations for the ethnic Chinese in Southeast Asia. Huang Luxia's *Malaysia. Chronological History of Huaqiao/Huaren* chronicles important dates and the historical evolution of Chinese immigration to the Malay Peninsula from the fifth century to the present day (the book ends with a record of events in the year 2004). Compiled from historical archives, as well as documents from libraries and the Internet, this lengthy and extended timeline on *Huaqioa/Huaren* in the Malay Peninsula (and later Malaysia) provides a useful guide for important events and personalities in the Malaysian Chinese history. Huang, whose previous publication includes *The Chinese in Malaysia* (《马来西亚的华人》), is at present a researcher at the Fujian Academy of Social Sciences. With this ambitious work, she attempted to record the significant events in the then Malay Peninsula to the present state of West and East Malaysia almost year by year. Events and personalities recorded ranged from the establishment of certain *Huiguan* in a locality and its founder (for example, in the year 1894, it was record that the Klang Qiongzhou Huiguan 巴生琼州会馆 was established, the main dialect was Hainanese, and its founder was Chen Wande 陈万德, p. 53) to the setting up of Tunku Abdul Rahman University by the Malayan Chinese Association in 2001. The length of the entries also ranges from one line (p. 164) to one-and-a-half pages (pp. 384–85).

There are a few outstanding features of the book. One, the documentation on the activities of the Chinese since the beginning of the twentieth century were necessarily more substantive than those before, given that large-scale immigration from China to the peninsula occurred only during the beginning of the twentieth century (events from 515 to 1800 take up 13 pages, 1801–1900 are covered in 44 pages, while the rest of the book records events from the 1900s to 2004). Explanations and details tend to be more extensive and clearer for those parts of the narrative where information is most available. Two, most of the sources tend to be secondary sources published in China. Very few of these sources used are primary sources published in Malaysia. Only in more recent years were local newspapers such as *Nanyang Siang Pau* 南洋商报, *Sin Chew Jit Poh* 星洲日报, *Lianhe Zaobao* 联合早报 and *Guanghua Ribao* 光华日报 used more extensively. Admittedly, newspapers are probably the most important source of information for a book of this genre, but other sources such as archival materials, publications by local organizations that were intended only for internal circulation etc. should also be consulted. Third, there is an over-emphasis on the historiography of East Malaysia *vis-à-vis* West Malaysia. The author displayed more fondness for the history of Sabah and Sarawak, as reflected in several entries made on the contributions of Huang Nai Shang (黄乃裳), a Chinese pioneer in the East Malaysian states. Events related to the Malayan Communist Party, whose membership was predominantly ethnic Chinese, were also highlighted.

While historical items are extensively recorded, the reader does not get a sense of the major strands of historical development of the Malaysian Chinese from the vast entries. First of all, what were the major milestones in Malaysian

Chinese history? The book does not seem to give the reader any clues. While Huang has written on Malaysian Chinese, her minimal contact with the community and lack of understanding of the real issues in Malaysia (and ethnic Chinese in Malaysia) become readily apparent to the initiated reader. The comprehensive time-line can certainly be broken up into several parts or segments (organized by century or historical turning point such as World War II, Malaya's independence, etc.), which would make certain events milestones in the historiography of the Malaysian Chinese. Secondly, sources used were sometimes unreliable; events/issues selected were too insignificant to deserve an entry, and the organization of entries too haphazard for a reader to register a sense of thematic development from the chronology. If the author had divided the events into social, cultural and political matters, it would have achieved much clarity. Thirdly, perhaps more pertinent to the theme of this chapter, is that the author approached the Malaysian Chinese history mainly from the perspective of mainland China, looking at the immigration movement of Chinese overseas mainly from the perspective of a scholar residing in China. Such sentiment is first demonstrated in the title of the book, *Huaqiao Huaren Biannianshi*. No doubt the political and social conditions during the early periods of Chinese immigration would qualify them to be called *huaqiao*, however, the developments after the Malaysia's independence in 1957 have certainly made the term outdated. While this chorological history of Malaysian Chinese has no ambition of making such a distinction (the entry on 31 August 1957 consisted of only one line about the independence of Malaya), it is still worth pointing out that Malaysian Chinese readers do read with a critical eye towards practical relevance and their deserving roles in the nation-building process. It may be asking too much of such a volume to address contentious questions of methodology, but the failure to confront directly its ultimate dependence on some form of "China-centric" analysis undercuts the efforts of other scholars searching for autonomous studies on ethnic Chinese in Southeast Asia.

Zeng Shaocong's *Studies in Contemporary Southeast Asian Chinese and Ethnic Relations* examines the social, economic, and political forces at work in Southeast Asia and their impact on the relations between Chinese communities and the local communities in the Philippines, Malaysia and Singapore. The first three chapters sketched the origins of Chinese immigrants in Southeast Asia, and traced the development of Chinese culture and traditions in the mainland. An encyclopaedic narrative of governmental policies towards the ethnic Chinese in the Philippines, Malaysia, and Singapore, the transformation of Chinese identity after World War II, and the changes in ethnic relations during the era of globalization follows. In the conclusion, the author returns to the theme of the history of Chinese immigration, offering yet again a historical overview of Chinese immigration in Southeast Asia.

The author consciously attempted to go beyond "the perspective of China", and utilized "the theories of ethnic policies and multi-nation-state and ethnic relations" (p. 41) in investigating the problem. The book did not disappoint those looking for an elaboration of methodology, as the author reviews the six groups of theoretical literature he employs in the study, which are: ethnology, international immigration, world system and globalization, international relations, demography, and social capital. While it is obvious that this book is a multi-disciplinary study, the emphasis is nevertheless on Chinese immigrants in a foreign land and their process of adaptation. In other words, it is still predominantly a study on Chinese immigration. However, an important attempt was made to analyse the interaction of the Chinese in Malaysia and the Philippines with the colonials, local authorities and the elected governments. Also interesting is the analysis on the Chinese new immigrants who congregated in these countries from the beginning of the 1990s.

Zeng's study is well researched and an academic account of the conduct of ethnic relations of the Chinese in Southeast Asia. However, its analysis did not go beyond "the perspective of China". This reviewer found painstaking attempts by the author to do so, but he has only half succeeded. As in most historical studies of the overseas Chinese, the approach of the author to regard these groups as immigrants has become the central theme (the independent variable), rather than an attempt to integrate local and indigenous histories in an analysis to produce an entirely different intellectual outlook. However, the author ought to be commended for his conscious effort to have moved in a direction that few PRC scholars have attempted so far. If Huang's study remains Sino-centric, then Zeng's work is a transition from "Sino-centricity" to a self-conscious consideration to go beyond such a perspective.

... TO "AUTONOMOUS NARRATIVE"

A critical intellectual leap to emphasize the local/indigenous Chineseness rather than the motherland's cultural Chineseness can be found in Qiu Gebing's, *Southeast Asian Chinese Secret Societies.* Based on a dissertation submitted to Nanjing University in 2000, the book is a study of the evolution, structure, organization and function of Chinese secret societies in Southeast Asia. The first chapter is on Chinese southward immigration and overseas Chinese communities, detailing the historical development of Chinese immigration to the South Seas and the historical push-pull factors for Chinese immigration. The second chapter provides an overview of Chinese secret societies in Southeast Asia, their origins, spatial distribution, organizational development, and their eventual demise in these countries towards the end of the twentieth century. Chapter three examines the composition of membership, leadership, management and rituals of these secret societies. Chapter four looks at the relations/connections between/among secret societies, their similarities and differences and conflicts. Chapter five analyses the relationship between the Chinese secret societies with the mainstream local Chinese community and the local governments. The final chapter concludes with an analysis of the changing roles and functions of these organizations.

The study throughout is logically organized with good introductions and conclusions to each chapter which tie the work together. Research findings are well-explained and are reflective of knowledge gained from extensive literature. Well-researched and building on pioneering works of Blythe, Comber and Mak Lau-fong, the study employs a perspective that is tightly glued to the local environments and historiography of the emergence and gradual transformation of Chinese secret societies. Their emergence was more a function of indigenous factors than mainland Chinese cultural traditions. While the origins of Chinese secret societies were traced (in the first chapter), it simply receded into the background in the subsequent analysis of their evolution in local societies and histories. This work not only represents a significant contribution to the study of Chinese secret societies in Southeast Asia, but also indicates the author's ability to go beyond the "Chinese perspective", linking the adaptation of the secret societies to local environments after they have been physically and perhaps psychologically disconnected from the motherland. Dynamics of indigenous forces and local cultural configurations were carefully considered and incorporated in the explanations to give the book a genuinely "objective" stance in its analysis.

Wu Xiao An's *Chinese Business in the Making of a Malay State, 1882–1941*, is unique in its genre. It is by far the best treatment of the Chinese business network in late nineteenth century Malaya. As the product of a doctoral dissertation presented at the University of Amsterdam in 1999, the book retains the intensity of a dissertation. As Heather Sutherland points out in the "Foreword", the book is a sign of "the growing maturity of this field [of Overseas Chinese studies]."[14] This is probably not an exaggeration. The author wrote: "[t]he purpose of this book is to link Chinese business networks and family studies to a larger framework considering issues of the state, region, ethnicity, migration and Southeast Asian modernization" (p. 1). Carl

Trocki, in reviewing the book, noticed that the study is "much broader than the simple story of Chinese Business in Kedah", as the author is really concerned about the "Southeast Asian transformation".[15]

The author shows a good mastery of the literature by citing many relevant sources in a few hundred footnotes, most of which contains several references to archival materials. It is significant that throughout the book, the author gives due consideration to the local history and the significance of indigenous factors that have engulfed the Chinese merchants in the northern Malay states of Kedah and Penang, and Southern Thailand. Mainland China receded into the background, and indeed appeared quite distant, as the author immersed himself in local Malay historical records and documentation.

Underpinning this historical perspective is the evolution of the local Chinese businesses *vis-à-vis* the Malay authorities in the states of Kedah and Penang. The reader is provided not only with insights into the Chinese business network as an alien institution, but also with a study of the political, social and commercial roles of the British colonial rulers, the Malay rulers, local clansmen, etc. One learns, for example, that the Sultan of Kedah (in 1888) often was at odds with wealthy Chinese Lim Leng Cheak in the use of a steam-powered rice mill in the Kota Star district for a period of twenty years (p. 125). The study of the complex configurations of local actors provides a unique perspective, and provides the reader with a comprehensive view of the Chinese businesses and their impact on the socio-political-cultural landscapes in the Malay States during the historical periods under study.

This book represents a move away from the myth that Chinese scholars of Southeast Asian Studies cannot utilize non-Chinese sources for their research.[16] By relying on a wealth of scholarly material in English and Chinese, the author clearly demonstrates that Malaysian Chinese histories could be unveiled with archival materials. It also highlights the crucial distinction that just because an author is PRC Chinese, it does not mean that the author is China-centric.

AUTONOMOUS HISTORY, AUTONOMOUS SOUTHEAST ASIAN STUDIES

The discussion on "Sino-centricity" in Southeast Asian Studies in the PRC, with a brief review of the four books mentioned above, inevitably raises the long-debated question in the field on autonomous history. David Marr, in his report on the visit by the Australian delegation to China in 1981, observed that at that time:

> "… most historians we met were preoccupied with what might loosely be called the Chinese influence in Southeast Asia. They seemed stunned whenever we urged them to take more seriously the autonomous histories of Southeast Asian Kingdoms, and to place their Chinese texts alongside local archaeological data, court chronicles, folk-lore compilations and linguistic reconstruction."[17]

That situation has probably changed. As far as the study of Southeast Asian Chinese is concerned, the intellectual momentum is towards a more autonomous narration of local histories, with ethnic Chinese as an integral and essential part of the story. Admittedly there are many works done by Chinese scholars which are still preoccupied with China-centric research, constructing the image of the Southeast Asian Chinese from their history and cultural roots. Although their studies or arguments presuppose careful empirical research, PRC scholars rarely conduct such research or propose how it might be conducted. Such approaches remain rooted in China-centric tenets of research. The gap between the demand and supply of empirical research is predictable in a field that appears to reward empiricism over theory-building, political correctness over scholarship. At the same time, good secondary accounts emerged in most cases, and the attempt to further investigate cases based on first-hand study has surfaced, at least in its nascent form. Undoubtedly, studies on overseas Chinese in Southeast Asia by PRC scholars have been facilitated by their competence in the language and culture. Their interest in the *huaqiao* is historical and their academic strength cannot be doubted. However, beyond the nationalistic and historical factor, one has to ask if there is a need to look at social science methodology seriously at the present stage of development.

In 1961, John Smail wrote the classic essay on the possibility of an autonomous history of Modern Southeast Asia in which he wondered whether it was possible to write a history of the Southeast Asian region from an angle different from the one the Europeans had used so far.[18] Smail's writings (and others such as John Legge and Harry Benda) acted as a catalyst for scholars later to embark on an intellectual path very different from their predecessors.[19]

I do not intend to review Smail's contributions to the discussion on autonomous history writing.[20] Suffice to say, Smail discerned four different approaches to history writing on Asia: straight colonial history, neo-colonial history, anti-colonial history, and autonomous history writing. He believed that only autonomous history — history written from the perspectives of the local — could do justice to the history of Asian society. Smail was inspired by the early historian Van Leur's works. While Van Leur argued that that

European and Asian powers kept each other in balance until roughly 1800, Smail took exception. He wanted to go beyond Asia and Europe centrism. He observed that that there had always been an autonomous history of Asia in which continuities were not disturbed and where alien cultures and norms were absorbed. A new form of history writing could be developed to surpass the cultural restraints of Western or Asian historians.[21]

As I survey the recent harvest of Southeast Asian Chinese studies in China, it has proven very difficult to ignore these culturally-bound limitations. It is clear that for geo-strategic and political reasons, scholarship on Southeast Asia (especially Southeast Asian Chinese) in the PRC has been much influenced by non-academic considerations. The cultural domains of China in the centre for these scholars have proved to be at times a constraint. It is argued, the urge to resist the notion and the use of "China perspective" as reflected in these studies is because they still operate within the frame of "national China" or "cultural China", through which imagines a space of the shared "Chinese" culture and communities that is perhaps emotionally nostalgic, but is nevertheless, extremely China-centred, and regards the ethnic Chinese in Southeast Asia to be the subordinates. Whether the phenomenon is related to cultural expansionism growing out of modern manifestations of Chineseness is unclear. However, it does appear that the mission of PRC scholars is fundamentally different from that of the home scholars.

In general, the mainstream works on Southeast Asian Chinese by PRC scholars have focused on the ethnic Chinese experience by emphasizing cultural relations from the point of view of the interests of mainland Chinese. They have lacked a theoretical perspective that is dynamic and is focused on the political economy of indigenous change. These PRC mainstream works were thus unprepared, methodologically and epistemologically, to deal with both the intellectual concerns of ethnic Chinese and the cultural and political needs of the community in the Southeast Asian context.

Even for the home scholars, when narrating the histories of the ethnic Chinese in Southeast Asia, they face additional challenges as the subject is often regarded a "non-indigenous" entity in the region. After all, the Chinese in Southeast Asia are immigrants or descendents of immigrants. Locating them in the autonomous histories of Southeast Asian nation-state requires scholars to distinguish between the native and non-native, colonial and non-colonial, indigenous and the non-indigenous. By categorizing the ethnic Chinese as a non-indigenous community has been a convenient way of studying the subject, but it offers no paradigmatic breakthrough in scholarship. In addition, home scholars acquire an "outsider within" posture, and seem to have, so far, nurtured an ambivalent consciousness to the very cultural mainstreams that nourish them. At the same time, however, they are also being marginalized in the indigenous academic setting which they have ironically claimed as their own.

Robert Taylor noted "the first search for an autonomous history of the region with a quest to write the narrative of the post-colonial states of Southeast Asia from their own individual perspectives."[22] He also noted that " ... the nationalist historiography saw the fruits of imperialism and nationalism as the template for describing the totality of history."[23] A "totality of history" for the Southeast Asian Chinese is only possible if there are different perspectives of history making it truly holistic, comprehensible and wholesome. Home scholars in the region have attempted to write "from their own individual perspective", but with only limited success. *The Chinese in Malaysia* edited by Lee Kam Hing and Tan Chee Beng,[24] and 马来西亚华人史新编 (*The New History of Malaysian Chinese*) edited by Lim Chooi Kwa, et al.,[25] are exemplary works in the autonomous history tradition, even if the contributors and the editors did not consciously approach the subject matter from that perspective. These home scholars' autonomous history writings are unique in their contribution to ethnic Chinese Southeast Asian Studies (in this case the Chinese in Malaysia) because of their conscious effort to read and interpret history in regard to the necessity and inevitable development of nationalism and cultural identity in the region, thereby offering a framework unlike that advocated by Hall and Smail.[26] These home scholars are ready to create a new autonomous methodology allowing ethnic Chinese to control knowledge about themselves.[27] It is important to bear in mind that "there is no implication that the work of Southeast Asian scholars is somehow more authoritative or authentic",[28] and that home scholars have "no privileged access to the truth and (are) equally open to debate."[29]

The rewards of greater attentiveness to the challenges of autonomous histories and social science methodology would be two: increased depth of the subject matter and empirically driven progress in our general understanding of Southeast Asian Chinese, and the larger field of Southeast Asian Studies. Scholars sceptical that ethnic Chinese case studies could yield any theoretical advance should still welcome the depth they would bring as their richness will certainly contribute to the theoretical development of the discipline. It is hard to read books such as those reviewed here without concluding that attention to autonomous histories and field research is a necessary condition of scholastic progress.

CONCLUSIONS

This review essay tries to ascertain if the historiography of Southeast Asian Chinese by these PRC scholars has indeed expressed such a perception of China-centric paradigm, and to what degree such intellectual orientation has changed over time. It argues that the dominant approach of "Sino-centricity" in Southeast Asian Studies have slowly moved to became less China-centred, and to a certain extent exhibited a standard of scholarship which can be labelled as social science-centred, which consciously or unconsciously displays the nascent essence of "autonomous narrative". The writing of autonomous history may not have penetrated mainstream awareness, but it has surely begun to show signs of progress.

The study of Southeast Asian Chinese has been a major focus by scholars in Chinese academic institutions. The proliferation of publications in recent years in the subject should not take the academic community by surprise. But the quality of some certainly did. Inasmuch as sufficient time has passed since the modern incarnation of Southeast Asian Studies in the PRC as an academic focus, what are we to make of its accomplishments, contributions, and shortcomings? The books by Huang, Zeng, Qiu and Wu represent only a fraction of the huge literature on the ethnic Chinese in Southeast Asia by PRC scholars in the last five years. Taken collectively the works provide a sense of transition and arrival. This short essay has been selective in its review of publications in the field, and makes no pretense that it is a comprehensive assessment about the entire spectrum of scholarship on Southeast Asian Chinese Studies in the PRC.[30] It is necessarily superficial, sporadic and incomplete; it is not intended as a critique or interrogation of reigning intellectual systems, but a humble invitation for discussion on the subject.

NOTES

1. Wang Gungwu, et al., *Southeast Asian Studies in China: A Report.* Research School of Pacific Studies, Australian National University, Canberra, 1981.
2. J.A.C. Mackie, "China Report", in Wang Gungwu, et al., pp. 10–22.
3. David Marr, "Chinese Study of Southeast Asia in Transition", in Wang Gungwu, et al., p. 34.
4. Ibid., p. 34.
5. Liao Shaolian, "Southeast Asian Studies in China", in *Southeast Asian Studies in Asia: An Assessment,* Conference-Workshop Proceedings, Asian Centre, University of the Philippines, 2003, pp. 53–58.
6. See Francis Lai, ed., *State of East and Southeast Asian Studies Since 1979 in China,*

Hong Kong and Singapore. Hong Kong: Centre for Asian Pacific Studies, Lingnan College, 1987.

7. Liu Hong, "Southeast Asian Studies in Greater China", *Kyoto Review of Southeast Asia*, no. 3 (March 2003).
8. Liao, op. cit., pp. 56–57.
9. See Abu Talib Ahmad and Tan Liok Ee, "Introduction", in *New Terrains in Southeast Asian History*, edited by Abu Talib Ahmad and Tan Liok Ee. Ohio University Press, 2003.
10. Eurocentricism in social science has been under attack for decades. Immanuel Wallerstein wrote: "It has been argued that social science expresses its Eurocentrism in (1) its historiography, (2) the parochiality of its universalism, (3) its assumptions about (Western) civilization, (4) its Orientalism, and (5) its attempts to impose the theory of progress." See his "Eurocentrism and its Avatars: The Dilemmas of Social Science", keynote address at ISA East Asian Regional Colloquium, "The Future of Sociology in East Asia", 22–23 November 1996, Seoul, Korea, co-sponsored by Korean Sociological Association and International Sociological Association, <http://fbc.binghamton.edu/iweuroc.htm>, accessed on 7 December 2005.
11. 中国学者"鲜见从东南亚或者世界范围的角度来观察新马华人问题"。张应龙"新时期新马华人研究评述 (1978–2000)", 收入李元瑾编《新马华人：传统与现代的对话》, 新加坡：南洋理工大学，中华语言文化中心，新加坡亚洲研究会，南洋大学毕业生协会, 2002.
12. 何启良,"拒绝点缀、建立主体：'马来西亚华人研究'的思考"，马来西亚吉隆坡华社研究中心主办,《马来西亚华人研究：新视野》研讨会，*吉隆坡星洲日报*, 2005年7月2日.
13. D.G.E. Hall, *A History of Southeast Asia*, 1955; reprinted, London: Macmillan, 1961. Quoted in Abu Talib Ahmad and Tan Liok Ee, "Introduction", in *New Terrains in Southeast Asian History*, edited by Abu Talib Ahmad and Tan Liok Ee. Ohio University Press, 2003, p. x.
14. Heather Sutherland, "Foreword", in Wu Xiao An, *Chinese Business in the Making of A Malay State, 1882–1941*. London: Routledge, 2003, p. xi.
15. Carl Trocki, "Book Review of Wu Xiao An, *Chinese Business in the Making of A Malay State, 1882–1941*". London: Routledge, 2003; *Journal of Southeast Asian Studies* 35, no. 3 (October 2004): 569.
16. Carl Trocki wrote: "He is among the first PRC scholars to publish a major study on Southeast Asian Chinese in English." Ibid., p. 569.
17. David Marr, "Chinese Study of Southeast Asia in Transition", in Wang Gungwu, et al., *Southeast Asian Studies in China: A Report*, op. cit., p. 34.
18. John Smail, "On the Possibility of an Autonomous History of Modern Southeast Asia," *Journal of Southeast Asian History* 2, no. 2 (1961): 73–105; reprinted in Laurie J. Sears, ed., *Autonomous Histories, Particular Truths: Essays in Honor of John R.W. Smail*. Madison: Wisconsin Monographs on Southeast Asia, 1993.
19. For example, the publication of *In Search of Southeast Asia* in 1971 by a group

of American scholars for the first time relegated the colonial masters in Asia to the background. David Joel Steinberg et al., *In Search of Southeast Asia; A Modern History*. Kuala Lumpur, Oxford University Press, 1971.

20. For this treatment, refer to Laurie J. Sears, ed., *Autonomous Histories, Particular Truths*, op. cit.
21. The above summary is taken from Leonard Blussé, "The VOC Records and the Study of Early Modern Asia", *IIAS Newsletter*, 10–11 December 1998.
22. Robert Taylor, "Introduction", in *Recalling Local Pasts: Autonomous History in Southeast Asia*, edited by Sunait Chutintaranond and Chris Baker. Chiang Mai, Thailand: Silkworm Books, 2002, p. 1.
23. Ibid., p. 2.
24. Lee Kam Heng and Tan Chee Beng, eds., *The Chinese in Malaysia*. Kuala Lumpur: Oxford University Press, 2000.
25. 林水檺，何启良，何国忠，赖观福合编. 《马来西亚华人史新编》，全三册 , Lim Chooi Kwa, Ho Khai Leong, Hou Kok Chung, Lai Kuan Fook (eds.). *A New History of Malaysian Chinese*. 3 volumes. Kuala Lumpur: Federation of Chinese Associations Malaysia, 1998.
26. Other works include: 林开忠著. 《建构中的"华人文化"：族群属性、国家与华教运动》 Lim Khay Thiong. *Constructing "Chinese Culture": Ethnicity, State and the Chinese Education Movement*. Kuala Lumpur: Centre for Malaysian Chinese Studies, 1999; 林廷辉 •宋婉莹 著. 《马来西亚华人新村五十年》 Lim Hin Fui. *Fifty Years of Malaysian Chinese New Villages*. Kuala Lumpur: Centre for Malaysian Chinese Studies. 2nd edition. 2002; 何国忠著. 《马来西亚华人：身份认同与文化的命运》 Hou Kok Chung. *The Chinese in Malaysia: Identity, Culture and Communal Politics*. Kuala Lumpur: Centre for Malaysian Chinese Studies, 2002. For a brief introduction of the centres for Chinese studies in Malaysia, see Wu Xiao An, "Centres for Chinese Studies in Southeast Asia", *Kyoto Review of Southeast Asia*, no. 3 (March 2003).
27. It should be noted that even among the home scholars, there are differences in the way the subject matter is approached. This could be a result of their different educational backgrounds. The English-educated scholars and the Chinese-educated scholars invariably write with different degrees of emotional involvement and intensity and hence their evidence, argument and interpretation of events and history can be quite different. See 潘永强："英文视野下的马来西亚华人", 载《华人政治思潮》, 吉隆坡：大将出版社, 2003.
28. Abu Talib Ahmad and Tan Liok Ee, "Introduction", in Abu Talib Ahmad and Tan Liok Ee, eds., *New Terrains in Southeast Asian History*. Ohio University Press, 2003, p. xi.
29. Ibid., p. xii.
30. After I have finished the essay, Leo Suryadinata brought to my attention this book 李安山编：《中国华侨华人学—学科定位与研究展望》(北京：北京大学出版社, 2006). The book is a collection of essays reviewing the state of scholarship on overseas Chinese studies in the PRC, and I find many themes

explored in the book relevant and pertinent to the central argument of my essay. Certainly the subject will require a revisit in the next few years given the lively pace of development in the field.

REFERENCES

Abu Talib Ahmad and Tan Liok Ee, eds., *New Terrains in Southeast Asian History*. Ohio University Press, 2003.

Chutintaranond, Sunait and Chris Baker, eds., *Recalling Local Pasts: Autonomous History in Southeast Asia*. Chiang Mai, Thailand: Silkworm Books, 2002.

Lai, Francis, ed., *State of East and Southeast Asian Studies Since 1979 in China, Hong Kong and Singapore*. Hong Kong: Centre for Asian Pacific Studies, Lingnan College, 1987.

Lee Kam Heng and Tan Chee Beng, eds., *The Chinese in Malaysia*. Kuala Lumpur: Oxford University Press, 2000.

Liu Hong. "Southeast Asian Studies in Greater China", *Kyoto Review of Southeast Asia*, no. 3 (March 2003).

Sears, Laurie J., ed., *Autonomous Histories, Particular Truths: Essays in Honor of John R.W. Small*. Madison: Wisconsin Monographs on Southeast Asia, 1993.

Southeast Asian Studies in Asia: An Assessment. Conference-Workshop Proceedings, Asian Centre, University of the Philippines, 2003.

Steinberg, David Joel, et al., *In Search of Southeast Asia; A Modern History*. Kuala Lumpur: Oxford University Press, 1971.

Wang Gungwu, et al. *Southeast Asian Studies in China: A Report*. Research School of Pacific Studies, Australian National University, Canberra, 1981.

Wu Xiao An. "Centers for Chinese Studies in Southeast Asia", *Kyoto Review of Southeast Asia*, no. 3 (March 2003).

李元瑾.《新马华人：传统与现代的对话》.新加坡：南洋理工大学，中华语言文化中心，新加坡亚洲研究会，南洋大学毕业生协会, 2002.

李安山编：《中国华侨华人学 — 学科定位与研究展望》.北京：北京大学出版社, 2006.

林水檺，何启良，何国忠，赖观福合编.《马来西亚华人史新编》，全三册.吉隆坡：马来西亚中华大会堂总会, 1998.

潘永强："英文视野下的马来西亚华人"，载《华人政治思潮》.吉隆坡：大将出版社, 2003.

7

Southeast Asian Studies in Yunnan: Achievements, Challenges and Outlook

Wang Shilu

Yunnan, a frontier province, shares border with Myanmar, Laos and Vietnam with a total boundary line of 4,060 kilometres, of which 1,997 km is with Myanmar, 710 km with Laos and another 1,353 km with Vietnam. It is adjacent to Thailand, Cambodia, Malaysia and Singapore with the linkage of routes. There are sixteen ethnic groups living across the border line where there are eleven national first-grade border ports with more than eighty passages leading to neighbouring countries. With its special geographic position and historical relations with Southeast Asian countries, Yunnan Province provides positive external conditions for its scholars to conduct Southeast Asian Studies. Therefore, since the founding of the People's Republic of China, the government departments concerned have attached growing attention to Southeast Asian Studies in Yunnan. As a result, the academic circle has gradually turned to systematic research on Southeast Asia compared with the past spontaneous studies. Since the establishment of the Institute of Southeast Asian Studies of Yunnan Academy of Social Sciences, Southeast Asian Studies in Yunnan have been raised to a higher level. The further acceleration of reform and opening up has brought unprecedented opportunities to the development of Southeast

Asian Studies in Yunnan in the form of increasing new academic achievements and expanding research groups. This chapter, based on the research results made by the Institute of Southeast Asian Studies of Yunnan Academy of Social Sciences, attempts to give a general evaluation on the history, status and outlook of Southeast Asian Studies.

A BRIEF HISTORY OF SOUTHEAST ASIAN STUDIES IN YUNNAN

Yunnan initiated its Southeast Asian Studies long ago. Even before the founding of the People's Republic of China, the academic institutions there had produced the odd publication. Fang Guoyu, professor at the Department of History in Yunnan University, and Zhang Fengqi were senior researchers conducting Southeast Asian Studies. They conducted thorough studies on the history of China-Southeast Asia relations and border issues with Myanmar, Laos and Vietnam.

Systematic studies began in the early 1950s when the Yunnan Institute of Southeast Asian Studies initiated research on China-Myanmar boundary and Myanmar issues. Since the establishment of the Yunnan Institute of Social and Historical Studies of Minority Nationalities in 1956, some researchers at the institute began to conduct specialized researches on Southeast Asia. In 1963, the Yunnan Institute of Social and Historical Studies of Minority Nationalities was renamed Yunnan Institute of Historical Studies under which the Division of Southeast Asian Studies was founded. The division began studies on the histories and nationalities of Myanmar, Thailand and three countries of Indochina. During the three years from its founding to "the Great Cultural Revolution", the division worked mainly in the following four areas:

1. Establishing a relatively comprehensive material system by collecting a great number of Chinese and English books on Southeast Asia from various sources, as well as subscribing to newspapers and periodicals;
2. Compiling historical materials on Southeast Asia in *Ershisishi [Twenty-Four Histories]*. Of the compiled materials, *The Abstracts of Historical Materials about Vietnam, Myanmar, Thailand and Laos Culled* from *Qingshilu [the True Records of Qing Dynasty]* was published by the Yunnan People's Publishing House in 1985;
3. Conducting surveys and interviews on overseas Chinese from Myanmar, Thailand and three countries of Indochina, as well as collecting a great number of materials on the studies of the overseas Chinese in Southeast Asia;

4. Translating some foreign language materials and works into Chinese, of which the important ones are *Biography of U Nu* and *Burma under Japanese Occupation*, etc.

Since the beginning of the "The Great Cultural Revolution" in 1966, the systematic pursuit of Southeast Asian Studies in Yunnan went into stagnation. In 1972, the Yunnan Institute of Historical Studies was reinstated. After the reinstatement of the institute, the Division of Southeast Asian Studies was established and the publication, *Southeast Asia Information*, was published. A number of researchers was recruited into the division, which laid the foundation for the future development of Southeast Asian Studies in Yunnan. By the late 1970s, scholars had published many research papers of considerable influence such as "*Whether the Conquest of the State of Dali by Kublai Khan Led to Large-scale Migration of the Thai to the South?*" by Du Yuting and Chen Lufan published in *History Studies* no. 2 (1978), "*Contributions of Overseas Chinese to Vietnam's Economic and Cultural Development*" by Qing Qinzhi published in *History Studies* no. 6 (1979), and "*Land Policy before the Liberation of Cambodia*" published in *History Studies* no. 10 (1979), etc.

As the policy of opening up and reform moved forward in 1981, people had an urgent need to know more about Southeast Asia. Under such circumstances, the local authorities approved the establishment of the Institute of Southeast Asian Studies of Yunnan Academy of Social Sciences, under which were the Division of Southeast Asian Studies and the Division of South Asian Studies. Since the establishment of the Institute of Southeast Asian Studies, a group of new researchers were recruited into the institute and the staff was expanded. In 1983, a quarterly journal *Southeast Asia*, which was based on *Southeast Asia Information*, was published. It was distributed both at home and abroad in 1984. Since the early 1980s, with the institute's renewed efforts and opportunities brought by the open and reform policy, Southeast Asian Studies in Yunnan have moved into a new period of development.

STATUS OF SOUTHEAST ASIAN STUDIES IN YUNNAN

After twenty years of development, Southeast Asian Studies in Yunnan, covering research achievements and the reinforcement of research contingents as well as the amassment of materials, have been elevated to greater heights.

Research Infrastructure

First of all, the research institutions have been expanded and reinforced. As Yunnan's opening up to Southeast Asia develops further, in particular, with

Yunnan's participation in the Lancang-Mekong Sub-region Co-operation and progress in the China–ASEAN Free Trade Area, increasing numbers of people have been caring about the development of Southeast Asia, especially of the five countries of mainland Southeast Asia. As a result, an enthusiasm for Southeast Asian Studies has developed in Yunnan Province. With the guidance of the Institute of Southeast Asian Studies and the promotion of organizations concerned, research institutions and researchers engaged in Southeast Asian Studies have grown. It is now in a phase where official departments concerned, universities, and professional research institutes work together to conduct thorough, systematic and in-depth studies on Southeast Asia (including ASEAN countries and regional or sub-regional cooperation institutions) at different levels.

In terms of research institutions, in addition to the Institute of Southeast Asian Studies of Yunnan Academy of Social Sciences, many institutions and organizations have established their own centres which could directly serve themselves in their works or teachings. The major institutions are the Institute of Southeast Asian Studies of the School of International Relations of Yunnan University; Institute of Southeast Asian Studies of the Department of History of Yunnan Normal University; Institute of International Trade Research of the Department of Commerce of Yunnan Province; Institute of Science Research of the Department of Science and Technology of Yunnan Province; Development Research Centre of the Yunnan Provincial Government; Policy Research Centre of the Yunnan Provincial Party Committee; Institute of Economic Studies of Dehong Dai and Jingpo Autonomous Prefecture of Yunnan, etc. Besides, some teachers from institutions such as the School of History and Culture, School of Economy, School of Development Studies, Centre for Studies of Chinese Southwest's Borderland Ethnic Minorities of Yunnan University; School of History and Administration, School of Tourism of Yunnan Normal University; Institute of Nationality Research, School of Southeast Asian Languages and Cultures of Yunnan Nationalities University have also been doing research on Southeast Asia. Yunnan Association of Southeast Asian Studies, a non-government organization, has done much in terms of academic exchanges and the improvement of Southeast Asian Studies in Yunnan. In terms of research contingents, there are at present over one hundred researchers who are directly or indirectly engaged in Southeast Asian Studies in Yunnan compared with forty or fifty researchers in the mid-1980s. In universities such as Yunnan University, Yunnan Normal University and Yunnan Nationalities University, more postgraduate students have been choosing Southeast Asia as their research direction. Yunnan University has doctoral courses in Southeast Asia Studies under the discipline of world history. Therefore, institutions of Southeast Asian Studies have been refreshed with qualified success.

Thus after more than twenty-five years, the Institute of Southeast Asian Studies has developed into a comprehensive institution with a pool of qualified researchers, and is a core institute in Yunnan carrying out research on Southeast Asia Studies. At present, Yunnan Institute of Southeast Asian Studies has twenty staff members, of whom eight are senior researchers. The divisions of the institute are as follows: Research Division on Thailand; Research Division on Myanmar; Research Division on Indochina; Research Division on Southeast Asian Politics and Economy; Reference Room; Editorial Office; and Administrative Office. The Institute of Southeast Asian Studies of Yunnan Academy of Social Sciences is therefore a special organ in Yunnan Province engaged in Southeast Asian Studies and one of the five research entities in mainland China.

Second, with the collection and amassment of a lot of materials, a comparatively comprehensive material system has been set up. There are about 40,000 volumes of reference books at present, among which about 30,000 volumes are in foreign languages such as English, Thai, Lao, Vietnamese, Russian, Japanese, French, etc. The institute subscribes to over a hundred foreign journals and eighty-odd domestic journals annually. It has established a long-term material-exchange relationship with many institutions both at home and abroad. Moreover, an efficient electronic information enquiry system has been established.

Thirdly, the publication of the academic journal, *Southeast Asia* (Quarterly), has provided a favourable channel to reflect the academic output. Since the publication of the first issue of *Southeast Asia* in 1983, eighty-six volumes (about 8.6 million words) have been published.

Main Fields of Study and Achievements

The main scope of Southeast Asian Studies in Yunnan include the countries of mainland Southeast Asia such as Thailand, Myanmar, Vietnam, Laos and Cambodia while research on Singapore, Malaysia, the Philippines, Indonesia, and regional issues are also focal points. The specialties involved are: international economy, international politics, international relations, historical studies and ethnology. The main fields of study comprise: (1) Economy of Southeast Asian countries; (2) Sub-regional cooperation in Southeast Asia; (3) Contemporary politics and international relations of Southeast Asia; (4) Histories of Southeast Asian countries; (5) Bilateral or multilateral relations between countries of mainland Southeast Asia and

Yunnan, as well as national cultures of Southeast Asian countries; (6) Economic and trade relations between Yunnan and Southeast Asian countries; (7) Yunnan's participation in the Lancang-Mekong Sub-region Cooperation and China-ASEAN Free Trade Area.

The Institute of Southeast Asian Studies of Yunnan Academy of Social Sciences, as one of the vigorous forces in Southeast Asian Studies in China and an important base for Southeast Asian Studies in Yunnan, has produced hundreds of academic works since its establishment. It is estimated that more than 40 books and 2,000 academic papers (about 60 million words altogether) have been published, of which over 90 papers were published in influential journals such as *Social Science in China, History Research, World History, Ethno-National Studies, Report on China's Borderland History and Geography Research, World Economy, World Economy and Politics, Overseas Chinese History Studies, Contemporary International Relations, South Asian Studies, Contemporary Asia-Pacific Studies* and *World Nationalities Studies*, and about 40 papers were published or reprinted in foreign journals. These academic results have played a positive role in advancing Southeast Asian Studies in China, particularly in Yunnan, and have exerted a favourable influence on society.

1. Comprehensive Studies on Contemporary Southeast Asian Politics and Economy

In order to serve the aim of opening up wider to Southeast Asia, the Institute of Southeast Asian Studies of Yunnan Academy of Social Sciences has compiled two series of books since the mid-1980s. One is the *Contemporary Southeast Asia* series in eleven volumes, which have been published successively by Sichuan People's Publishing House since 1992. The series covers every country of Southeast Asia and ASEAN, and makes a comprehensive introduction and analysis of the geography, nature, history, politics, economy and foreign affairs of Southeast Asian countries. The other is the *Economy of Contemporary Southeast Asia* series in seven volumes, published successively by Yunnan People's Publishing House since 1996. The series covers every country of Southeast Asia and provides a systematic introduction and analysis of the economic development of Southeast Asia since the 1990s. The two series have become one of the most valuable reference books in the field. Since 2000, the Institute of Southeast Asian Studies has set to compile and publish the *Annual Report on Southeast Asian Development*, as part of the *Yunnan Blue Papers* series. Three volumes compiled by Professor Wang Shilu have been published by Yunnan People's Publishing House since 2003.

2. Studies on International Relations and Regional Cooperation of Southeast Asia

The international relations and regional cooperation of Southeast Asia are Yunnan scholars' focal points in recent years. Some researchers have put enormous efforts in studies on ASEAN, and the internal and external relations of Southeast Asian countries. Hundreds of papers have been published, and the main books published are: *From ASEAN to Greater ASEAN: Studies on 30 years of Development of ASEAN*, written by Wang Shilu, Wang Guoping (Beijing: World Affairs Press, 1998), *ASEAN and the Asia-Pacific Entering into the 21st Century: Development Trends of ASEAN and Its Implications for the Asia-Pacific* by Wang Shilu, Wang Guoping (Contemporary World Publishing House, 1999); *Southeast Asia and China Entering into the 21st Century*, by He Shengda, Ma Yong, and Wang Shilu (Yunnan University Press, 1997); *ASEAN and China at the Turn of the Century* by He Shengda and Chen Minghua (Yunnan Nationalities Publishing House, 2001); and *Contemporary International Relations of Southeast Asia*, compiled by Ma Jinqiang (World Affairs Press, 2000), which is a textbook for master's degree courses in international relations.

Other scholars have done in-depth research on China-Southeast Asian relations. For example, Professor Zhu Zhenming offers original views on Sino-Malaysia relations and Sino-Thailand relations and has published several papers. Nowadays, he is researching on the post-war history of China-Southeast Asia relations.

3. Origin of Thai Nationality and Races in the State of Nanzhao

From the end of the nineteenth century till the early years of the twentieth century, Western scholars successively gave rise to the viewpoints that the Thai race originated somewhere from northern Sichuan Province to southern Shanxi Province, or that Altay Shan Mountains and Nanzhao Kingdom had been a state founded by the Thai people, which greatly influenced the international academic circles. In spite of Chinese scholars questioning these viewpoints, they were written into the historical books published in the West or Southeast Asia, and were circulated internationally for nearly one hundred years. Since the mid-1970s, Yunnan scholars have conducted in-depth and systematic research on races in the state of Nanzhao and on the origin of the Thai race. As a result, they have published a large number of research papers both at home and aboard. Early in 1978, *History Studies* published a paper on "Whether Kublai Khan's Conquest of the Dali Kingdom Gave Rise to the mass migration of the Thai People to the South" by Du Yuting and Chen Lufan, who pointed out that the concept of "Massive Migration" originated from some Western scholars' "arbitrary creation based on a bit of false appearance". Political and academic circles in Thailand attached great importance to the paper. The former Thai Prime Minister Kukrit Pramoj, who translated the English paper into Thai and serialized it on *SiamRath*, advocated in his review that "the paper deserves (the) attention of historians" and "some historians (have) come to be suspicious of the viewpoint that Thai people originated from the North", hence Thai academic circles began to reassess the viewpoint accepted by them for nearly one hundred years.

Yunnan scholars, who were mainly from the Institute of Southeast Asian Studies, published a series of research papers, and those that deserve recommending are: *Whence Came the Thai Race? — On the Homeland of the Thai People, The Fallacy of the So-called "Seven Southerly Migrations of the Thai People": A Specific Analysis, The Nanzhao Kingdom: A State Not Founded by the Thai People, A Preliminary Analysis of the Important Cultural Relics of the Nanzhao and Dali Kingdoms, More on Whether Kublai Khan's Conquest of the Dali Kingdom Gave Rise to the Mass Migration of the Thai People to the South.* These papers were edited into a bilingual Chinese-English edition entitled *Whence Came the Thai Race? — An Inquiry*, published by the International Cultural Publishing Company of China. Professor Chen Lufan agreed that "the Nanzhao Kingdom was not founded by the Thai people" and further put forward that the Thai race originated from the south of Yunnan and the ravines and flats of the north of mainland Southeast Asia, findings which had a great influence on the political and academic circles of Thailand. Meanwhile, Professor Xie Yuanzhang also made an in-depth research on the origin of the Thai people. He published some papers such as *Viewing the Origin of Thai Race from the Use of Stele of Sukhonthai* (the first issue of *Southeast Asia*, Kunming, 1983), *Influence and Significance of Chinese Culture on the Ancient Cultures of the Thai and Dai Peoples* (*Southeast Asia*, no. 1, Kunming, 1989), *More on the Influence and Significance of Chinese Culture on the Ancient Cultures of the Thai and Dai Peoples* (*Southeast Asia*, no. 3, Kunming, 1990). He put forward different views on the origin of the Thai people, which held that the ancestors of the Thai and Dai peoples had been likely living in China's territory and under the direct rein of Chinese feudal dynasties. The current Thai and Dai peoples in Southeast Asia and Yunnan immigrated from the south of China more than one thousand years ago. Professor He Shengda's paper, *The Origin and Ruin of the Theory of That the 'Nanzhao Kingdom was Founded by the Thai Race'* (published in *Social Science in China*, no. 3, 1990) drew the attention of the academic circle. Based on past research, the paper held that the theory that "the Nanzhao Kingdom was Founded by the Thai Race" was concocted by Western scholars at the end of the nineteenth century and circulated for a long time because it then served the imperialists' aggression against China and also catered to the "Thai chauvinism" mentality among Thailand's ruling classes at that time. In addition, researchers made deficient scientific researches on the theory during the end of the nineteenth century till the early years of the twentieth century. In recent decades, research by scholars at home and abroad have shown that the theory, as an academic point of view, is meaningless now.

Yunnan scholars' major achievements on the issue mentioned above were compiled into *The Proceedings of the Studies of the Origin of Thais and Nanzhao Kingdom* in three volumes (about 1.2 million words), published by Chinese Ancient Books Publishing House in May 2005.

The publications mentioned above promoted heated discussions and brought about further studies on the origin of Thai nationality and races in the state of Nanzhao from the 1980s to 1990s.

4. Studies on the History of Southeast Asia

In the past four decades, Yunnan scholars have attached great importance to researches into the history of Southeast Asia and the history of Thailand, Myanmar and Vietnam. Since the setting up of the Institute of Southeast Asian Studies, research into the history of Southeast Asia in Yunnan has entered into a new age.

Of the studies on the history of Southeast Asian region, Yunnan scholars have published large numbers of writings and books, among which the important ones include: *Essentials of Southeast Asian History* edited by professor Wang Mintong (published by Yunnan University Press, 1994), which was popular as a textbook for Master's degree courses in college; *The Post-War History of Southeast Asia*, written by professor He Shengda (published by Yunnan University Press, 1995), was about the history of Southeast Asian development from 1945 to 1994. Another of his books, *A Cultural History of Southeast Asia* (published by Yunnan People's Publishing House, 1996,) was the first book written by a Chinese scholar to inquire into the history of the development of Southeast Asian cultures systematically; *Studies on History of Foreign Relations of Southwest China* by professor Shen Xu (Yunnan Fine Arts Publishing House, 1994) probed into the historical relations between the southwest of China and Southeast Asia while focusing on "the Southern Silk Road "; The *Cambridge History of Southeast Asian* edited by Negolas Tarlyn, was translated into Chinese by scores of Yunnan scholars led by professor He

Shengda (published by Yunnan People's Publishing House, 2003) which has enriched the studies on Southeast Asian history in China.

On the history of Thailand, which include fields such as the succession of the kingdoms, society, nature, the history of Sino-Thailand relations, as well as reform movements in Thai history, dozens of writings, papers and translations have been published, the most valuable of which is the translation of *Yonok Chronicle* compiled by the Thai historian, Phaya Prajakit-koracak (巴差吉功札). The important writings are: *A Mystery in the History of Sino-Siamese Relations: Whether or Not King Ramkhamhaeng has been to China?* by Zou Qiyu (*World History*, no. 5, 1980), *A Preliminary Inquiry of the Thai Social Nature in Modern Times* by Ma Xiaojun (*World History*, no. 5, 1987). Professor He Shengda published his papers "*On the Guiding Ideology on Chulalongkorn Reform*", and "*Chulalongkorn Reform and Modernization of Thailand*" in journals such as *Southeast Asia, Social Science in China*, and *World History*. He did a systematic analysis and review of Chulalongkorn reform, which had been an important influence on the history of Thailand.

Regarding the history of Myanmar, some scholars at the Institute of Southeast Asian Studies have conducted thorough researches on the history of succession of the kingdoms of Myanmar, the history of Burmese nationalities and foreign relations, Sino-Myanmar relations as well as the land issue of Myanmar in modern times, and have written and translated a number of writings and papers. Of the collated and translated writings, the most valuable are *Burmese Politics and General Ne Win* written by Burmese scholar Maung Maung and *The History of Burma* by Burmese historian Maung Tin-Aung. Professor He Shengda wrote a monograph, namely, *The History of Burma*, published by People's Publishing House in 1992. Moreover, he published numerous papers in journals like *World History, Southeast Asia* and *Social Science in Yunnan*, etc. The paper *on the Characteristics of the Federal Society of Burma* was carried in *Social Science in Yunnan* and later reprinted by *Xinhua Digest*.

Of the studies on the history of Vietnam (including Sino-Vietnam relations), some scholars at the Institute of Southeast Asian Studies have worked arduously translating and collating piles of materials, which have yielded many valuable research results, of which the most important translations are: *Villages of Vietnam* written by Vietnamese scholars Nguyen Huong Phon (阮鸿峰), The Time of King Hung by Van Tam (文新). Others include: *A Brief History of Vietnam, Preliminary Exposition on Imperial Examination System* by Jin Xudong (*Southeast Asia*, no. 3, 1986, *Kunming*), *Contributions of Overseas Chinese to the Economy and Cultural Development of Vietnam* (*Historical Studies*, no. 6, 1979).

In terms of the history of Laos, Professor Shen Xu has carried out an in-depth research, publishing papers on the ancient history of Laos and its nationalities. His book *History of Laos* (about 300,000 words) was published by Yunnan University Press in 1990.

5. Studies on Ethnic Issues in Southeast Asia

In the last ten years, Yunnan scholars have studied ethnic issues in Southeast Asian nations, policy towards ethnic groups living across the border linking Yunnan with Southeast Asia, and inter-ethnic relations. They have translated large numbers of materials and published papers and books. The important books are as follows: *Nationalities living across the Borderline between Yunnan and Southeast Asia* by Shen Xu and Liu Zhi (Yunnan Nationalities Publishing House, 1988); *Nationalities of Mainland Southeast Asia* by Qin Qingzhi and Zhao Weiyang (Yunnan People's Publishing House, 1990); *Inspiration and Choice: Studies on Nationalities of Neighbouring Countries and Yunnan's Opening up* by Liu Zhi (Yunnan Nationalities Publishing House, 1994); *Studies on Contemporary Nationalities Living across the Borderline and Eradicating Sources of Drugs Outside China* by Sun Wei (Yunnan Nationalities Publishing House, 2001), *Studies on Sources of Drugs Outside Yunnan* by Ma Shuhong (Yunnan Nationalities Publishing House, 2001); *From Yunnan to Assam — Reinvestigation and Reconstruction of the History of Thai-Dai People* by He Ping (Yunnan University Press, 2001), etc. In addition, a group of scholars from the institutions or departments of Southeast Asian Studies of Yunnan University, Yunnan Nationalities University and Yunnan Academy of Social Sciences have performed researches and published many writings on relations between the ethnic groups in Yunnan and Southeast Asian countries.

6. Studies on Economic Relations between China (Yunnan) and Southeast Asia

In the last ten years, Yunnan scholars have placed much more emphasis on China's (Yunnan's) opening up to Southeast Asia. Focusing on the issues as the Lancang-Mekong Sub-region Cooperation and Yunnan's participation in the China-ASEAN Free Trade Area as well as Yunnan's economic and technological cooperation with ASEAN countries, especially with Vietnam, Laos, Cambodia, Myanmar, and Thailand, Yunnan scholars have researched and written papers, research reports and books which could be significant towards policy-making on Yunnan's opening up to and its economic cooperation with Southeast Asia. Several research results have attracted great attention among academic circles and relevant departments in Yunnan and elsewhere in China. Some of the research results worth mentioning are papers such as: *Economic Cooperation between the Southwest of China and Southeast Asia in 1990s*; *Studies on the Comprehensive Development of the Lancang-Mekong River*; *Studies on the Construction of China-ASEAN FTA and Yunnan's Opening Up*, etc. The main books are: *The Danube of the East: Studies on the Development of the Lancang-Mekong River Basin* by Ma Shuhong (Yunnan People's Publishing House, 1996); *Construction of China-ASEAN FTA and Yunnan's Opening Up to Southeast Asia* by He Shengda (Yunnan People's Publishing House, 2003); *Participating in Building Up of China-ASEAN FTA and Yunnan's Development* by Liu Zhi (China Book Press, 2004); *The Great Southwest and Cooperative Development of the Lancang-Mekong Sub-Region* by Li Yigan (Yunnan Nationalities Publishing House, 2001); *Studies on Yunnan-Shanghai Joint Participation in the Lancang-Mekong Sub-region Cooperation* by Li Yigan (Yunnan Nationalities Publishing House, 2001); *Pan-Asian Railway: Studies on Singapore-Kunming Railway* by Li Ping (Yunnan Nationalities Publishing House, 2000). Of particular note is that an increasing number of people, including professional research fellows, teachers of universities and graduates or doctors, have participated in the research on China (Yunnan)'s economic relations with Southeast Asia. Their research fields involve trade and investment, construction of transport networks, and cooperation in the development of energy, human resource, science and technology, tourism, and combating drugs.

INTERNATIONAL ACADEMIC EXCHANGE

As the opening up and reforms develop further, the institutions of Southeast Asian Studies in Yunnan have increased links and exchanges with their international counterparts. Taking the Institute of Southeast Asian Studies of Yunnan Academy of Social Sciences as an example, since its establishment twenty-five years ago, about twenty academic groups have been dispatched to Thailand, Australia, Singapore, Japan, France, the Philippines, Myanmar, Laos, and Vietnam on academic trips or visits. The researchers of the institute have independently conducted academic activities in almost all Southeast Asian countries (except Indonesia, Brunei, and East Timor), the United States and many countries in Europe. In turn, several hundreds of foreign scholars came to Yunnan for academic exchanges and investigations every year, and the institute has hosted visiting and exchanging scholars from thirty-odd countries, including former Thai premier Chuan Leekpai, former Thai ambassador to China De Wongna (德汶纳), Singaporean former ambassador to China Huang Wanqing, Indian former ambassador to China, the American consul-general at Chengdu, the former Myanmar consul-general at Kunming and the Vietnamese consul-general at Kunming. In addition, scores of researcher of the institute have been sent to the United Kingdom, France, Thailand, the United States, Singapore, India, Japan, Laos, Vietnam and Myanmar for further studies.

Yunnan Institute of Southeast Asian Studies often holds international conference and invites international counterparts for academic exchanges. In May 1990, the institute hosted the Fourth International Conference on Thai studies in Kunming. Over 450 scholars, including some 250 foreign participants, attended the conference. Other major international academic conferences held by the institute were the International Symposium on China-Vietnam Economic Cooperation co-hosted by the Institute of Trade Studies of the Ministry of Trade of Vietnam in July 2001, Kunming; The Second International Symposium on China-Vietnam Economic Cooperation co-hosted by the Institute of Trade Studies of the Ministry of Trade of Vietnam in October 2002, Hanoi; Construction of China-ASEAN FRA and the Opening Up of the Southwest China: The Sixth International Symposium of Cooperative Development System of Asia-Southwest China Continental Bridge funded by Hong Kong Society of Asia Pacific 21 in November 2003, Kunming; The International Forum on China-Vietnam Cross Border Trade Fair co-hosted by the Foreign Trade and Economic Cooperation Bureau of Hong He Prefecture of Yunnan in November 2003, Hekou, Yunnan; International Symposium on Dai-Thai Nationalities and Cultures co-hosted by Yunnan Institute of Southeast Asian Studies in Kunming, December 2004. These dynamic academic exchanges have enhanced communions between Yunnan scholars and their international counterparts.

THE MAJOR FOCUSED ISSUES

At present, Yunnan scholars have focused their attention on the following issues:

Economic issues:

1. The revival of Southeast Asian economy in the wake of the Asian financial crisis;
2. Economic modernization of the four ASEAN newer members;
3. Construction of the China-ASEAN Free Trade Area.

Political issues:

1. Democratization and modernization of the six former ASEAN countries;

2. Development of the political situation in Myanmar;
3. Construction of the socialist countries of Vietnam and Laos.

Security issues:
1. Terrorism in Southeast Asia and anti-terror actions;
2. Maritime Security in Southeast Asian (represented by sea-lane security in the Straits of Malacca);
3. Disputes over Spratly Islands;
4. Non-traditional security issues in Southeast Asia;
5. Big powers and regional security in Southeast Asia.

Religious culture:
1. The religious culture and characteristics of Southeast Asian nationalities;
2. The cultural industry of ASEAN and external cooperation.

Regional cooperation:
1. Economic, security, social and cultural integration of ASEAN;
2. "ASEAN+3" cooperation and East Asian cooperation;
3. ASEAN-Japan and ASEAN-South Korea cooperation;
4. Construction of the China-ASEAN FTA;
5. The Lancang-Mekong Sub-region Cooperation;
6. Security cooperation in Southeast Asia.

Big powers and Southeast Asia:
1. China and Southeast Asia;
2. The United States and Southeast Asia;
3. Japan and Southeast Asia;
4. EU and Southeast Asia;
5. India, Australia, and Southeast Asia.

We believe that in-depth research into the issues above will be of positive significance towards promoting cordial relations between China and Southeast Asian countries and pushing forward China's opening up to Southeast Asia.

OPPORTUNITIES AND CHALLENGES

Southeast Asian Studies in Yunnan have laid a solid foundation for further development and by all accounts had noteworthy achievements. However, the future development of Southeast Asian Studies will face opportunities as well as challenges. The future looks bright, as conditions are ripe for better Southeast Asian Studies in Yunnan.

First, Yunnan has geographical advantage to conduct Southeast Asian Studies. As mentioned above, Yunnan is situated in the southwestern part of China and shares borders with Vietnam, Laos and Myanmar, with the boundary line extending over 4,000 kilometres. Because of the same origin of the nationalities and mountains and rivers, they have maintained a close relationship since ancient times. The geographical advantage has provided Yunnan scholars with convenient conditions to carry out Southeast Asian Studies. For example, Yunnan scholars can find out what is happening in neighbouring countries through field study in border areas, and they can even conduct field studies when travelling in border areas.

Second, the Institute of Southeast Asian Studies of Yunnan Academy of Social Sciences, as a core force in Southeast Asian Studies, has established close ties with a dozen research institutions and universities in Southeast Asian countries, especially in Thailand, Laos, Vietnam, Myanmar, Singapore and the Philippines. For example, it has conducted cooperative research with the Institute of Asian Studies of Chulalongkorn University of Thailand.

Third, as China opens up further, Yunnan Province will play a unique role in the Lancang-Mekong Sub-region Cooperation and building up of the China-ASEAN FTA. Meanwhile, people have an urgent need to know more about Southeast Asia, thus providing new opportunities for the enhancement of Southeast Asian Studies in Yunnan. The province has also given priority to Southeast Asia in its opening up to the outside world. At present, there is a "Southeast Asia boom" in Yunnan Province, which on the one hand, has propelled the authorities at different levels to pay more attention to Southeast Asian Studies and support it with manpower and material resources, and on the other hand, it has been an encouragement for the institutions and researchers to conduct Southeast Asian Studies.

Fourth, the institutions of Southeast Asian Studies in Yunnan, as mentioned above, have had a good number of researchers with high qualifications. They have expanded academic ties with their counterparts abroad; therefore, they are capable of achieving more in Southeast Asian Studies.

Fifth, so far, the achievements in Southeast Asian Studies in Yunnan have been acknowledged by society and have exerted growing influence at home and abroad. Provided the relevant research institutions are strengthened continuously and supported financially, Southeast Asian Studies in Yunnan will be elevated to even greater heights.

In spite of the achievements in Southeast Asian Studies in Yunnan as well as the favourable opportunities for development, its future development will face a lot of problems, difficulties and challenges, of which the major ones are as follows:

1. Some researchers in the research institutions are less qualified and incapable of meeting a higher requirement, which are shown as follows: firstly, the researchers have inadequate professional knowledge and theories; secondly, the researchers do not have a good mastery of foreign languages and thus have difficulties in external exchanges; thirdly, they desire quick success and instant benefits, so that many of them have no clear research field and become "Jack-of-all-trades".
2. Since"the social demands" of Southeast Asian Studies are large, some so-called new forces of Southeast Asian Studies have suddenly come to the fore resulting in many mediocre research works. As a result the general level of Southeast Asian Studies has suffered and there are few research results of high quality.
3. Insufficient inputs and backward infrastructures have limited the further development of Southeast Asian Studies in Yunnan. Because of the shortage of research outlays, research institutions are unable to purchase more foreign language books and facilities, and most researchers have little chance to go abroad for further studies or attending academic conference, which will inevitably affect the research work.
4. Because of the poor remunerations, scores of researchers left their research work and took on other kinds. People with high qualifications are unwilling to undertake Southeast Asian Studies professionally. Since remuneration for university faculties and civil servants have been raised largely, a growing number of researchers have gone into the universities and government departments, which is shaking the stability of the research contingent.

If the above-mentioned problems are not paid attention to, they will undoubtedly have an exert unfavourable impact on the development of Southeast Asian Studies in Yunnan.

8

Southeast Asian Studies in China and Taiwan: A Comparative Perspective

Samuel C.Y. Ku

INTRODUCTION

Southeast Asia is closely linked with the Chinese society, not only because of a great number (more than thirty million) of ethnic Chinese in the region but also because of its multilateral connections with China. Historically speaking, China and Southeast Asia started interactions which could be traced back to as early as 111 B.C. when China took over Vietnam during the Han dynasty. Both parties expanded bilateral contacts since Admiral General Cheng Ho's voyages to Southeast Asia during the Ming dynasty in the fifteenth century.[1] China and Southeast Asia have gradually strengthened various interactions since the late nineteenth century when more Chinese immigrated to Southeast Asia due to China's internal chaos and the economic opportunities in this part of the world. Geographically speaking, Southeast Asia has long been regarded as China's rear door or the neighbour in the South. It is particularly true for the people in China's provinces of Guangdong, Guangxi and Yunnan, because peoples (particularly minority ethnic groups) over there often migrate from one area to another, regardless of the concepts of borders and territories of the modern nation-state.

Culturally speaking, in addition to the minority ethnic groups along the borders of China and Vietnam, Laos and Myanmar where these minority groups share similar cultures, ethnic Chinese (mainly Cantonese, Fujiannese, Hainanese, and Hakkanese) have also appeared in all countries in Southeast Asia since the late seventeenth century, making Chinese culture significant in the local countries. Economically speaking, the minority groups in the north of mainland Southeast Asia and the above four ethnic Chinese groups along the coast of the South China Sea have already established a long economic history with the local people and among themselves. Politically speaking, it was since the late Ching dynasty that the Chinese Government began to be officially in touch with Western colonial powers, and China began to establish counselor offices in a number of Southeast Asian countries after the Republic of China (ROC) was established in 1911.

Given these close connections between China and Southeast Asia, the study of Southeast Asia in China only began in the early twentieth century, much late than the beginning of bilateral interactions of the two sides. Due to the great contribution of the overseas Chinese in Southeast Asia to the creation of the ROC in 1911, then National Jinan University established the Department of Nanyang (Southeast Asia) Cultural and Educational Affairs in1928,[2] the first of its kind in China. Since then, Southeast Asian Studies began to become a field in China's social sciences, although it was seriously affected, to some extent terminated, later in the 1940s and 1950s due to the political and social turbulence in China. Due to the implementation of China's open-door policy, the China Southeast Asian Studies Association was established in 1979, and scholars in China started again to concentrate and later to expand the study on Southeast Asia.

When the ROC government fled to Taiwan in late 1949, it continued the policy of promoting the study and education of overseas Chinese. Yet, there were only a few scholars, mainly born in the mainland, who were doing studies on Southeast Asia in general and overseas Chinese in particular, in the 1960s and 1970s. During the first three decades after the ROC government moved its seat to Taiwan, Southeast Asian Studies on the island was actually situated at the periphery in academics. It was since the late 1980s when Taiwanese businessmen started to engage their business in Southeast Asia, that government officials and scholars also began to pay attention to Southeast Asian Studies.

Accordingly, the study of Southeast Asia was reactivated on both sides of the Taiwan Strait since the late 1980s, and scholars from both China and Taiwan began to engage in the study of Southeast Asia. Yet, few studies have been conducted on the comparison of Southeast Asian Studies across the Taiwan Strait. This chapter tries to fill this vacuum, making a comparison on Southeast Asian Studies between the two sides of the Taiwan Strait. Therefore, this is not an academically oriented paper; rather, it aims to promote the understanding of Southeast Asian Studies in both China and Taiwan. While conducting the comparison from four perspectives, this chapter will also initiate some academic thinking on the study of Southeast Asia for scholars from both Taiwan and China.

HISTORICAL BACKGROUND

When the ROC government established the first Southeast Asia-oriented institute in National Jinan University in 1928, it also began to establish cultural and social connections with overseas Chinese in Southeast Asia and the study of Southeast Asia as well. Later, the development of Southeast Asian Studies in China was, unfortunately, not rosy at all due to a series of factors, including the war against Japan's invasion from the mid-1930s to the mid-1940s, the Chinese civil war between the Chinese Nationalists and the Chinese Communists in the latter half of the 1940s, China's instability in the 1950s, and the chaos resulting from the Cultural Revolution throughout the 1960s to the early 1970s.

When the People's Republic of China (PRC) was established in October 1949, the study of Southeast Asia was certainly not a priority on the agenda of the PRC. It was until 1956 when Nanyang (Southeast Asia) Institute, the first of this kind after the creation of the PRC, was established in Xiamen University,[3] that the PRC began to pay attention to the studies on overseas Chinese and Southeast Asia. The institute, however, was shut down during the Cultural Revolution mainly because any overseas connection was taboo during the period, not to mention the studies on overseas Chinese and Southeast Asia that were associated with the capitalist world. However, the Nanyang Institute resumed functioning in 1972 at the end of the Cultural Revolution. When the PRC initiated the open-door policy in 1979, the institute, co-existing with the Centre for Southeast Asian Studies,[4] was gradually expanded in the studies on overseas Chinese specifically and Southeast Asia in general.

In 1996, the Nanyang Institute was reorganized under a new name — the Research School for Southeast Asian Studies (still co-existing with the

Centre for Southeast Asian Studies), which was authorized to increase the number of researchers and administrative staff. In September 2000, the Centre and the school were assigned by the Ministry of Education as among the research bases in Humanities and Social Sciences in China. This has empowered the centre to recruit more researchers (currently more than thirty full-time researchers) and receive more graduate students seeking to obtain master degrees and doctoral degrees. The Centre for Southeast Asian Studies in Xiamen University is now the largest and most reputable academic institute on the study of Southeast Asia in China.

As for Jinan University in Guangzhou, it did not continue the study of overseas Chinese after the founding of the Department of Nanyang (Southeast Asia) Cultural and Educational Affairs in1928; rather, it was only until 1960 when the Institute of Southeast Asian Studies was established that Jinan University began to pay attention to the study of the overseas Chinese and countries in the region of Southeast Asia. Similar to the one in Xiamen University, the institute in Jinan University did not develop much in the 1960s and 1970s; it was only since the early 1980s that the institute began to grow and expand. Currently, the institute has more than twenty full-time researchers and receives graduate students pursuing their master degrees and doctoral degrees.

The other two institutes involved in Southeast Asian Studies in southern China, that is, the Institute of Southeast Asian Studies in Yunnan Academy of Social Sciences and the Institute of Southeast Asian Studies in Guangxi Academy of Social Sciences, share similar stories in their development. Taking the one in Yunnan Academy of Social Sciences as an example, it was originally established in 1963 as a research team under the Yunnan Department of History, which was shut down during the Cultural Revolution. When the Yunnan Department of History resumed functioning in 1972, the research team on the study of Southeast Asia also started operating again. As China opened its door to the world in late 1979, the first group of students studying Southeast Asian history also enrolled in the Yunnan Department of History. Two years later in 1981, the Institute of Southeast Asian Studies was officially established at Yunnan Academy of Social Sciences. In 1983, the institute established an academic journal — *Southeast Asia Quarterly*, the first of its kind in China. The institute continues to expand in the 1990s, and it now has more than twenty full-time researchers.

In central China, the Shanghai Academy of Social Sciences, created in 1958, helped to establish the Institute of Asia-Pacific Studies in 1990. The institute consists of four research divisions, and Southeast Asian Studies is one of them. With only twelve full-time researchers and covering a variety of subjects, the study of Southeast Asia is not a major focus of this institute.

In northern China, the study of Southeast Asia started a little late. At the Institute of Asia-Pacific Studies in the Chinese Academy of Social Sciences, there is a Centre for Asia-Pacific Economic Cooperation Organization and East Asian Cooperation, which covers research on Southeast Asia. Although this is not an institutionalized centre, it has been active in publicizing its working papers and monographs on a number of issues about Southeast Asia. Also in Beijing, the Institute of Overseas Chinese and Overseas Chinese History Studies was established in 1981.[5] This institute is not specifically concentrated on Southeast Asian Studies, but it covers the study of overseas Chinese in Southeast Asia. In addition, Peking University established the Center for Southeast Asian Studies in August 2002, which is an inter-disciplinary and inter-departmental organization. This centre is also the first institute specifically on the study of Southeast Asia in northern China.

As for Southeast Asian Studies in Taiwan, it actually started quite early since the mid-1950s, mainly because of the legacy of the ROC government's policy towards overseas Chinese in Southeast Asia and the relationship between the ROC and its diplomatic partners in the region, including Vietnam, Thailand, Malaysia, and the Philippines.[6] The academic community of Southeast Asian Studies in Taiwan was not yet established, however, in the first four decades after the ROC government fled to Taiwan in 1949. There were only a few scholars, mostly born in the mainland, who were doing studies on Southeast Asia, but they were in different universities and academic institutes. It was in the mid-1990s that Taiwan's community of Southeast Asian Studies was established, because of the creation of two graduate institutes.

The first one is the Graduate Institute of Southeast Asian Studies at Tamkang University, which was established in August 1996, the first of its kind in Taiwan. This institute receives twelve to fifteen graduate students pursuing a master's degree each year since its creation. With only four to five faculty members, the institute at Tamkang University has produced more than fifty graduates who have already received a master's degree. One year later in August 1997, National Chi Nan University (NCNU) in Nantou County also established the Graduate School of Southeast Asian Studies. With more resources than the one in Tamkang University, the one in NCNU has also established a Centre for Southeast Asian Studies, which recruits teaching staff from other departments in the university, promoting joint research projects and activities on Southeast Asia.

In addition to these two universities, National Sun Yat-sen University (NSYSU) in Kaohsiung and National Cheng Kung University (NCKU) in

Tainan also established a Centre for Southeast Asian Studies at the turn of the century, respectively. Unlike the above two institutes that receive graduate students, the two in southern Taiwan are research-oriented centres that do not receive regular students nor have regular researchers. However, both NSYSU and NCKU have a couple of Southeast Asian specialists teaching in different graduate institutes in the College of Social Sciences, which receives regular graduate students pursuing their master's degrees or doctoral degrees. It is in this way that the two schools in the south also have a small community for Southeast Asian Studies.

Finally, Taiwan's Academia Sinica established the Programme for Southeast Asian Area Studies (PROCEA) in September 1994 under the leadership of Professor Michael Hsin Huang Hsiao. Although PROCEA was not authorized to receive regular graduate students, it was the first research-oriented institution specifically for Southeast Asian Studies in Taiwan. PROCEA was merged with another programme into the Asia-Pacific Research Programme (APARP) in January 2002, and was re-organized again in January 2003, under the new name — The Centre for Asia-Pacific Area Studies (CAPAS). CAPAS is now one of the six centres in the Research Centre for Humanities and Social Sciences, established in July 2003 in Academia Sinica. Although CAPAS now has a wider research scope, Southeast Asian Studies remain as a priority on its agenda. Compared with the two centres in southern Taiwan, CAPAS is empowered with regular budget, full-time researchers and administrative staff. Accordingly, both PROCEA and CAPAS have played a key role in the study of Southeast Asia in Taiwan since 1994.

In short, the development of Southeast Asian Studies in both China and Taiwan has to do with political manoeuvering and policy changes on both sides. When China implemented the open-door policy in 1979, the study of Southeast Asia was restored on the mainland. The ROC government initiated the Southward Policy in early 1994, which also pushed the creation of PROCEA in Academia Sinica in September 1994, followed by other institutes in Taiwan.

ACADEMIC COMMUNITY

Academic community is the foundation for the development of all disciplines in humanities and social sciences because it serves as a base of academic exchanges for scholars and students who have common research interests. During the period of unstable years in the 1950s, 1960s, and 1970s, both China and Taiwan did not establish an academic community for the study of Southeast Asia.

After the revival of Southeast Asian Studies in both China and Taiwan, academic communities of Southeast Asian Studies across the Taiwan Strait have also been established. China first established the Chinese Association of Southeast Asian Studies in 1979, which includes most institutes and scholars who are engaged in Southeast Asian Studies on the mainland. After its creation, the association has been holding conferences, although they are not held annually. Since the five major institutes on Southeast Asian Studies are in southern China, including Xiamen University, Jinan University, Sun Yat-sen University,[7] Yunan Academy of Social Sciences and Guangxi Academy of Social Sciences, the first five conferences were held in the South.

The sixth conference was held in Beijing in 2001, the first time in northern China, which contributed to the establishment of the Centre for Southeast Asian Studies in Peking University in August 2002. The Sixth Conference on Southeast Asian Studies in Beijing attracted more than one hundred scholars to attend, and more than seventy papers were presented at the conference. Accordingly, the academic community on Southeast Asian Studies in China has relatively consolidated, laying the foundation for the exchange of scholars and students who are interested in Southeast Asian Studies.

Regarding Taiwan's academic community for Southeast Asian Studies, it started much later than that in China. Yet, annual conference on Southeast Asian Studies has been regularly held in Taiwan since 1999. The first one was organized by Professor Michael Hsiao's PROCEA, which was co-sponsored by the other four Southeast Asia-related institutes and centres in Taiwan, as indicated earlier. It should be noted that each institute alternately holds the annual conference since 1999. The Graduate School of Southeast Asian Studies of National Chi Nan University took its turn to hold the most recent one (the seventh of this kind) in April 2005 and more than sixty papers were presented at the conference. This is the second time that the National Chi Nan University held this conference; so did PROCEA and Tamkang University a couple of years ago. The Centre for Southeast Asian Studies of National Cheng Kung University is scheduled to hold the 2006 Conference of Taiwan Southeast Asian Studies in Tainan, which will be the first time for the NCKU to hold such a conference.

In another significant development, the Taiwan Association of Southeast Asian Studies was established in Nantou in April 2005 during the Seventh Conference of Taiwan Southeast Asian Studies. The creation of Taiwan's Association of Southeast Asian Studies is already half a century after the ROC moved its seat of government to Taiwan. It should be noted also that the annual conference on Southeast Asian Studies is the first area studies-related association that holds regular conferences in Taiwan. Although other area studies associations may hold conferences irregularly, the size of these conferences is not comparable to the one on Southeast Asian Studies. This is to say that the academic community of Southeast Asian Studies is now the largest area studies-oriented community in Taiwan.

RESEARCH SCOPES

The study of Southeast Asia is inter-disciplinary in nature, covering a variety of disciplinarians such as politics, economics, history, sociology, anthropology, language, liberal arts, and so on. To study Southeast Asia, scholars would firstly get in touch with countries in the region, which can be approached on the basis of individual country, or a comparative study on two or more countries, or the entire region as a unit. Putting these two variables together, one will find it is very difficult and complicated to study Southeast Asia, similar to other area studies. Given these difficulties, scholars who are interested in Southeast Asian Studies still have to start from a specific discipline in a specific country or a few countries if necessary. For a research institution, it may focus on one discipline in one or a few countries; it may also cover a wider scope in a few disciplines in most, or all of, the countries in Southeast Asia.

For scholars in both China and Taiwan, the study of overseas Chinese was the first topic when both sides started Southeast Asian Studies in the mid-twentieth century, which has continued to the present. This is mainly because of the legacy from the creation of the first Southeast Asia-related institute in 1928. Although Southeast Asian Studies were suspended later because of the turbulence in China, the study of overseas Chinese continued. When Southeast Asian Studies were restored in China, the study of overseas Chinese, including history, immigration, economic development, etc. remained the most popular topic in most major universities in southern China, including Xiamen University, Jinan University, Sun Yat-sen University, Guangxi Academy of Social Sciences and Yunnan Academy of Social Sciences.

The scope of Southeast Asian Studies in both China and Taiwan began to expand since the early 1990s. The Centre for Southeast Asian Studies at Xiamen University presents the best example in China. Since it resumed operation in 1972, the centre has expanded its scope on Southeast Asian Studies from overseas Chinese to Southeast Asian history, Southeast Asian culture, Southeast Asian religions, etc. As the centre was re-organized into the Research School for Southeast Asian Studies in 1996, its organization had expanded at the same time. The school now includes four institutes, that is, the Institute of Southeast Asian Politics and Economics, Institute of Overseas Chinese Studies in Southeast Asia, Institute of International Relations in Southeast Asia, and Institute of Southeast Asian Religion History and Culture. These four institutes basically reflect the scope of Southeast Asian Studies in Xiamen University, which means that their researchers cover a variety of disciplines, including political science, economics, sociology, anthropology, and history.

Regarding the countries covered in the Research School for Southeast Asian Studies, researchers there have covered almost all countries in Southeast Asia; some of them are even specialized in China's relations with Southeast Asia as a whole. In addition, due to its status as one of the key research bases in humanities and social sciences in China, the School now has become the largest Institute on Southeast Asian Studies in China in terms of the number of researchers, student population (roughly 100 graduate students enrolled), and the size of the library (more than 42,000 books) as well.

As for the rest of the institutes involving Southeast Asian Studies in China, they have also expanded the scope in the study of Southeast Asia since the early 1990s, with similar comprehensive coverage on Southeast Asia. The Institute of Southeast Asian Studies in Yunnan Academy of Social Sciences is probably a little different, because its research scope covers only four Southeast Asian countries that share borders with Yunnan province, that is, Vietnam, Laos, Thailand, and Myanmar. In addition, Yunnan Academy of Social Sciences and Guangxi Academy of Social Sciences, due to the advantages of geographic proximity, are also famous for their studies on minority ethnic groups along the borders between China and the above four Southeast Asian countries. These two institutes have been famous for their expertise in the study of minority ethnic groups.

It should be noted that most Southeast Asia-oriented institutes in China have recently concentrated on the study of regional economic cooperation and integration, including such topics as "ASEAN+1", "ASEAN+3", Joint Development Projects on the Mekong River, and so on. Clearly, this has to do with the recent development of free trade area in the region. The Institute of Southeast Asian Studies in Guangxi Academy of Social Sciences, for example, recently published the *China-ASEAN Yearbook* in November 2004, the first of its kind by the institute. The Institute of Southeast Asian Studies in Yunnan Academy of Social Sciences even designates China-ASEAN Free Trade Area as one of the eight research areas of the institute.[8] The Institute of Asia-Pacific Studies in the Shanghai Academy of Social Sciences has recently received a big project from China's National Foundation for Social Sciences

Research to conduct research on Asia-Pacific economic cooperation and China's strategy on the Asia-Pacific economic cooperation.

As for Taiwan, CAPAS in Academia Sinica has the widest research scope on Southeast Asian Studies in Taiwan. Since its creation, PROCEA has published numerous monographs and books, covering a variety of topics, including middle classes in Southeast Asia, Taiwan's investment in Southeast Asia, Taiwan enterprises in Southeast Asia, a series of Vietnamese studies, a series of Malay and Islam studies, a series of studies on Singapore, the Philippines, and Thailand, and so on. It should be noted that the authors of these publications are mainly from outside, rather than its own regular research staff. These external researchers were using the research grants from either PROCEA or APARP or CAPAS. This is the key reason that CAPAS can produce so many publications in such a short period of time. In other words, CAPAS does not concentrate on a specific subject in a specific Southeast Asian country; rather, its research scope is based on the nature of the research grants. Because it has a regular budget and a few full-time staff,[9] CAPAS is likely to continue to play a key role in the study of Southeast Asia in Taiwan.

The research scopes of the two teaching institutes in Taiwan is mainly based on the research interests of their own full-time faculty members. The Graduate School of Southeast Asian Studies in National Chi Nan University, for example, now has six full-time faculty members with specializations in human resource management in Southeast Asia, Chinese immigration history, comparative politics and ethnic politics in Southeast Asia, Taiwanese enterprises in Southeast Asia, overseas Chinese in Southeast Asia, and Indochina studies.

The Institute in Tamkang University now has five full-time faculty members, whose research interests include Southeast Asian Chinese and related issues, labour migration in Southeast Asia, comparative politics in Southeast Asia, regional economic development and integration, teaching Bahasa Malaysia, etc. The one in Chi Nan University has better advantages for its research, since it is empowered by another independent Center of Southeast Asian Studies, an inter-departmental institution. With the same leadership, the institute and the centre usually work together and are able to mobilize more resources from both inside and outside of the university.

Regarding the two centres in the South, their research scope is also based on the expertise of their faculty members. Compared with the above two teaching institutes, these two centres are quite small because there is only one key scholar in these two centres respectively. Professor Samuel C.Y. Ku, a political scientist, leads the one in National Sun Yat-sen University, whereas the one in National Cheng Kung University is directed by Professor Jen-Jaw

Song, a sociology-trained scholar with a research interest in political economy in Southeast Asia.

The advantage of these two centres, however, is that both Professor Ku and Professor Song regularly receive graduate students from the institutes they are affiliated with, and their research scope is expanding as they instruct students working on different topics of their theses. The weakness of these two centres, however, is that they are not stable in the future development because they, without having regular budget and regular full-time staff, are not institutionalized. Once there are financial and personnel problems, these two centres are likely to be dissolved.

INTERNATIONAL LINKAGES

Building international linkages is crucial for academic institutions if they desire to promote their research to the international academic community. Regarding international linkage, it at least includes three perspectives. The first one is to hold regular, or at least occasional, international conferences or symposiums, so that international scholars with similar research interests would have the opportunity to share their research results with local scholars. The second one is to exchange scholars among institutions with the exchange agreements or other cooperation programmes, so that scholars would have the opportunity to visit each other, either for temporary teaching assignments or for joint research projects. The final one is to send exchange students to other institutions, which is also possible among institutions with official agreements so that institutions would accept exchange students and recognize the credits they take in the host schools.

When China started to redevelop Southeast Asian Studies in the early 1980s, it focused on the stability of domestic research and academic development. It was not until the early 1990s that the five major Southeast Asian-oriented institutions in southern China began to build international connections. Xiamen University is the most prominent one, especially since it was assigned as one of China's key state research base in the humanities and social sciences in 1996. The Centre of Southeast Asian Studies in Xiamen University has not only held occasional international conferences, but also dispatches its scholars overseas, whether they be visiting scholars or conducting research projects overseas. As for exchange students overseas, this is something that Xiamen University needs to strengthen. The centre is also home to two organizations, that is, the China Association of Southeast Asian Studies, and the China Branch of the World Association of Chinese Studies. Accordingly,

Xiamen University has good reasons to expand its international linkages on the study of Southeast Asia.

When Sun Yat-sen University in Guangzhou shut down its Institute for Southeast Asian Studies, Jinan Unviersity becomes the only other one that receives graduate students in China. Similar to the one in Xiamen University, the Institute of Southeast Asian Studies in Jinan University occasionally holds international conferences and also assigns their faculties overseas for academic exchanges and cooperation, but the frequency of such international exchanges is lower than its competitor in Xiamen University.

Regarding the other two institutes in Yunnan Academy of Social Sciences and Guangxi Academy of Social Sciences, they do not receive graduate students. They do not often hold international conferences either. It should be noted, however, that the institute at Yunnan Academy of Social Sciences held an international conference on Thai studies in May 1990, which attracted the participation of more than 250 international scholars and more than 200 domestic scholars. Due to its geographic proximity, the institute at Yunnan Academy has close ties with its counterparts in Thailand, Myanmar, and Laos, whereas the institute in Guangxi is proud of its academic connections with its counterparts in Vietnam. The one in Yunnan Academy is even more active in assigning its researchers overseas (for example, more than twenty international group visits) on either visiting scholarships or to conduct joint research projects.[10]

As for the Institutes in Taiwan, CAPAS in Academia Sinica is credited with the widest scope in its international connections due to its frequently holding international symposiums and assigning projects to international scholars. Since the creation of PROCEA, the predecessor of CAPAS, in 1994, CAPAS has been actively building academic connections with institutions in Southeast Asia, Australia, the United States and even some European countries. Because it receives regular and sufficient budget, CAPAS has regularly published monographs and books for domestic and international scholars who receive research grants from the centre. It is in this way that CAPAS continues to maintain its broader linkages with international scholars who have similar research interests in Southeast Asian Studies.

The two teaching Southeast Asia-oriented institutes do not have strong international connections as compared with CAPAS, although they occasionally invite international scholars to give a seminar there. For example, Professor Benedict Kerkvliet of National Australian University and Professor Anthony Reid of National University of Singapore had been invited to give a seminar at the institute at National Chi Nan University.[11] So far, these two institutes have not yet held international conferences, although they often hold domestic conferences and symposiums. In addition, these two institutes encourage their graduate students to go to Southeast Asia for field studies if necessary, and their instructors sometimes accompany their students to visit Southeast Asia. In addition, some individual faculty members in these two institutes have quite good connections in Southeast Asia. Dr. Pei-hsiu Chen of National Chi Nan University, for example, has on-going research on Thailand for some time, whereas Dr. Juo-yu Lin, a journalist-turned scholar, has visited most countries in the region.

Regarding the two centres in southern Taiwan, the one at National Sun Yat-sen University established international connections a little earlier than the one at National Cheng Kung University. Professor Samuel C.Y. Ku of National Sun Yat-sen University has relatively good academic connections in Southeast Asia; he often travels to academic institutions in the region. In the last couple of years, Professor Ku initiated a few exchange agreements and memorandums between National Sun Yat-sen University and several key universities in Southeast Asia, including University of the Philippines, University of Malaya, Chulalongkorn University, University of Indonesia, etc. In addition, the centre, under Professor Ku's leadership, has organized two international conferences, that is, one in March 2004 on the "Changes and Challenges in China and Southeast Asia" and the other one in May 2005 on "Political Reforms in Taiwan and Vietnam".

Professor Jen-jaw Song of the National Cheng Kun University in Tainan also often visits academic institutions in Southeast Asia, and he sometimes takes his students to do field studies in the region. Recently, the NCKU, under the leadership of President Chiang Kao, is planning to establish a platform for some key universities between Taiwan and Southeast Asia. It is likely that the NCKU has the potential to expand its international linkages for the study of Southeast Asia.

CONCLUSION

Having made a comparison on Southeast Asian Studies between China and Taiwan, this chapter concludes with the following five points. First of all, both China and Taiwan need to expand the scope of Southeast Asian Studies. Although both sides have started the study of overseas Chinese quite early in the mid-1920s, probably even earlier than European and American scholars, Southeast Asian Studies actually cover many other subjects, including local economies, social interactions among different ethnic groups, local politics and policies, etc. Up to the present, the study of overseas Chinese (including overseas Taiwanese) still dominates Southeast Asian Studies across the Taiwan Strait. The rationale for this is because of the language advantage for scholars in both China and Taiwan. As the new century evolves, both China and Taiwan should make efforts to study the local issues in Southeast Asia, in order to make Southeast Asian Studies more native and more comprehensive. Although some institutions have already moved towards this direction, scholars in both China and Taiwan need to strengthen local studies, covering different disciplines and exploring as many countries as possible in Southeast Asia.

Secondly, language training should be strengthened for scholars in both China and Taiwan. While a command of the Chinese language is already an advantage for scholars across the Taiwan Strait, to learn a local language is also imperative to promote the study of Southeast Asian Studies. Both China and Taiwan have scholars who are doing local studies and conducting field works in Southeast Asia, but only a few of them are proficient in the local languages. In the past few decades, a number of Western scholars, such as Professor William Liddle of the Ohio State University, have set up good examples, because their expertise in Southeast Asian Studies are empowered by their proficiency in the local languages, including Bahasa Indonesia, Thai, Vietnamese, and Filipino. This is something fundamental to keep the study of Southeast Asia going.

Thirdly, comparative study is another important field that scholars across the Taiwan Strait need to explore. Southeast Asia is characterized by its varieties, not only in ethnicity, but also in culture, religion, politics, economics, history, and so on. While some countries may share a similarity in one thing, they may differ in other things. Thailand and Vietnam, for instance, share a similar Buddhist religion, but they are different in language, colonial experience, and minority ethnic groups. That is to say, in order to enrich the study of Southeast Asia, scholars from Taiwan and China are obligated to engage in comparative studies on Southeast Asia.

Fourthly, scholars from China and Taiwan should be more active in engaging the global community of Southeast Asian Studies. This means English publications or Chinese-translated English works by scholars across the Taiwan Strait should be encouraged and strengthened. When students are taking courses on Southeast Asia in the West, they are required to read, assigned by their instructors, a great deal of English readings mostly written by Western scholars, and only some of them were written by scholars with a Chinese background. Certainly, there are a number of Southeast Asia-born Chinese scholars who have successfully achieved the study of Southeast Asia and have been recognized worldwide. There are few China-born and Taiwan-born scholars, however, whose works on Southeast Asian Studies are internationally recognized. While China-born and Taiwan-born scholars have gradually won recognition in China studies in the international academic community, scholars across the Taiwan Strait are obligated to play a role in Southeast Asian Studies, at least in this part of the world.

Finally, both China and Taiwan have already established an academic community for Southeast Asian Studies, but both sides have not yet established a platform for bilateral academic exchanges on Southeast Asian Studies. While scholars of Southeast Asian Studies have already established a community in the region as well as in the world, scholars across the Taiwan Strait should also make efforts to establish a community for Chinese scholars who are engaged in Southeast Asian Studies. If possible, scholars proficient in the Chinese language are also encouraged to join this community. To make this dream possible, the Centre and the School of Southeast Asian Studies of Xiamen University, with sufficient resources and support from China's central government, should play such a role. While the centre is already home to the China Association of Southeast Asian Studies and China Branch of the World Association of Chinese Studies, the centre should move forward and take the lead to organize a global Chinese community for Southeast Asian Studies.

NOTES

1. General Cheng Ho of Ming Dynasty led a Treasure Fleet, consisting of 62 ships, as his first voyage to Southeast Asia in 1405 and completed another six voyages to Southeast Asia in the next 28 years. General Cheng Ho's second voyage was from 1407 to 1409, the third one from 1409 to 1411, the fourth one from 1413 to 1415, the fifth one from 1417 to 1419, the sixth one from 1421 to 1422, and the last voyage was from 1431 to 1433. He was believed to have died on the return trip in 1433. For details about Cheng Ho, see Louise Levathes, *When China Ruled the Sea*. New York: Simon & Schuster, 1994.
2. Jinan School was originally created in Nanjing in 1906 for the purpose of promoting Chinese culture and education overseas, and later was moved to Shanghai under a new name — National Jinan University in 1927 during the reign of the Nationalist government. In September 1949, National Jinan University was merged into Fudan University and Jiaotong University. After the Chinese Communists took over the mainland, Jinan University, the new name of the school, was re-established in Guangzhou in 1958.
3. The creation of the Nanyang Institute was actually sponsored by the Central Committee of Overseas Chinese Affairs.
4. This means the Institute and the Center share similar personnel and offices.
5. This Institute is under the guidance of China's Association of Returned Overseas Chinese, which began to publish a quarterly based Overseas Chinese History Studies since 1988.

6. The ROC government had a Consul General office in Kuala Lumpur till 1974 when the Malaysian government exchanged diplomatic recognition with the PRC on 31 May 1974.
7. There was an Institute for Southeast Asian Studies at the Sun Yat-sen University in Guangzhou, but, unfortunately, it was closed down in 2003.
8. For details, please visit the website of the Yunnan Academy of Social Sciences.
9. CAPAS now has only one full-time researcher, two adjunct researchers (co-appointments with other institutes in Academia Sinica), and two administrative assistants.
10. For details, please visit the website of the Institute at <http://www.sky.yn.gov.cn/big5/xkdept/readinfo.asp?ID=0104> (4 August 2005).
11. They both were there in April 2004, attending a special symposium on Southeast Asian Studies in National Chi Nan University.

9

Understanding the Chinese Overseas: Changing Themes and Evolving Approaches[1]

Liu Hong

Nearly thirty-five million ethnic Chinese now live outside mainland China, Hong Kong, Macao and Taiwan. Known collectively as "Chinese overseas", they are a crucial force in the socio-economic transformations of modern China and the countries they reside and in the processes of cross-national interaction. Viewed from the perspective of international migration, they are one of the most dynamic immigrant and ethnic minorities. Despite a steady growth of interest in diasporic Chinese societies, relevant writings are scattered across scholarly journals,[2] while some pioneering studies are out of print and hard to find. By re-examining the central themes of some representative works published in the last seven decades and reflecting upon the changing genealogies of the field, I hope readers can gain a deeper understanding of Chinese communities overseas in different historical periods and geo-cultural settings.

While by no means a comprehensive survey of relevant scholarship, this essay sketches the main trajectories and themes in Chinese international migration, meaning "the departure from Chinese soil for the purpose of living and working abroad with the likelihood of settlement", whether or not the settlement was intended.[3] It also reviews the changing approaches to these themes in spatial and temporal perspectives. The chapter goes on to provide an overview of these main approaches and connects them thematically and in other ways, and suggests additional references. Although this article is not specifically concerned with the status of overseas Chinese studies in the PRC *per se*, many issues discussed here have also been closely scrutinized by scholars in China, whose important efforts have collectively contributed to the field's emergence and maturation. This essay, therefore, can be read comparatively with other chapters in this volume dealing with Overseas Chinese studies in the PRC.

TRAJECTORIES AND THEMES

The Chinese have had a long history of living and working outside China — a concept that is in itself a historical construct. The first account of Chinese emigration dates back to the Qin and Han dynasties (221 B.C.–220 A.D.), but not until the mid-nineteenth century did Chinese start to leave on a massive scale. This exodus had two principal causes: The socio-economic dislocations brought about by Western intrusion and the deteriorating imperial order in late Qing China; and the growth in demand for cheap labour and for merchants to serve as middlemen between the Westerners and Southeast Asian indigenes.

Later migration can be divided into three main phases. In the first period (the 1850s–1950), large numbers of Chinese, mainly from Guangdong and Fujian in South China, left for Southeast Asia. Up to the end of World War II, most considered themselves *Huaqiao* (Chinese sojourners or overseas Chinese), whose political loyalty and cultural orientation were towards China (in the form of a civilization, an ancestral hometown or *qiaoxiang*, or a nation-state). They were the generation of *luoye guigen* ("fallen leaves return to their roots"), a reference to Chinese who stayed loyal to their native places and wished (usually in vain) to return to them.

In the second period (1950–80), new ethnic Chinese identities emerged and people began to emigrate for different reasons and in different ways from in the past. An increasing number of Chinese living overseas were born locally, and the inflow of migrants virtually ceased after the founding of the People's Republic of China (PRC) in 1949. The *Huaqiao* gradually became *Huaren* (ethnic Chinese or Chinese overseas), who owed their political allegiance to their countries of residence. They were the generation of *luodi shenggen* ("falling to the ground and striking root"), a reference to the new pattern of permanent settlement abroad and renunciation of Chinese citizenship, while privately preserving a Chinese lifestyle and Chinese cultural values. Chinese now emigrated in large numbers from Hong Kong, Taiwan, and Southeast Asia. Unlike in the previous century, most went to North America, Australia, Western Europe, and Japan.

In the third and most recent period (1980–the present), new migrants originating in the PRC began to make up a greater proportion of overall Chinese emigration. The diasporic Chinese communities themselves have also undergone tremendous changes, due to continuing localization processes, accelerating globalization, and the emergence of China as a regional and potentially a world power.

This summary of Chinese emigration highlights central themes in an understanding of Chinese overseas, including the importance of different historical phases, differing patterns of adaptation in a range of political and geographical settings, linkages — political, economic, and symbolic — with the hometown or homeland, and the networks that connect Chinese overseas and their communities. A multi-dimensional perspective is essential for exploring these themes and processes.

First, by viewing Chinese overseas in the context of developments both in China and in their places of settlement, their complexities and characteristics are more easily captured. Second, it is essential to approach Chinese communities overseas from an inter-disciplinary angle. Social science theories and methods help to understand the Chinese diaspora, whose study is at the intersection of the humanities and social sciences. Approached creatively, its marginality is its strength. Studies of the Chinese diaspora can also be enriched by the broader study of international migration and associated theories, including issues such as identity, multi-culturalism, cosmopolitanism, networks, and ethnicity. Third, it is necessary not only to examine the impact on diasporic Chinese societies of China as a political entity and symbolic representation but also to analyse the diaspora's role in political and economic change in China since the end of the nineteenth century. The Chinese overseas also play a role in interactions between China and their countries of residence. Finally, although Chinese overseas are a product of the eras of empire and the nation-state, at the same time they constantly cross national borders and defy the imposition of an identity based purely on territoriality, so they must be conceptualized in a transnational framework. Their mentality is one of both "here" and "there", a characteristic that is often overlooked in state-centric histories.

The changing configurations and multi-dimensionality of Chinese overseas make scholarly inquiry daunting as well as exciting. It is exciting because the field affords numerous opportunities to reconstruct the tortuous journeys undertaken by Chinese in search of a better life. Chinese communities overseas are a magnet for inter-disciplinary projects. Studying them, however, is at the same time daunting, for the diversity of their social, cultural and political settings is impossible to grasp without a broad mastery of languages, histories and power relations. Collective work by scholars from different disciplinary and cultural backgrounds is the most effective means of tackling this diversity and fathoming its underlying unity.

This anthology aims to comprehend this multi-dimensionality by bringing together in one place some of the more representative writings published in English over the last seventy years. Apart from the usual criteria of academic merit and analytical rigour, special consideration is given to disciplinary and geographical factors, comparative analysis, transnational awareness, the blending of empiricism with larger theoretical discourses, and inter-disciplinarity. The anthology includes sections on the historical evolution of Chinese communities overseas with a focus on the second half of the twentieth century, when such communities underwent fundamental change, including hybridization. In terms of geography, besides articles on common institutional and cultural patterns among global Chinese communities, the volumes focus chiefly on communities in Southeast Asia, North America, Europe, and Australia. A salient feature of the collection is Chinese transnationalism, viewed from different disciplinary and geo-cultural perspectives. The contributors include both Chinese and non-Chinese. The essays are mostly from leading journals of the humanities and social sciences published in North America, Europe, Japan, Singapore, and China. Some are from edited volumes, and a small number are extracted from monographs, especially in the case of early publications vital for shaping our view of the Chinese overseas. Readers may find the statistics (and interpretations) of some selections dated, for they reflect the knowledge, political concerns, and dominant paradigms of their time, as such, they can also be seen as historical documents in their own right and chapters in the evolving genealogy of the field.

The complexity of diasporic Chinese history and the richness of its scholarship cannot be fully captured in an anthology of this sort. Many representative works and authoritative accounts are excluded for lack of space. To remedy this shortcoming, I have provided additional bibliographical references for some key themes. Readers may also wish to consult recent bibliographical works[4] as well as the invaluable *Encyclopedia of the Chinese Overseas* edited by Lynn Pan of the Chinese Heritage Centre in Singapore and the massive twelve-volume *Encyclopedia of Chinese Overseas* under the general editorship of Zhou Nanjing of Peking University.[5]

STRUCTURE AND VARIATIONS

Conceptualizing and Historicizing Chinese International Migration

This volume deals with the conceptualization, history, demography, and spatial distribution of Chinese migration, including the changing paradigms of its study. The section on "Conceptualization" begins with a chapter on the historical patterns of Chinese migration by Wang Gungwu, doyen of the field over the last half-a-century.[6] His essay describes the characteristics and inter-relations of four major players in Chinese migration and overseas settlement since 1800: The *Huashang* (Chinese trader), the *Huagong* (Chinese labourer or "coolie", a term generally considered to be derogatory), the *Huaqiao* (Chinese sojourner), and the *Huayi* (descendant of migrants). Arguing that the "powerful and indestructible" *Huashang* pattern has been basic to Chinese migration since ancient times, Wang draws our attention to the profound spatial differences between Chinese migration to Southeast Asia and to the countries of European settlement in the Americas and Australasia.

While Wang Gungwu is a historian by training and mainly researches Southeast Asia, Paul C.P. Siu is a sociologist working on the first-generation Chinese in North America.[7] Using the frameworks of George Simmel's "stranger" and Robert Park's "marginal man", Siu conceptualizes "the Chinese sojourner" up to the 1950s as someone who "clings to the culture of his own ethnic group as in contrast to the bicultural complex of the marginal man. Psychologically he is unwilling to organize himself as a permanent resident in the country of his sojourn. When he does, he becomes a marginal man." He identifies the dilemmas a sojourner faced in deciding whether to stay abroad or return home, a problem centrally related to "the success or failure of the job [of making money in the new land] — he would not like to return home without a sense of accomplishment and some sort of security. But this state is psychologically never achieved". This movement back and forth forms an integral part of the sojourner's life. "The sojourner stays on abroad, but he also never loses his homeland tie."

The chapter by Philip Kuhn[8] begins with the origins of Chinese migrant institutions within China itself since the sixteenth century and examines the foreign environments into which Chinese migrated and the community structures they developed, giving special attention to the flexible adaptation and recombination of cultural templates. He argues that the Chinese migrant ecosystem has functioned as "a spatially extended system that overspreads geophysical and administrative boundaries". This ecosystem, furthermore, acted through a network of corridors, which made possible the continued recruitment of new migrants through exchanges of information and patronage. In an attempt to formulate a comparative framework in understanding Chinese migration, Kuhn proposes "an historical ecology", a narrative deals with migrants' adaptation to changing environments over historic time on a worldwide scale. Writing at the threshold of the twenty-first century and drawing on a wide range of data about global Chinese communities, Adam McKeown[9] aims to reconceptualize Chinese diasporas and identifies two traditions in scholarly writings, one that emphasizes the adaptive nature of Chinese social and cultural organizations and their contributions to the national histories, another that stresses "the enduring love, patriotism, connections, and contributions of Chinese their homeland". He criticizes the fragmentation created by "nation-based perspectives" and advocates a "diasporic perspective" that highlights the "global connections, networks, activities, and consciousnesses that bridge these more localized anchors of reference".

The section on "Historical Evolution and Changing Demography" deals with the definition of "Chinese overseas", a much contested subject. It is generally agreed that "Chinese overseas" refers to ethnic Chinese who live outside mainland China, Hong Kong, Taiwan and Macau "but acknowledge their Chinese origins, or are so regarded by demographers."[10] Some earlier writings include the populations of Hong Kong and Macau in their statistics, partly because of their unique place in the mental and geographical maps of Chinese diasporans. Confining his definition of "overseas Chinese" to two kinds of people, international migrants (whether they change their nationality or not) and their descendants, Zhu Guohong[11] provides a detailed historical survey of the origins and processes of Chinese international migration using Chinese-language sources. He divides the history of Chinese migration into five stages and examines the processes in light of changes in the motivation for emigration, typologies of migration, and the distribution of the emigrating population. This perspective provides a contrast to earlier Western scholarship that tended to pay greater attention to colonial policies.[12]

Labour migration was a main factor in Chinese international migration between 1850 and 1950. "A Survey of Chinese Emigration" prepared by the International Labour Organization[13] deals with the characteristics and statistics of Chinese emigration in the first half of the twentieth century. Apart from discussing push-and-pull factors, it also describes the measures taken by receiving governments to restrict Chinese immigration and the Chinese Government's attempts to protect its subjects abroad, thus highlighting the importance of power relations in emigration. The next two chapters describe the changing demography of Chinese overseas since the end of World War II. Using statistics and surveys provided by the Overseas Chinese Affairs

Commission in Taipei in the mid-1960s, the geographer Sen-Dou Chang[14] examines the overall distribution of Chinese overseas and their occupational changes. According to him, the Chinese overseas were more numerous in the tropical than in the mesothermal regions, on islands or along coasts than in the interior of continents, and in urban than in rural areas. They worked primarily in restaurant, retail trade, agriculture, handicrafts and small industry, and mining in the mid-twentieth century. The data for the chapter on "The Global Distribution of the Overseas Chinese around 1990"[15] derive from the *Overseas Chinese Economic Year Book* published in Taiwan, as well as from the national censuses of concerned countries. The chapter reports thirty-seven million Chinese overseas in 1990. (However, these figures include Hong Kong and Macau [approximately 6.1 million] and should be used carefully.) Apart from listing the demographic statistics of countries with a large number of Chinese, this survey provides useful data on population growth in the developed and developing regions and changes in the distribution of Chinese population between 1948 and 1990. The proportion of Chinese living in Southeast Asia has steadily declined, while that of industrialized nations has grown, a trend that has continued over the last fifteen years. (The latest demographic survey of Chinese overseas put their number at nearly thirty-three million in 1997, excluding Hong Kong and Macau.[16])

Studies on Chinese overseas have undergone paradigm shifts since the 1950s, when the field first began to take shape and grow in a climate of nationalism and Cold War. The chapters in the section on "Research Frameworks and Approaches" are concerned with changing perspectives on the Chinese diaspora. The main approach of scholars like G. William Skinner[17] in the 1950s and 1960s was in terms of assimilation theory. Refuting popular myths about the "unchanging Chinese", Skinner conceptualized Chinese assimilation in Thailand as a process when "the immigrant's descendant identifies himself in almost all social situations as a Thai, speaks the Thai language habitually and with native fluency, and interacts by choice with Thai more often than with Chinese". In a similar vein, Bernard Wong[18] defined assimilation as a process whereby "immigrants discard the cultural traits of their land of origin and acquire those of their host country through intermarriage, participation in the institutions of the host society on primary group levels, internalization of the values of the larger society, and adoption of their behaviors and attitudes." His work in Peru and the United States led him to conclude that the Chinese in Lima were more assimilated than in New York. While Skinner emphasized the role of politics in explaining the successful assimilation of the Chinese in

Thailand, Wong also identified structural and environmental factors as the key variables in accounting for the differences.

By the 1980s, the assimilationist thesis had come under increasing criticism for its one-sidedness and uni-directionalism.[19] In one of the first essays on diasporic Chinese identities, Wang Gungwu[20] had argued that modern Southeast Asian Chinese tend to assume multiple identities. He elaborated four types of identity that have a central bearing on the minds and hearts of Chinese in the region: National, class, ethnic, and cultural. Some of his views have been subsequently refined and revised, but this essay generated much interest and debate. L. Ling-Chi Wang[21] takes the critiques of the assimilationist and loyalty paradigms a step further. Arguing that the sole focus of these paradigms is "on the racial difference and conflict between the dominant Euro-Americans and the Chinese minority" and that it is "simplistic, unidimensional, biased and incomplete", he proposes an alternative paradigm under which "racial exclusion or oppression and extraterritorial domination converge and interact in the Chinese American community, establishing a permanent structure of dual domination and creating its own internal dynamics and unique institutions".

Cultural studies and scholarly discourses on the relationship between knowledge and power have given a new impetus over the past decade to the debate on Chinese identity. A fundamental issue at the heart of Chinese diaspora, Chineseness, has been treated with greater theoretical rigour than in the past. Instead of focusing on Chinese communities in specific locales, these studies are more concerned with conceptual and theoretical issues. Rey Chow[22] makes a critique of the field of China study — particularly the study of Chinese languages, literatures and cultures, but she also argues that "the habitual obsession" with Chineseness has given rise to a cultural essentialism that draws an imaginary boundary between China and the world. It is one of several attempts to tear down the barriers between the study of China and of the diaspora. According to her, "in the controversies over cultural identity, the signs of the times are that the diasporic is fast becoming the norm." In a similar effort to elucidate Chineseness, Ien Ang explores the limiting conceptual and political implications of diaspora discourse and argues that just like nations, "diaspora are not natural, always-already existing entities but 'imagined communities'." The transnationalism of the Chinese diaspora, she points out, is "actually nationalist in its outlook, because no matter how global in its reach, its imaginary orbit is demarcated ultimately by the closure effected by the category of Chineseness itself". Questioning the rigid division between Chinese and non-Chinese, she proposes a return to the hybridizing context of the global cities as "points of destination for large numbers of migrants from many different parts of the world" and argues for bringing out the intrinsic contradiction of the concept of diaspora, thus constituting "the space of diaspora's undoing".

Ien Ang[23] has problematicized not only Chineseness but the approaches to it, including transnationalism. Since the mid-1990s, transnationalism has made big inroads into migration studies, especially in studies on the Latino communities of the United States. Transnationalism is usually defined as "the processes by which immigrants form and sustain multi-stranded social relations that link together their societies of origin and settlement.... An essential element is the multiplicity of involvements that transmigrants sustain in both home and host societies." More specifically, transnational studies are concerned with "a growing number of persons who live dual lives: Speaking two languages, having homes in two countries, and making a living through continuous regular contact across national borders."[24] Recent theoretical reformulation has, on the other hand, claimed that the connections linking "here" and "there" are contingent outcomes subject to multiple political constraints.[25] The chapter by Aihwa Ong and Donald Nonini[26] — and the collection they co-edited — has been highly influential in shaping our understanding of modern Chinese transnationalism, which is grounded in the "culturally distinctive domain within the strategies of accumulation of the new capitalism — both Chinese and non-Chinese — emerging over the last two decades in the Asia-Pacific region." Conceptualizing modern Chinese transnationalism as a "third culture" that "arise[s] when groups face problems of inter-cultural communication at first hand and confront the necessity of continually moving back and forth between different cultures, each to some extent spatially defined," they demonstrate the centrality of the Chinese diaspora's transnational mobility and its flexible strategies in negotiating with "modern regimes of colonial empires, postcolonial nation-states, and international capitalism". This path-breaking work has inspired a number of recent studies and points toward new and exciting directions in future research. Transnational studies have gained much ground over the past decade, as evidenced by recent studies on the Chinese press,[27] religion,[28] and migration.[29]

Modern Chinese transnationalism must be understood in the context of linkages between China as a nation-state and the diaspora. Prasenjit Duara[30] explores "the ways in which nationalist ideologies sought to contain and domesticate a variety of transnational phenomena in East Asia that potentially ran counter to the sovereign interests of the nation-state in the first half of the twentieth century". He examines the different strategies employed by the Qing imperial state, revolutionary republicans, and the reformists, including

Pan-Asianism, Han radicalism, and Confucian culturalism, in their engagement with the Chinese overseas (particularly in Southeast Asia and North America). This contact led to the politicization of the Chinese overseas, who came to play an increasingly important role in China.

China, to be sure, has more than one face. "China is not just another nation-state in the family of nations," observed Lucian Pye; instead, it is "a civilization pretending to be a state".[31] This reconstructed China has ramifications for the Chinese overseas. Tu Weiming's conceptualization of "Cultural China"[32] is another attempt to go beyond the geographical and cultural boundaries that have shaped the study both of China and of Chinese overseas. Accordingly to Tu, Cultural China can be examined in terms of a continuous interaction of three symbolic universes: Societies populated predominantly by cultural and ethnic Chinese, which include mainland China, Taiwan, Hong Kong and Singapore; Chinese communities throughout the world; and individuals "who try to understand China intellectually and bring their conceptions of China to their own linguistic communities". While this conception is controversial, it points to the dynamic flows of Chinese cultures on a global scale and the formation of new identities as a result of their interactions. The increasing economic integration of ethnic Chinese societies has reinforced symbolic interactions in the cultural arena. Together with its political ramifications, it is at the heart of the equally controversial "Greater China" concept.[33] Wang Gungwu's chapter[34] reminds us that this concept must be employed cautiously and that history provides a useful angle from which to understand contemporary evolutions. After a judicious examination of the changing political attitudes of different types of Chinese overseas toward the Chinese state, he concludes that while there are those who are narrowly concerned with China's resurgence and those who are narrowly concerned with the survival of ethnic Chinese communities overseas, the rise of Greater China has had a profound impact on Chinese lives and the regions they inhabit. Again, China's inseparability from the Chinese diaspora and the cultural linkages that bind them leads to an exploration of institutions that have had a long-standing and lasting impact upon diasporic Chinese and their homeland connections, themes central to Volumes Two and Four.

Culture, Institutions and Networks

A number of institutions have played a key role in shaping diasporic Chinese societies. Chinese culture is a main element in these institutions and the transnational networks that bind them. The second volume of *The Overseas Chinese* starts with a section on "Chinese Family and Clanship", seen as the foundation of Chinese society, and their transformations in foreign settings. Ta Chen (1892–1975), who obtained his Ph.D. in sociology from Columbia University and taught at Tsinghua University in the 1920s/1930s, was a pioneer in the study of overseas Chinese and their hometown linkages. His chapter[35] deals with the family system in emigration and how the joint management of its resources and rigid control of individual family members was influenced by legal and social codes. He illustrates his arguments with concrete examples of the "dual family system", meaning the establishment and maintenance of two families, one in South China's emigrant communities and another in the diasporic settlements of the Nanyang (Southeast Asia). The dual family system differed from class to class — in upper, middle and lower class families — but its chief function remained the perpetuation of the family tree and economic inter-dependence. The husband enjoyed much authority, just as in the traditional family, but women played a larger role in the emigrant community and often had to manage family affairs in the absence of the household head. Tien Ju-kang,[36] who obtained his Ph.D. in anthropology from the London School of Economics in 1948 and did field work in Sarawak, describes the clans, a surname group comprising a large number of dispersed localized sub-clans whose members may or may not be able to trace their origins to a single founding ancestor. He finds that "the intricate network of surname relationship" played an important social and economic role and highlights the changes that took place in clans overseas, including a greater sense of mutual solidarity and a larger economic role. Unlike in China, where seniority counted most, the leadership among Chinese clans in Sarawak was based on personal qualities and high economic status.[37]

For the overseas Chinese community, the family is not only cultural and social but profoundly economic. "The essence of Chinese economic organization is familism," according to Siu-lun Wong's seminal essay.[38] He argues that Chinese family firms are not necessarily small, impermanent, and conservative and identifies four phases of their development: Emergent, centralized, segmented, and disintegrative. Subsequent studies have pointed out that Chinese familism must be understood in different socio-political structures and that prevailing political discourses have also played a part in shaping it.[39] While the concept of the family as a cohesive unit is normally linked with the notion of family members living under one roof, family dispersal is as old as human migration, a phenomenon well documented by Ta Chen and others. The wave of globalization at the end of the twentieth century further transformed the diasporic Chinese family. In his chapter on Hong Kong's "astronaut families", Chan Kwok Bun[40] makes two main arguments: The dispersing of the patrilineal Chinese family is often a rational family decision to preserve the family and "families split in order to be together translocally"; and these spatially dispersed families constitute strategic nodes of an ever-expanding transnational field that produces the emerging Chinese cosmopolitan.[41]

Voluntary associations are a central pillar of diasporic Chinese societies. Voluntary association is usually defined as "any public, formally constituted, and non-commercial organization of which membership is optional, within a particular society",[42] but Chinese voluntary associations are somewhat different. As Gary Hamilton argues, "[v]oluntary associations are clubs with members, with precise organizational boundaries, with some kind of governing body and specific purpose, and with written duties and responsibilities for the members. Chinese associations, however, are not so clear-cut as these, and are not so well defined and neatly bounded. Rather, these Chinese groups focus on the relationships that bind members into a common identity and that form a moral community out of which a sense of duty and obligation arises."[43] The section on "Voluntary Associations" begins with Edgar Wickberg's chapter.[44] On the basis of a comparative study of Chinese in Southeast Asia and North America, he provides a useful overview of overseas Chinese adaptive organizations that help new immigrants (and older ex-migrants) meet their initial basic needs — housing, jobs, and social support. Over the past 150 years, Chinese migrants' needs have changed from housing and employment to new opportunities and hometown connections; and from new opportunities and hometown connections to concerns about their children's need for Chinese education, in language or culture or both. He also examines the changing role of the *huiguan* (an association based on place of origin in China or common surname).[45]

The chapter by Maurice Freedman,[46] a pioneer in the anthropological study of Chinese overseas, is a classic work on immigrant associations in nineteenth century Singapore and elsewhere.[47] Freedman examines connections built on the principles of locality, dialect, surname, and occupation and finds that there were both continuities and changes in the overseas settings. Secret societies in late Qing China were a main precedent for these associations.[48] Anti-Manchuism was their *raison d'être* in China, but it became less so in Singapore, where secret societies served as "a means both of insulating the Chinese from outside interference, and of balancing the relations between the segments of a relatively closed Chinese community". Lawrence Crissman's theory of the segmentary structure of urban overseas Chinese communities, based on data from Southeast Asia and North America,[49] offers a generalized model for understanding diasporic Chinese social organization. While emphasizing the multiplicity and situationality of Chinese ethnicity, Crissman points out that the Chinese community is not homogenous and is divided into a number of sub-communities, or segments, in terms of dialect and geographical origin. These segments are interlocking, overlapping and fluid. The leadership of Chinese segmentary communities is based on wealth and prestige. "Overseas Chinese communities", concludes Crissman, "are plutocracies in which wealth breeds prestige and power". This leadership pattern represented a major departure from that in China. As Wang Gungwu has demonstrated, in traditional China *shi* (scholar-officials) were at the top of the social and political hierarchy and *shang* (merchants) were either at the bottom (in the ideal type) or below the *shi* (in reality). Among Chinese in colonial Southeast Asia, on the other hand, "commerce and shop-keeping were the only sources of wealth open to them.... Thus, there were broadly speaking only two divisions in overseas Chinese society — merchants and those who aspired to be merchants."[50]

Chinese voluntary associations are primarily designed to meet immigrants' needs in specific geographical locales, but their transnational activities should not be overlooked. Hong Liu's chapter[51] is concerned with an unprecedented surge in globalizing activity by overseas Chinese voluntary associations starting in the early 1980s, embodied in their frequent and large-scale gatherings; the formation of permanent international associations; and, most importantly, the extensive and creative use of such meetings and institutions to facilitate business and socio-cultural networks (both within the diaspora and between the diaspora and the homeland). It argues that the globalization of overseas Chinese associations represents a re-working of structural and cultural relationships in a multi-dimensioned global space. As a strategy of historical regeneration, social survival, economic expansion, and cultural revitalization, it deeply influences patterns of modern Chinese transnationalism and socio-economic developments in China and has created a new synergy between the global and the local.

Overseas Chinese business networks and entrepreneurship has been the subject of scholarly and popular discourse over the last two decades.[52] Two different approaches have emerged, one culturalist and the other structuralist, to explain diasporic economic activities. More recently, what I called a "revisionist turn" has emerged, characterized by an attempt to go beyond the established dichotomy.[53] The section on "Networks and Entrepreneurship" opens with Jamie Mackie's chapter,[54] which is an early examination of overseas Chinese business success and entrepreneurial capacity. Most of the writings he surveyed are on Southeast Asia, but he places his findings in the larger context of immigrant entrepreneurship, including its links with values, motivations and socio-political structures. All these issues have been at the center of the debate on entrepreneurship ever since the heyday of Weberian and Schumpeterian scholarship in the early twentieth century.[55]

I mentioned earlier that studies on the Chinese diaspora have been international in scope and researchers from different disciplines and national backgrounds have contributed to the field. Well-known for his innovative work on the Chinese tributary system in East Asia, Takeshi Hamashita[56] has brought Japan's sinological tradition and rich source materials to the attention of scholars outside Japan.[57] Instead of relying on the conventional unit of analysis that focuses on the country or national economy, his chapter looks at overseas Chinese financial networks at the intersection of region and ethnicity, with a special emphasis on the extensive trade triangle of Inchon-Shanghai-Osaka/Kobe. After its opening by the West in the 1850s, Japan created economic ties with other parts of East Asia by using the long-established commercial networks set up by Chinese merchants and overseas Chinese.[58] Gary Hamilton[59] questions the conventional wisdom that attributes the so-called economic miracle of East and Southeast Asia in the 1980s/1990s to the role of state, market, and culture. He argues that Chinese capitalism is not confined to precisely defined geographic boundaries and calls for a more historically grounded analysis. Chinese capitalism rests on a form of social organization that is "legitimated through kinship principles and is not dependent on a system of political economy". These principles nurture business networks that "are extremely flexible and that give Chinese entrepreneurs a comparative advantage in demand-responsive settings".[60]

The fourth section, "A Question of Culture", collects writings on factors that have helped shape the worldviews and mentality of Chinese overseas. It begins with a chapter on the role played by newspapers in Hong Kong in the making of diasporic Chinese consciousness. Historically, Hong Kong has served as a major port of emigration and a nexus of Chinese diaspora.[61] Elizabeth Sinn[62] shows that the Chinese press in Hong Kong in the late nineteenth century was a prime source of information on the Chinese abroad. By describing the suffering of compatriots overseas, highlighting the commonality of their experience, and underlining their ties with the homeland, it created in readers' minds "a transnational entity that we now call the Chinese diaspora". This reformulation of the Chinese diaspora coincided with the making of the *Huaqiao* and the emergence of a "New Asia" in socio-political discourse, pointing up the relationship between ethnicity and region.[63]

Religion has played an important part in the imagining by Chinese emigrants, especially those of earlier generations, of the outside world and served as "cultural capital" linking them with the ancestral homeland.[64] In an anthropological study on the Chinese in Southeast Asia, Tan Chee Beng[65] examines forms and structures of Chinese religions, including Buddhism. He argues that these religions, characterized by polytheism and syncretism and in the realm of folk religions, were fundamental in creating Chinese identities. Education is another agency. Tan Liok Ee[66] looks at Chinese schools in Malaysia, the most comprehensive Chinese-language educational system outside mainland China, Hong Kong, and Taiwan. She finds that the schools survived both by joining the national school system and by providing an alternative to it. As a result of demographic, socio-cultural, economic and political factors in the transition from immigrant society to membership of an independent nation-state, the Chinese culture of education remains resilient.

The gender issue in Chinese emigration has received increasing attention in recent years. Quite a few studies have appeared on Chinese immigrant women, particularly in North America.[67] An obstacle to such research has been the paucity of accounts by Chinese women themselves, yet another "people without history" (to quote Eric Wolf). Judy Yung[68] argues that oral history "allows ordinary folks like my subjects to speak for themselves, fill in historiographical gaps, and challenge stereo-types, as well as validate their lives". She concludes on a hopeful note: "Chinese women have always had to be inventive in order to survive, adapt, and contribute to the well-being of their families, community, and country."

Chinese representation and self-representation is another strand of scholarship in this field of study. Such representations happen principally in films, music, literary works, and socio-political commentaries.[69] Caroline Hau[70] looks at representations of Chinese in Filipino nationalist thought and notes a constant tension between efforts to identify Chinese as part of the Philippine nation-state and to hold them at arm's length from it. She not only "calls attention to the marginalization of the Chinese, and the way it is principally expressed in terms of the suppression or subornation of a minority to the majority" but examines the mechanisms by which "the selective inclusion and exclusion of the Chinese helped enable precisely a political community to be imagined as Filipino". This relationship between power, knowledge and the representation of Chinese as "aliens" is not confined to the Philippines. *The Chinese in Indonesia*, a commentary on ethnic Chinese in Indonesia by the country's leading intellectual, Pramoedya Ananta Toer (1926–2006), is similarly intertwined with the politics of the Sukarno regime and the changing perceptions of the Indonesian state and the PRC.[71]

Chinatown is inevitably shaped by the culture, ethnicity, and political authority of the host society. In North America, it is typically characterized as "a concentration of Chinese people and economic activities in one or more city blocks which forms a unique component of the urban fabric [and] is basically an idiosyncratic oriental community amidst an occidental urban environment". Kay Anderson,[72] however, goes beyond this conventional approach and presents Chinatown instead as "a social construction with a cultural history and a tradition of imagery and institutional practice that has given it a cognitive and material reality in and for the West". It is, she argues, "an idea that belongs to the 'white' European cultural tradition". Her analysis of municipal policies and landscape planning in Vancouver and of intellectual discourses on Chinatown shows how it is embedded in white Europeans' sense of difference between immigrants from China and themselves. Chinatown's internal politics and transnational linkages with China in the twentieth century were further ingredients in the making of Chinese urban communities in the West.[73]

Chinatown is not only an idea and image but a place of residence and work, stretching in some cases even to an industrial sector. By means of extensive surveys and statistical analyses, Min Zhou and John Logan[74] examine New York City's Chinatown, one of the oldest in North America. Defining it as an ethnic enclave that creates opportunities for its members unavailable to them in the larger society, Zhou and Logan find that education, labour-market experience, English-language ability, and other forms of human capital enable male workers in the ethnic enclave to increase their earning power. However, gender discrimination in the enclave labour market means that human-capital returns are minimal for female enclave workers.

Communities Across the Globe

While the first two volumes look mainly at the Chinese diaspora as a whole, the third volume presents specific studies of ethnic and immigrant Chinese communities in different regional and national environments and the strategies they have adopted to cope with them. Themes such as identity, Chineseness, and gender discussed in the earlier volumes also feature here. It is not possible to cover ethnic and diasporic Chinese communities everywhere, so I have chosen to focus on Southeast Asia and North America. This choice is made also in recognition of changing demographic and scholarly trends. Southeast Asia was the main destination of Chinese emigration until the 1950s, when it was replaced by North America and other industrialized nations. However, some 80 per cent of Chinese overseas still live in Southeast Asia. The rise of cultural studies and ethnic studies in the United States and other Western countries has gradually led to the integration of ethnic Chinese into these new fields of enquiry.[75]

The section on Southeast Asia starts with the work of G. William Skinner,[76] whose analysis of diasporic Chinese societies combined a social science approach with sinological knowledge. He argues that Chinese and indigenous cultures achieved a new and stable socio-cultural synthesis in the "intermediate creolized societies" of Southeast Asia. Skinner's comparative approach is complemented by the regional perspective developed by Carl Trocki[77] in his study of Chinese enterprise in the eighteenth and nineteenth centuries. Trocki shows that Chinese enterprise predated the colonial presence, that there was much transnational mobility, and that *kongsis* or shareholding partnerships were the main organizational structure of Chinese business. Claudine Salmon[78] reappraises the Chinese contribution in Southeast Asia. Instead of focusing on Chinese as exploitative "middlemen", she calls attention to various neglected aspects of Chinese enterprise, including technological assistance, financial support, and other forms of know-how in the period before and after the coming of the Westerners. The previous three chapters deal with the pre-colonial and colonial eras, when Chinese openly identified with China, as a civilization and nation-state. Fundamental changes took place in the post-colonial and postwar era after 1945, when indigenous nation-states emerged in Southeast Asia. Leo Suryadinata captures these changes and creates conceptual tools with which to study the new realities. Refuting terms such as "overseas Chinese" and "Chinese overseas", he prefers to call Chinese in the region Southeast Asians and examines both their self-perceptions and indigenous perceptions of them. Government policies have also played a role in shaping Chinese national identities, which remain fluid.[79]

Unlike most Southeast Asian regimes, which tend to homogenize ethnicity and portray it as a potential threat to national unity, North America, Australia, and New Zealand are migrant states committed to a policy of multi-culturalism and a general tolerance for ethnic diversity.[80] These new regimes emerged late in the twentieth century and were predated by systems that discriminated on grounds of "race", particularly against Chinese migrants. This institutional racism was a major determinant in the evolution of the identity, occupational patterns, and changing relationships of ethnic and immigrant Chinese with local state authorities and the ancestral homeland. L. Ling-Chi Wang[81] argues that Chinese identity in the United States was shaped not only by dominant ideas of assimilation (in the United States) and loyalty (to China) but also by ideas that evolved from actual encounters between Chinese and Euro-Americans. Their interplay led to the formation of five types of identity, based on sojourning, assimilation, accommodation, ethnic pride, and alienation. Sucheng Chan's[82] case study contrasts strikingly with Skinner's conceptualization of the creolized Chinese society in colonial Southeast Asia. According to Chan, second-generation Chinese Americans served as "one of the most important socializing agents in Chinese American communities" and strove to become Americans and to be treated as such. Unlike their Sino-Southeast Asian counterparts, Chinese Americans sensed irreconcilable differences between "American" and "Chinese" cultures and agonized over how to choose between them.[83]

Peter Li[84] traces the experiences of the Chinese in Canada between 1858 and 1930 and contends that their occupational choices were constrained by market conditions (including the demand for cheap labor) and institutional racism. Ethnic business emerged as a means of coping with a hostile environment.[85] Li's historical approach to ethnic stratification differs from traditional studies which tend to emphasize on psychological and cultural difference. Katharyne Mitchell[86] takes the story of Chinese immigration to North America up to the end of the twentieth century, when the transnational mobility of people and capital reached new heights. Citing the example of an influential voluntary organization formed by immigrant entrepreneurs from Hong Kong, she explores the intricate relationship between transnationalism, neo-liberalism in Canada, and Chinese networks. She highlights the need to ground Chinese transnationalism in the national political economy, in itself a product of global transformation.

Although most European countries are not migrant states in the same way as the United States, Canada, Australia, and New Zealand, they nevertheless became a prime destination of Chinese immigration in the late twentieth century. Frank Pieke[87] argues that Chinese immigration to Europe is a largely neglected topic, even though it dates back to the mid-nineteenth century. By the late 1990s, there were more than half a million Chinese in Europe. Pieke calls for comparative studies and theory-building, and proposes a Europe-wide instead of a nation-bound approach. In the meantime, nation-based studies of ethnic and immigrant Chinese communities will help lay a solid foundation for pan-European comparisons. Gregor Benton's[88] meticulously documented study questions currents in transnational studies that stress contemporaneity, economics, and elites and argues that transnational practices and institutions are "as old as Chinese immigration to Britain". In addition to building diasporic links with compatriots elsewhere, the transnational world of the Chinese in Britain has "several intersecting layers, corresponding to sub-ethnic, political, and class divisions".

The experience of Chinese in Australia and New Zealand is strikingly similar to that of those in North America, in that racist immigration policies played a big role in shaping their communities. C.Y. Choi's chapter[89] on the 1901 Commonwealth Immigration Restriction Act analyses the moment of birth of the White Australia Policy, which survived for decades. The act required immigrants to undergo a dictation test in a European language. Australia's Chinese population decreased by more than two-thirds mainly as a result, from more than 30,000 in 1901 to about 9,000 in 1947. The policy also precipitated the urbanization of the Chinese population and a concomitant switch from mining and farming to commercial and industrial pursuits. The inflow of large numbers of new migrants did not resume until the 1970s, when Chinese from Southeast Asia, China, and Hong Kong started to arrive.[90] In the new wave, women outnumbered men. Dissatisfied with the migration paradigms that "are conceptually represented as economically and male driven", Jan Ryan[91] examines the new patterns of Chinese immigration to Australia from the angle of gender and class. Manying Ip[92] surveys the evolution of Chinese in New Zealand in the light of changing immigration policies. She provides a demographic and employment profile of the community and analyses its coping strategies, intra-diasporic linkages, identity changes, and cultural revival since the 1990s.[93]

The final section of the third volume presents writings about Chinese communities in other regions. These communities are smaller, both proportionately and absolutely, than those we have considered up to now. Even so, studies on them add to our understanding of the diaspora.[94] Talking about the Chinese in Mexico and Peru, Evelyn Hu-Dehart[95] shows that "as field hands and laborers, truck farmers, merchants, shopkeepers, artisans and manufacturers, pioneers and frontiersmen, the Chinese have made significant contributions to the economic and infrastructural development of Latin America and the Caribbean".[96] As for the Chinese in Japan, although there has been a big increase of studies on them, most writings are in Japanese or Chinese.[97] Richard Friman[98] focuses on the transformation of Chinese migration to Japan by highlighting the instrumental role of immigration policies and enforcement patterns. Some Chinese went in through the front door, legally, while others entered through the side door on student and trainee visas or through the back door as illegal immigration, to help meet the Japanese demand for unskilled labour.[99]

In her chapter on Hakka ethnic identity in Calcutta, Ellen Oxfeld[100] explains that ethnic identity is a matter not simply of how a group chooses to define itself but of how others define it. Ethnic identity is dialogical or reflexive, "created, maintained, and reaffirmed through a continuous set of oppositions between one's own group and others". She focuses on three elements in the establishment and maintenance of Hakka identity in Calcutta: "State and national politics, an ethnically differentiated and stratified economy, and a host society with a religious system based on the symbolic opposition of purity and impurity". The final chapter, by Karen Harris,[101] is about the Chinese in South Africa, a community that has a long history of struggle and transnational interactions ignored both by South African historians and writers on the Chinese diaspora.[102] Harris describes the history of the Chinese in South Africa as "a legacy of inequality, inconsistency and interstitial existence". They suffered more or less the same racial discrimination as other coloured populations, but their small numbers and distinctive culture allowed them to escape the worst rigours of apartheid and "to lead a sometimes precarious existence in the interstitial spaces between a ruling while elite and a large, mainly laboring class, black majority".

Homeland Ties and Agency of Interactions

The history of the Chinese overseas is intertwined with their changing ties with the ancestral hometown/land. While China's own transformations shaped Chinese emigration, the diaspora has in its turn influenced the development of modern China. Chinese overseas have also played a role in political and economic relations between China and their countries of residence. The writings in this fourth volume deal with two related issues: The long-standing linkages between Chinese overseas and their homeland and the contribution by Chinese overseas to China's economic growth; and the diaspora's role in interactions between China and other places.

The first section on "*Qiaoxiang* and Beyond" deals with the role of Chinese overseas in the *qiaoxiang* (ancestral hometowns) and beyond. The *qiaoxiang* are primarily in South China, especially Guangdong and Fujian.[103] Ta Chen[104] compares an emigrant community with a non-emigrant one. In an ethnographical study, he examines how the emigrant community's livelihood was influenced by its sojourners overseas, including by way of remittances. Madeline Hsu[105] describes the sojourners' role in transforming the homeland, and their own transformation in the process. She focuses on the role of *qiaokan*, "magazines written and published locally and distributed to Taishanese [a sub-ethnic group originated from Taishan in Guangdong] internationally with the goal of nurturing a sense of connection to Taishan among émigrés and their descendants." She concludes that through these *qiaokan*, "Taishanese at home articulated a vision of community in which Taishanese abroad continued to play vital roles in their *guxiang* [hometown] by employing their superior access to capital and technology overseas to invest in the economy and well-being of Taishan."

While most studies on the *qiaoxiang* focus on Guangdong and Fujian, where the overwhelming majority of emigrants to Southeast Asia and North America originate, many ethnic Chinese in Europe are migrants or the descendants of migrants from the more northerly province of Zhejiang. Li Minghuan[106] writes about Wenzhou, which claims to have some 250,000 compatriots living outside of China, more than 65 per cent of them in Europe. Poverty is no long the main motive for emigration. The post-Mao economic reforms have raised the standard of living and of expectation. Like Ta Chen, Li identifies a distinct "culture of migration" in the Zhejiang *qiaoxiang*, whose people see "getting rich in Europe" as their common destiny. Chinese overseas have contributed crucially to China's rapid economic development since the late 1970s. The benefits have spread beyond the traditional *qiaoxiang*.[107] Paul Bolt[108] describes the efforts of the Chinese state to attract diasporic investors and the investors' enthusiastic response. He concludes that while the Chinese "tribe" is still overshadowed by the Chinese state, the state has gained greatly from its diasporic connections.

Interactions between state and diaspora began more than a century ago. The section on "The State, Local Politics, and Overseas Chinese Nationalism" begins with Michael Godley's[109] examination of the Qing campaign to modernize pre-1911 China using overseas Chinese capital and skills. In the closing decades of the nineteenth century, policy switched from protecting Chinese labourers overseas to "the encouragement of renewed contracts with the motherland to the outright exploitation of overseas experience and wealth". The switch had far-reaching implications. Using Singapore and Malaya as examples, Yen Ching-Hwang[110] traces the emergence of overseas Chinese nationalism at the turn of the twentieth century. An extension of Chinese nationalism, overseas Chinese nationalism was brought into being by the efforts of Qing officials and of the reformists and revolutionaries who visited Southeast Asia. External threats to China's sovereignty heightened this nationalist sentiment. A strong concern for China's fate was a main characteristic of overseas Chinese nationalism.

Wang Gungwu[111] debunks the portrayal of ethnic Chinese either as non-political or as a serious political threat to the peoples they live among.

Chinese groups are not static communities with solid and indestructible features; instead, they are "agents of change", heterogeneous, mobile, and dynamic. Wang identifies three major groups among overseas Chinese: Group A is predominantly concerned with Chinese national politics and its international ramifications; Group B with local community politics; Group C with the politics of non-Chinese hierarchies, whether indigenous, colonial, or nationalist.[112] In a comparative study of Jews in Central Europe and Chinese in Southeast Asia in the modern period, Anthony Reid[113] examines the "creative and vulnerable role" of both groups of outsiders in dynamic processes of change. Reid's chapter, which distinguishes between "blood" and "civic" nationalism, compares the transitions through which both entrepreneurial minorities passed: Their rise as key brokers for the expanding state; their emancipation; and their espousal of nationalism. William Callahan's chapter[114] is another comparative study of the interactions between multiple identities and the production of domestic and international politics. Neo-nationalists in both China and Thailand use diasporic Chinese as a resource to reconstruct a nationalist self and a foreign Other. The diversity of "Chineseness" is articulated in different economic and cultural spaces, while diasporas are "a symbolic resource in the production of cosmopolitanism, nationalism, and localism".

The Chinese overseas have played an important role in the economic and diplomatic interactions between China and their places of residence. The third section of this volume, "Ethnic Factor and the Political Economy of Diplomacy", begins with the chapter by Man-houng Lin on Taiwanese merchants' role in the modern economic transformation of East Asia, a largely neglected issue.[115] Their economic activities in Japan and Asia were shaped by Chinese merchants' cultural networks and Japanese political economy. "When the cultural network functions, we can see the autonomy of Taiwanese or overseas Chinese merchants," she concludes. "And where the Japanese political-economic force exerts influence, we can see the subordination of the Taiwanese or the overseas Chinese merchants."

Stephen Fitzgerald[116] deals with PRC policies toward the Chinese overseas, especially in the Cold War era, when the "Chinese problem" was at first a diplomatic liability and then (after the end of the Cultural Revolution) became an asset.[117] Fitzgerald argues that Chinese policies after 1956 were based on a "high degree of sensitivity to the attitudes and emotions of indigenous Southeast Asians, and a well-informed and realistic appraisal of the situation in Southeast Asia and the complexities of the Overseas Chinese problem", which in turn demonstrated Beijing's "capacity for rational foreign policy action". With a growing ethnic Chinese population in the United

States and increasing importance of Sino-American relations, the role of Chinese as "a bridge across the Pacific" has arisen as a topic of debate and scholarly inquiries.[118] Lucie Cheng[119] analyses the role played by Chinese Americans in forming linkages between the United States and the Asia-Pacific region and how they themselves have been affected by such linkages. The triangular relationship between the United States, China, and Chinese Americans is also discussed. In building bridges to China, Chinese Americans both contribute to globalization and challenge it. Their identities, local and transnational, are transformed by the start of the "Pacific Century".

The final section of this anthology, "Chinese New Migrants at the Turn of the Centuries", looks at the so-called new Chinese migrants, or *xin yimin*. These are the people who have emigrated since the late 1970s, either permanently or as sojourners. New migrants are of four main types: Students-turned-immigrants (who study abroad but stay on after graduating), chain migrants (who join kin already settled overseas), emigrating professionals (who emigrate to the West using their educational credentials and professional experiences), and illegal immigrants (who go overseas without papers or overstay after their visas run out).[120] Mette Thunø[121] traces two policies changes that have redefined the Chinese state's relationship with the new migrants: The PRC's recognition of Chinese citizens living abroad as a patriotic force in the late 1970s, and its decision to call upon the "cultural and national loyalties to China [of recent Chinese migrants and ethnic Chinese] regardless of citizenship".[122]

Whereas Thunø deals with macro-level policy changes and their ramifications, Xiang Biao[123] examines issues in the Chinese authorities' management of emigration flows, including exit control, diaspora policy, student migration, labor export, regulations on emigration agencies and human smuggling. The Chinese authorities use emigration to enhance China's international integration.

The anthology closes with my own preliminary observations on the uncertain future of new Chinese migrants and their homeland ties.[124] It is often said that overseas Chinese nationalism had died out by the 1950s, when China-centred allegiances gave way to local identities. This chapter analyses the revival of overseas Chinese nationalism and puts it in historical perspective. It argues that overseas Chinese nationalism is concerned with China's economic prosperity, cultural regeneration, and national unification. This nationalism is reactive and has an embedded tension with transnationalism, which reduces its centrality and intensity. As a result, it is unlikely to become a unified ideology or a centrally led movement like in the 1930s.

NOTES

1. This is a slightly revised version of the introduction to Liu Hong, ed., *The Chinese Overseas* (Routledge Library of Modern China), four volumes (London and New York: Routledge, forthcoming, 2006). The author is grateful for the help of many colleagues who have provided thoughtful suggestions and comments throughout the preparation of this work, particularly Wang Gungwu, Gregor Benton, Hamashita Takeshi, Philip Kuhn, Min Zhou, and Adam McKeown. Needless to say, this author is solely responsible for the shortcomings of the interpretations and criteria of the selection.
2. Some examples are: *The China Quarterly, The Journal of Asian Studies, International Migration Review, Diaspora, Comparative Study in Society and History, Journal of Southeast Asian Studies, Ethnic and Racial Studies, Identities, Journal of Asian Business, Amerasia,* and *Journal of Asian American Studies.* The newly launched *Journal of the Chinese Overseas,* edited by Chinese Heritage Centre in Singapore and published by Singapore University Press on behalf of the International Society for the Studies of Chinese Overseas (ISSCO), made its debut in May 2005 and is the only internationally refereed journal devoted exclusively to the studies of Chinese overseas.
3. Wang Gungwu, "Patterns of Chinese Migration in Historical Perspective", originally published in R.J. May and W.J. O'Malley, eds., *Observing Change in Asia: Essays in Honour of J.A.C. Mackie.* Bathurst, NSW: Crawford House Press, 1989, pp. 33–48. Reprint in Wang Gungwu, *China and the Chinese Overseas.* Singapore: Times Academic Press, 1991, pp. 3–21.
4. Some relevant bibliographies include Zeng Yiping and Chen Li-niang, eds., *Huaqiao Huaren Wenti Yanjiu Wenxian Suoyin (1980–1990)* [*Index to Periodical Articles on the Overseas Chinese (1980–1990)*]. Xiamen: Xiamen University Press, 1994; *Bibliography on Overseas Chinese.* Tokyo: Institute of Developing Economics, 1996; Gao Weinong and Shi Cangjin, eds., *Zhongguo de Huaqiao Huaren Yanjiu (1979–2000): Dui Ruogan Huaqiao Huaren Yanjiu Qikan Zaiwen de Zhaiping* [*The Studies of Chinese Overseas in China (1979–2000): Annotated Comments on Periodical Articles*]. Beijing: Zhongguo Huaqiao Chubanshe, 2002; Xu Bin, ed., *Huaqiao Huaren Yanjiu Zhongwen Shumu* [*Bibliography of Chinese Books on Overseas Chinese Studies*]. Xiamen: Xiamen University Press, 2003.
5. Lynn Pan, ed., *Encyclopedia of the Chinese Overseas.* Singapore: Archipelago Press, 1998; Cambridge: Harvard University Press, 1999. *Huaqiao Huaren Baike Quanshu* [*Encyclopedia of Chinese Overseas*] was published in Beijing by Zhongguo Huoqiao Chubanshe between 1998 and 2001; see in particular Zhou Nanjing and Hong Liu, et al., eds., *Zhuzuo Xueshu Juan* (*the Volume on Scholarly Works and Theories on the Chinese Overseas*) (2001), which includes brief introductions on relevant publications in major languages and local languages, profiles of major scholars and research institutions in the field as well as changing theoretical discourses about the Chinese overseas.

6. Wang Gungwu, "Patterns of Chinese Migration in Historical Perspective". For a comprehensive survey of Wang Gungwu's role in the evolution of the field, see Philip Kuhn, "Wang Gungwu: The Historian in His Time", in *Power and Identity in the Chinese World Order: Festschrift in Honour of Professor Wang Gungwu*, edited by Billy K. L. So, John Fitzgerald, Huang Jianli, and James K. Chin. Hong Kong: Hong Kong University Press, 2003, pp. 11–31; Hong Liu and Gregor Benton, "Introduction", in *Diasporic Chinese Ventures: The Life and Work of Wang Gungwu*, edited by Benton and Liu. London: Routledge, 2004, pp. 1–9.
7. Paul C.P. Siu, "The Sojourner", *American Journal of Sociology* 58, 1 (1952), pp. 34–44. On Siu's contribution to the historiography of Chinese Americans, see Franklin Ng, "The Sojourner, Return Migration, and Immigration History", *Chinese America: History and Perspective 1987*. San Francisco: Chinese Historical Association of America, 1987, pp. 53–71; Adam McKeown, "The Sojourner as Astronaut: Paul Siu in Global Perspective," in *Re/Collecting Early Asia America*, edited by Josephine Lee, Imogene L. Lim, and Yuko Matsukawa. Philadelphia: Temple University Press, 2002, pp. 127–42.
8. Philip A. Kuhn, "Toward an Historical Ecology of Chinese Migration", unpublished manuscript.
9. Adam McKeown, "Conceptualizing Chinese Diasporas, 1842 to 1949", *Journal of Asian Studies* 58, no. 2 (1999): 306–37.
10. Wang Gungwu, "Greater China and the Chinese Overseas", *The China Quarterly* 136 (1993): 926–48.
11. Zhu Guohong, "A Historical Demography of Chinese Migration", *Social Sciences in China* 12, no. 4 (1991): 57–91.
12. See for example one of the earliest scholarly treatises on the Chinese overseas, Frederick W. Williams, "The Chinese Immigrants in Further Asia", *American Historical Review* 5, no. 3 (1900): 503–17. See also Victor Purcell, *The Chinese in Southeast Asia*. London: Oxford University Press, 1951 and Sybille Van Der Sprenkel, "V.W.W.S. Purcell: A Memoir," in *Studies in the Social History of China and South-East Asia: Essays in Memory of Victor Purcell (26 January 1896–2 January 1965)*, edited by Jerome Ch'en and Nicholas Tarling. Cambridge: Cambridge University Press, 1970, pp. 1–20. For a study of early Chinese settlement in the region, see Chang Pin-tsun, "The First Chinese Diaspora in Southeast Asia in the Fifteenth Century," in *Emporia, Commodities and Entrepreneurs in Asian Maritime Trade, c. 1400–1750*, edited by Roderich Ptak and Dietmar Rothermund. Stuttgart: Franz Steiner Verlag, 1991, pp. 13–38.
13. International Labour Organization, "A Survey of Chinese Emigration", *International Labour Review* 60 (1950), pp. 289–301.
14. Sen-dou Chang, "The Distribution and Occupation of Overseas Chinese", *Geographical Review* 58, no. 1 (1968): 89–107.
15. Dudley Poston, Jr., Michael Xinxiang Mao, and Mei-yu Yu, "The Global

Distribution of the Overseas Chinese around 1990", *Population and Development Review* 20, no. 3 (1994): 631–45.

16. For the latest demographic survey of the Chinese overseas in various countries, see Laurence J.C. Ma, "Space, Place, and Transnationalism in the Chinese Diaspora", in *The Chinese Diaspora: Space, Place, Mobility, and Identity*, edited by Laurence J.C. Ma and Carolyn Cartier. Lanham: Rowman & Littlefield Publishers, Inc., 2003, pp. 1–49.
17. G. William Skinner, "Chinese Assimilation and Thai Politics," *Journal of Asian Studies* 16, no. 2 (1957): 237–50.
18. Bernard Wong, "A Comparative Study of the Assimilation of the Chinese in New York City and Lima, Peru", *Comparative Studies in Society and History* 20, no. 3 (1978): 335–58.
19. Wang Gungwu suggests that "this approach [assimilation] tells us little about the social dynamics of the group when it acts as a community. It also fails to take into account the history and traditions that guide that community's actions". Wang Gungwu, *The Chinese Overseas: From Earthbound China to the Quest for Autonomy* (Cambridge: Harvard University Press, 2000), p. 40. See also Chan Kwok Bun and Tong Chee Kiong, "Positionality and Alternation: identity of the Chinese of Contemporary Thailand," in *Alternate Identities: The Chinese of Contemporary Thailand*, edited by Tong and Chan. Leiden and Singapore: Brill and Times Academic Press, 2001, pp. 1–8.
20. Wang Gungwu, "The Study of Chinese Identities in Southeast Asia", in *Changing Identities of the Southeast Asian Chinese since World War II*, edited by Jennifer W. Cushman and Wang Gungwu. Hong Kong: Hong Kong University Press, 1985, pp. 1–21. Wang Gungwu acknowledged later that his earlier conceptualization of Chinese identities had been somewhat influenced by the nation-state framework and had presented the issue from the perspective of the new nation-state in Southeast Asia. He points out that it is imperative to give greater attention to the fluidity of Chinese identities and the role of China in the evolution of diasporic Chinese identities. Wang Gungwu, "Zai lun haiwai huaren de shenfen rentong", [Reassessing Overseas Chinese Identities], in *Haiwai huaren yanjiu de dashiye yu xin fangxiang: Wang Gengwu jiaoshou lunwen xuan* [*Macro-perspectives and New Directions in the Study of Chinese Overseas: Selected Essays of Wang Gungwu*], edited by Hong Liu and Huang Jianli. Singapore: Global Publishing Inc., 2002, pp. 97–116. Another important work on the issue of Chinese identity published in the 1980s is Linda Lim and Peter Gosling, eds., *The Chinese in Southeast Asia*. Singapore: Maruzen Asia, 1983; see in particular, Peter Gosling, "Changing Chinese Identities in Southeast Asia: An Introductory Review", in *Chinese in Southeast Asia,* vol. 2, *Identity, Culture and Politics*, pp. 1–15.
21. L. Ling-chi Wang, "The Structure of Dual Domination: Toward a Paradigm for the Study of the Chinese Diaspora in the United States", *Amerasia Journal* 21 (1995): 149–67.

22. Rey Chow, "Introduction: On Chineseness as a Theoretical Problem", in *Modern Chinese Literary and Cultural Studies in the Age of Theory: Rethinking a Field*, edited by Chow. Durham: Duke University Press, 2000, pp. 1–25.
23. Ien Ang, "Undoing Diaspora: Questioning Global Chineseness in the Era of Globalization", in idem., *On Not Speaking Chinese: Living between Asia and the West*. London and New York: Routledge, 2001, pp. 75–93.
24. Linda G. Basch, Nina Glick Schillier, and Christina Blanc-Szanton, *NationsUnbound: Transnational Projects, Post-colonial Predicaments, and De-terrirorialized Nation-States*. Langhorne, PA: Gordon and Breach, 1994, p. 6; Alejandro Portes, Luis E. Guarnizo and Patricia Landolt, "The Study of Transnationalism: Pitfalls and Promise of an Emergent Research Field", *Ethnic and Racial Studies* 22, no. 2 (1999): 217–37.
25. Roger Waldinger and David Fitzgerald, "Transnationalism in Question", *American Journal of Sociology* 109, no. 5 (2004): 1177–95.
26. Donald Nonini and Aihwa Ong, "Chinese Transnationalism as an Alternative Modernity", in *Ungrounded Empires: The Cultural Politics of Modern Chinese Transnationalism*, edited by Ong and Nonini. New York: Routledge, 1997, pp. 3–33.
27. Special issue on "Transnationalism and the Chinese Press", *China Review* 4, no. 1 (2004).
28. Special issue on "Modern Chinese Religious Transnationalism", *European Journal of East Asian Studies* 2, no. 2 (2003). See also Yoshiko Ashiwa and David L. Wank, "The Globalization of Chinese Buddhism: History, Network, and Transnationalism in the Twentieth Century", *International Journal of Asian Studies* (July 2005).
29. Frank Pieke, Pàl Nyiri, Mette Thunø, Antonella Ceccagno, *Transnational Chinese: Fujianese Migrants in Europe*. Stanford: Stanford University Press, 2004.
30. Prasenjit Duara, "Transnationalism and the Predicament of Sovereignty: China, 1900–1945", *American Historical Review* 102, no. 4 (1997): 1030–51.
31. Cited in Tu Wei-ming, "Cultural China: The Periphery as the Center", in *The Living Tree: The Changing Meaning of Being Chinese Today*, edited by Tu. Stanford: Stanford University Press, 1994, p. 17.
32. Ibid.
33. Harry Harding, "The Concept of 'Greater China': Themes, Variations and Reservations", *The China Quarterly* 136 (1993): 660–86. For a recent re-evaluation of the concept of Greater China and its relevance to the Chinese diaspora, see William Callahan, *Contingent States: Greater China and Transnational Relations*. Minneapolis: University of Minnesota Press, 2004.
34. Wang Gungwu, "Greater China and the Chinese Overseas".
35. Ta Chen, "The Family", in idem, *Emigrant Communities in South China: A Study of Overseas Migration and Its Influence*. New York: Institute of Pacific Relations, 1940; reprint: New York: AMS Press, 1978, pp. 118–48.
36. Tien Ju-kang, "Clanship", in idem., *The Chinese of Sarawak: A Study of Social*

Structure. London: London School of Economics Monographs on Social Anthropology, no. 12, 1953, pp. 21–35.

37. For a comparative view of Chinese clanship and leadership in Southeast Asia, see G. William Skinner, *Leadership and Power in the Chinese Community of Thailand*. Ithaca: Cornell University Press, 1958; Chinben See, "Chinese Clanship in the Philippine Setting", *Journal of Southeast Asian Studies* 12, no. 1 (1981): 224–47; and C.F. Yong, *Chinese Leadership and Power in Colonial Singapore*. Singapore: Times Academic Press, 1992.
38. Wong Siu-lung, "The Chinese Family Firm: A Model", *British Journal of Sociology* 36, no. 1 (1985), pp. 58–72.
39. For some discussions of changing discourse on family in Chinese economic development, see Susan Greenhalgh, "De-Orientalizing the Chinese Family Firm", *American Ethnologist* 21, no. 4 (1994): 746–75; M. K. Whyte, "The Chinese Family and Economic Development: Obstacle or Engine?" *Economic Development and Cultural Change* 45, no. 1 (1996): 1–30; Arif Dirlik, "Critical Reflections on 'Chinese Capitalism' as Paradigm", *Identities* 3 (1997): 303–30.
40. Chan Kwok Bun, "A Family Affair: Migration, Dispersal, and the Emergent Identity of the Chinese Cosmopolitan", *Diaspora* 6, no. 2 (1997): 195–214.
41. For constructive formulations of cosmopolitanism in the context of both China and diasporic Chinese, see Leo Ou-fan Lee, "On the Margins of the Chinese Discourse: Some Personal Thoughts on the Cultural Meaning of the Periphery", in *The Living Tree*, edited by Tu Weiming, pp. 221–44; Chan Kwok Bun, "Imagining/Desiring Cosmopolitanism", *Global Change, Peace & Security* 15, no. 2 (2003): 139–56.
42. Gordon Marshall, *Oxford Concise Dictionary of Sociology*. Oxford: Oxford University Press, 1994, p. 557.
43. Gary Hamilton, "Competition and Organization: A Reexamination of Chinese Business Practices", *Journal of Asian Business* 12, no. 1 (1996): 18.
44. Edgar Wickberg, "Overseas Chinese Adaptive Organizations, Past and Present", in *Reluctant Exiles? Migration from Hong Kong and the New Overseas Chinese*, edited by Ronald Skeldon. Hong Kong: Hong Kong University Press, 1994, pp. 68–84.
45. These are the two major types of Chinese voluntary associations, and another major typology is occupational association, especially the chamber of commerce that has played key political and social roles. For some representative discussions of Chinese associations in China and overseas, see Bryna Goodman, *Native Place, City, and Nation: Regional Networks and Identities in Shanghai, 1853–1937*. Berkeley: University of California Press, 1995; Wang Tai-peng, *The Origins of Chinese Kongsi*. Petaling Jaya: Pelanduk Publications, 1996; Li Minghuan, *"We Need Two Worlds": Chinese Immigration Associations in A Western Society*. Amsterdam: Amsterdam University Press, 1999; Him Mark Lai, "Chinese Organizations in America Based on Locality of Origin and/or Dialect-Group Affiliation, 1940s–1990s", *Chinese America: History and Perspective 1996*. San

Francisco: Chinese Historical Society of America, 1996, pp. 19–75. For some treatment on the Chinese chamber of commerce, see Theresa Chong Carino, *Chinese Big Business in the Philippines: Political Leadership and Chang*. Singapore: Times Academic Press, 1998; Hong Liu, "Organized Chinese Transnationalism and the Institutionalization of Business Networks: the Singapore Chinese Chamber of Commerce and Industry as a Case Analysis", *Southeast Asian Studies* 37, no. 3 (1999): 392–417. A less studied aspect of diasporic Chinese associations is class-based organizations, which may undermine ethnic identities (especially among poor immigrants) but help forge a diasporic internationalism among workers. See for example, Renqiu Yu, *To Save China, To Save Ourselves: The Chinese Hand Laundry Alliance of New York*. Philadelphia: Temple University Press, 1992; and Gregor Benton, *Chinese Abroad and the Workers of the World: Studies in Diasporic Internationalism, 1917–1945* (unpublished manuscript).

46. Maurice Freedman, "Immigrants and Associations: Chinese in Nineteenth Century Singapore", *Comparative Studies in Society and History* 3, no. 1 (1960): 25–48.
47. For some discussions of Chinese associations in Singapore in the twentieth century, see Vincent Wing Chung Ng, "Urban Chinese Social Organization: Some Unexplored Aspects in *Huiguan* Development in Singapore, 1900–1941", *Modern Asian Studies* 26, no. 3 (1992): 469–94; Cheng Lim Keak, *Social Change and the Chinese in Singapore*. Singapore: Singapore University Press, 1985; and Hong Liu, "Chapter 2: Internal Structure of Singapore Chinese Society: Changes and Continuities", in Hong Liu and Sin-kiong Wong, *Singapore Chinese Society in Transition: Business, Politics and Socio-economic Change, 1945–1965*. New York: Peter Lang Publishing, 2004, pp. 45–86.
48. David Ownby and Mary Somers Heidhues, eds., *"Secret Societies" Reconsidered: Perspectives on the Social History of Modern South China and Southeast Asia* (Armonk: M.E. Sharpe, 1993).
49. L.W. Crissman, "The Segmentary Structure of Urban Overseas Chinese Communities", *Man* 2, no. 2 (1967): 185–204. His subsequent attempt along this direction also includes data from Australia, see Lawrence W. Crissman, George Beattie, and James Selby, "The Chinese in Brisbane: Segmentation and Integration," in *The Overseas Chinese: Ethnicity in National Context*, edited by Francis L.K. Hsu and Hendrick Serrie. Lanham: University Press of America, 1998, pp. 87–114.
50. Wang Gungwu, "Traditional Leadership in a New Nation: The Chinese in Malaya and Singapore", in *Leadership and Authority: A Symposium*, edited by Gehan Wijeyewardene. Singapore: University of Malaya Press, 1968, p. 210. William Skinner's study of Chinese elite in Thailand has also led him to conclude that "Business success, wealth, and effective control of the important economic institutions of the community are all prerequisites for civic positions of high authority". Skinner, "Overseas Chinese Leadership: Paradigm for a Paradox", in Wijeyewardene, ed., *Leadership and Authority*, pp. 191–207; see

also Andrew Wilson, *Ambition and Identity: Chinese Merchant Elites in Colonial Manila, 1880–1916*. Honolulu: University of Hawaii Press, 2004.

51. Hong Liu, "Old Linkages, New Networks: The Globalization of Overseas Chinese Voluntary Associations and Its Implications", *The China Quarterly* 155 (1998), pp. 582–609.
52. For an anthology on this subject, see R. A. Brown, ed., *Chinese Business Enterprise in Asia*, 4 volumes (London: Routledge, 1995). Some recent representative literature includes Chan Kwok Bun, ed., *Chinese Business Networks: State, Economy and Culture* (Singapore: Prentice Hall, 2000); Henry Wai-chung Yeung and Kris Olds, eds., *Globalisation of Chinese Business Firms*. London: Macmillan, 2000; Edmund Terence Gomez, and Hsin-Huang Michael Hsiao, eds., *Chinese Business in South-East Asia: Contesting Cultural Explanations, Researching Entrepreneurship*. Surrey: Curzon Press, 2001 and *Chinese Enterprise, Transnationalism, and Identity*. London: RoutledgeCurzon, 2004; and Thomas Menkhoff and Solvay Gerke, eds., *Chinese Entrepreneurship and Asian Business Networks*. London: RoutledgeCurzon, 2002.
53. I have used the term "revisionist turn" in my review of Gomez and Hsiao, eds., *Chinese Business in South-East Asia*, in *ASEAN Economic Bulletin* 19, no. 3 (2002): 348–50, and discussed the topic more thoroughly in the chapter entitled "Paradigm Shifts in the Studies of Asian Chinese Business Networks", in Liu Hong, *Zhanhou Xinjiapo Huaren Shehui de Shanbian: Bentu Qinghuai, Quyu Wangluo, Quanqiu Shiye* [*The Transformation of Chinese Society in Postwar Singapore: Localizing Processes, Regional Networking, and Global Perspective*]. Xiamen: Xiamen University Press, 2003, pp. 179–211 and Hong Liu, "Chinese New Migrants and Transnational Entrepreneurship: The Sino-Singaporean Experience in Comparative Perspective", paper presented at the University of California Pacific Rim Conference "A New Breed of Chinese Entrepreneur in the Pacific Rim? Culture, Organizational Imperatives, and Globalization". Hong Kong University of Science & Technology, 21–22 May 2004.
54. J.A.C. Mackie, "Overseas Chinese Entrepreneurship", *Asian-Pacific Economic Literature* 6 (1992), pp. 41–64.
55. For some general overview on entrepreneurship, see Howard Aldrich and Roger Waldinger, "Ethnicity and Entrepreneurship", *Annual Review of Sociology* 16 (1990): 111–35; Patricia H. Thornton, "The Sociology of Entrepreneurship", *Annual Review of Sociology* 25 (1999): 19–46; Richard Swedberg, ed., *Entrepreneurship: The Social Science View*. Oxford: Oxford University Press, 2000; and Casson, Mark, *The Entrepreneur: An Economic Theory*. Second edition. Cheltenham: Edward Elgar, 2003.
56. Hamashita Takeshi, "Overseas Chinese Financial Networks and Korea", in *Commercial Networks in Modern Asia*, edited by S. Sugiyama and Linda Grove. Surrey: Curzon, 2001, pp. 55–70.
57. Yang Chien-chen and George L. Hicks, eds., *A Bibliography of Japanese Works on the Overseas Chinese in Southeast Asia, 1914–1945*. Hong Kong: Asian Research

Service, 1992; *Bibliography on Overseas Chinese*. Tokyo: Institute of Developing Economics, 1996, lists Japanese-language publications on the Chinese overseas, which are also reflected in *Kakyo Kajinsikenkyu no Genzai* [*The Status of Overseas Chinese Historical Studies*], edited by Iijima Wataru. Tokyo: Kyukosensho, 1999. Some of Hamashita's relevant work in English include "The Intra-regional System in East Asia in Modern Times", in *Network Power: Japan and Asia*, edited by Peter Katzenstein and Takashi Shiraishi. Ithaca: Cornell University Press, 1997, pp. 113–35; "Competing Political Spaces and Recreating Cultural Boundaries in Modern East Asia: Regional Dynamism and the Maritime Identity of Asia", in *China and Southeast Asia: Changing Social-Cultural Interactions*, edited by Melissa Curley and Hong Liu. Hong Kong: Center of Asian Studies, University of Hong Kong, 2002, pp. 27–38; and Giovanni Arrighi, Takeshi Hamashita, and Mark Selden, eds., *The Resurgence of East Asia: 500, 150 and 50 Year Perspectives*. London: Routledge, 2003.

58. An important study of the dynamic interactions between (Chinese) networks and Western/Japanese enterprises in modern China is Sherman Cochran, *Encountering Chinese Networks: Western, Japanese, and Chinese Corporations in China, 1880–1937*. Berkeley: University of California Press, 2000.
59. Gary Hamilton, "Overseas Chinese Capitalism", in *Confucian Traditions in East Asian Modernity*, edited by Tu Wei-ming. Cambridge: Harvard University Press, 1996, pp. 328–42.
60. Gary Hamilton also edits the ground-breaking work, *Business Networks and Economic Development in East and Southeast Asia*. Hong Kong: Centre of Asian Studies, University of Hong Kong, 1991; see also Hamilton, *Commerce and Capitalism in Chinese Societies*. New York: Routledge, 2005. For some relevant discussions along the lines of culture, market and capitalism, see Timothy Book and Hy V. Luong, eds., *Culture and Economy: The Shaping of Capitalism in Eastern Asia*. Ann Arbor: University of Michigan Press, 1997; and Robert W. Hefner, ed., *Market Cultures: Society and Values in the New Asian Capitalisms*. Singapore: Institute of Southeast Asian Studies, 1998.
61. One of the most important studies that place Hong Kong in the centre of Chinese international migratory system is Ronald Skeldon, ed., *Reluctant Exiles? Migration from Hong Kong and the New Overseas Chinese*. Armonk: M.E. Sharpe, 1994; see also Elizabeth Sinn, "*Xin Xi Guxiang*: A Study of Regional Associations as a Bonding Mechanism in the Chinese Diaspora. The Hong Kong Experience", *Modern Asian Studies* 3, no. 2 (1997): 375–97.
62. Elizabeth Sinn, "Beyond *Tianxia*: The *Zhongwai Xinwen Qiribao* (Hong Kong 1871–1872) and the Construction of a Transnational Chinese Community", *The China Review* 4, no. 1 (2004): 89–122.
63. See for details Wang Gungwu, "The Origin of Hua-Ch'iao", in Wang Gungwu, *Community and Nation: China, Southeast Asia and Australia*. St Leonards, NSW: Asian Studies Association of Australia in association with Allen & Unwin, 1992, pp. 1–10; Hong Liu, "Sino-Southeast Asian Studies: Toward an Alternative

Paradigm", *Asian Studies Review* 25, 3 (2001), pp. 259–83; and Rebecca E. Karl, *Staging the World: Chinese Nationalism at the Turn of the Twentieth Century*. Durham: Duke University Press, 2002.

64. Kuah Khun-eng, *Rebuilding the Ancestral Village Singaporeans in China* (Aldershot: Ashgate, 2000); Tan Chee-Beng, "Chinese Ethnological Field: Anthropological Studies of Chinese Communities Worldwide", in idem., *Chinese Overseas: Comparative Cultural Issues*. Hong Kong: Hong Kong University Press, 2004, pp. 9–30.
65. Tan Chee-Beng, "The Study of Chinese Religions in Southeast Asia: Some Views", in *Southeast Asian Chinese: The Socio-Cultural Dimension*, edited by Leo Suryadinata. Singapore: Times Academic Press, 1995, pp. 139–64.
66. Tan Liok Ee, "Chinese Schools in Malaysia: A Case of Cultural Resilience", in *The Chinese in Malaysia*, edited by Lee Kam Hing and Tan Chee-Beng. Kuala Lumpur: Oxford University Press, 2000, pp. 228–54.
67. Some representative works include Rey Chow, *Writing Diaspora: Tactics of Intervention in Contemporary Cultural Studies*. Bloomington: Indiana University Press, 1993; James A. Geschwender, "Ethnicity and the Social Construction of Gender in the Chinese Diaspora", *Gender and Society* 6, no. 3 (1992): 480–507; Kap Hsin-sheng, ed., *Nativism Overseas: Contemporary Chinese Women Writers*. Albany: State University of New York Press, 1993; Sharon K. Hom, ed., *Chinese Women Traversing Diaspora: Memoirs, Essays, and Poetry*. New York: Garland Pub., 1999; and Jiemin, Bao, *Marital Acts: Gender, Sexuality, and Identity among the Chinese Thai Diaspora*. Honolulu: University of Hawaii Press, 2005.
68. Judy Yung, "Giving Voice to Chinese American Women: Oral History Methodology", in idem., *Unbound Voices: A Documentary History of Chinese Women in San Francisco*. Berkeley: University of California Press, 1999, pp. 511–26.
69. For example, *Overseas Chinese Figures in Cinema* (Hong Kong: Urban Council, 1992); Xiao-huang Yin, *Chinese American Literature since the 1850s*. Urbana: University of Illinois Press, 2000; Frederick Lau, "Performing Identity: Musical Expression of Thai-Chinese in Contemporary Bangkok", of Social Issues in Southeast Asia 16, no. 1 (2001): 37–69; Shen Yuanfang, *Dragon Seed in the Antipodes: Chinese-Australian Autobiographies*. Melbourne: Melbourne University Press, 2001. See also relevant chapters in Roger Bromley, *Narratives for a New Belonging: Diasporic Cultural Fictions*. Edinburgh: Edinburgh University Press, 2000; Harry M. Benshoff and Sean Griffin, *America on Film: Representing Race, Class, Gender, and Sexuality at the Movies*. Malden, MA: Blackwell Pub., 2004; and Caroline S. Hau, *On the Subject of the Nation: Filipino Writings from the Margins, 1981–2004*. Manila: Ateneo de Manila University Press, 2004.
70. Caroline S. Hau, "Alien Nation", in idem., *Necessary Fictions: Philippine Literature and the Nation, 1946–1980*. Manila: Ateneo de Manila University Press, 2000, pp. 133–76.
71. Hong Liu, "Pramoedya Ananta Toer and China: The Transformation of a

Cultural Intellectual", *Indonesia* 61 (1996): 119–43; Sumit Mandal, "Pengantar: Orang Asing Yang Tidak Asing: Bahasa Pramoedya yang Mengganggu Mengenai Orang Tionghoa Indonesia" [Introduction: Strangers who are not Foreign: Pramoedya's Disturbing Language on the Chinese of Indonesia"], in Pramoedya Ananta Toer, *Hoakiau di Indonesia* [*The Chinese in Indonesia*]. Jakarta: Garba Budaya, 1998 [1960], pp. 1–30.

72. Kay Anderson, "The Idea of Chinatown: The Power of Place and Institutional Practice in the Making of a Racial Category", *Annals of the Association of American Geographers* 77, no. 4 (1987): 580–98.
73. See for example, Min Zhou, *Chinatown: The Socioeconomic Potential of an Urban Enclave*. Philadelphia: Temple University Press, 1992; Hsiang-Shui Chen, *Chinatown No More: Taiwan Immigrants in Contemporary New York*. Ithaca: Cornell University Press, 1992; Yong Chen, *Chinese San Francisco, 1850–1943: A Trans-Pacific Community*. Stanford: Stanford University Press, 2000; Peter Kwong, *Chinatown, New York : Labor and Politics, 1930–1950*. New York: New Press, 2001; Adam McKeown. *Chinese Migrant Networks and Cultural Change: Peru, Chicago, Hawaii, 1900–1936*. Chicago: University of Chicago Press, 2001; and Flemming Christiansen, *Chinatown, Europe: An Exploration of Overseas Chinese Identity in the 1990s*. London: Routledge, 2003.
74. Min Zhou and John R. Logan, "Returns on Human Capital in Ethnic Enclaves: New York City's Chinatown", *American Sociological Review* 54, no. 5 (1989): 809–20.
75. The shift of scholarly focus is evident in China as well. A survey of 6,175 academic articles dealing with the ethnic Chinese in specific regions published between 1980 and 2003 reveals that 57 per cent of them are concerned with Southeast Asia and 16 per cent with the United States, which have a combined total of 73 per cent. See Xu Yun, "Zhongguo Dalu Huaqiao Huaren Yanjiu de Wenxian Jilian Fenxi Baogao" [A Statistical Analysis of Articles about the Chinese Overseas published in Mainland China], *Huaqiao Huaren Lishi Yanjiu* [Studies in Overseas Chinese History], no. 4 (2004), pp. 7–17.
76. G. William Skinner, "Creolised Chinese Societies in Southeast Asia", in *Sojourners and Settlers: Histories of Southeast Asia and the Chinese*, edited by Anthony Reid. Sydney: Allen & Unwin, 1996, pp. 51–93.
77. Carl A. Trocki, "Boundaries and Transgressions: Chinese Enterprise in Eighteenth- and Nineteenth-Century Southeast Asia", in *Ungrounded Empires: The Cultural Politics of Modern Chinese Transnationalism*, edited by Aihwa Ong and Donald Nonini. New York: Routledge, 1997, pp. 61–85.
78. Claudine Salmon, "The Contribution of the Chinese to the Development of Southeast Asia: A New Appraisal", *Journal of Southeast Asian Studies* 12, no. 1 (1981): 260–75.
79. Leo Suryadinata, "Ethnic Chinese in Southeast Asia: Overseas Chinese, Chinese Overseas or Southeast Asians?" in *Ethnic Chinese as Southeast Asians*, edited by Leo Suryadinata. Singapore: Institute of Southeast Asian Studies 1997, pp.

1–24. For changing approaches to Southeast Asian Chinese in the recent decades, see also the observations by two veteran researchers, John Clammer, *Diaspora and Identity: The Sociology of Culture in Southeast Asia*. Selgangor: Pelanduk Publications, 2002; Tan Chee Beng, *Chinese Overseas: Comparative Cultural Issues*. Hong Kong: Hong Kong University Press, 2004.

80. For a detailed analysis of nation-state and migrant state and their implications for the ethnic Chinese, see Wang Gungwu, "Nationalism, Ethnicity and the Asia-Pacific", *Public Policy* 2, no. 2 (1998): 13–36.
81. L. Ling-chi Wang, "Roots and the Changing Identity of the Chinese in the United States", in *The Living Tree: The Changing Meaning of Being Chinese Today*, edited by Tu Weiming. Stanford: Stanford University Press, 1994, pp. 185–212.
82. Sucheng Chan, "Race, Ethnic Culture, and Gender in the Construction of Identities among Second-Generation Chinese Americans, 1880s to 1930s", in *Claiming America: Constructing Chinese American Identities during the Exclusion Era*, edited by K. Scott Wong and Sucheng Chan. Philadelphia: Temple University Press, 1998, pp. 127–64.
83. For some recent discussions of new generation Chinese American identity, see Josephine M.T. Khu, ed., *Cultural Curiosity: Thirteen Stories about the Search for Chinese Roots*. Berkeley: University of California Press, 2001; Andrea Louie, *Chineseness across Borders: Renegotiating Chinese Identities in China and the United States*. Durham: Duke University Press, 2004. See also Him Mark Lai, *Becoming Chinese American: A History of Communities and Institutions*. Walnut Creek: Altamira Press, 2004.
84. Peter Li, "A Historical Approach to Ethnic Stratification: The Case of the Chinese in Canada, 1858–1930", *Canadian Review of Sociology and Anthropology* 16, no. 3 (1979): 320–32.
85. For the latest development of ethnic business in Canada, see Eric Fong, Chiu Luk and Emi Ooka, "Suburban Spatial Distribution of Ethnic Businesses", *Social Science Research* 34, no. 1 (2005): 215–35.
86. Katharyne Mitchell, "Transnationalism, Neo-liberalism, and the Rise of the Shadow State", *Economy and Society* 30, no. 2 (2001): 165–89.
87. Frank Pieke, "Introduction", in *The Chinese in Europe*, edited by Gregor Benton and Frank Pieke. London: Macmillan Press, 1998, pp. 1–17.
88. Gregor Benton, "Chinese Transnationalism in Britain: A Longer History", Studies in Power and Culture 10, no. 3 (2003): 347–75.
89. C.Y. Choi, "Chinese Migration 1901–47: Under the Commonwealth Immigration Restriction Act 1901", in idem., *Chinese Migration and Settlement in Australia*. Sydney: Sydney University Press, 1975, pp. 36–54.
90. Christine Inglis, "The Chinese in Australia", *International Migration Review* 6, no. 2 (1972): 266–81; James E. Coughlan, "The Changing Characteristics of Chinese Migrants to Australia during the 1980s and Early 1990s", in *The Last Half Century of Chinese Overseas*, edited by Elizabeth Sinn. Hong Kong: Hong Kong University Press, 1998, pp. 299–345.

91. Jan Ryan, "Chinese Women as Transnational Migrants: Gender and Class in Global Migration Narratives", *International Migration* 40, no. 2 (2002): 93–114.
92. Manying Ip, "Chinese Immigrants and Transnationals in New Zealand: A Fortress Opened", in *The Chinese Diaspora: Space, Place, Mobility, and Identity*, edited by Laurence J.C. Ma and Carolyn Cartier. Lanham: Rowman & Littlefield Publishers, Inc., 2003, pp. 339–58.
93. For an earlier discussion of Chinese identity in the country, see Kwen Fee Lian, "The Sociopolitical process of Identity Formation in an Ethnic Community: The Chinese in New Zealand", *Ethnic and Racial Studies* 11, no. 4 (1988): 506–32.
94. For example, David Yen-ho Wu, "To Kill Three Birds with One Stone: The Rotating Credit Associations of the Papua New Guinea Chinese", *American Ethnologist* 1, no. 3 (1974): 565–84.
95. Evelyn Hu-DeHart, "Coolies, Shopkeepers, Pioneers: The Chinese of Mexico and Peru (1849–1930)", *Amerasia Journal* 15, no. 2 (1989): 91–116.
96. For some historiographical survey on the Chinese in Latin America, see Evelyn Hu-Dehart "From Area Studies to Ethnic Studies: The Study of the Chinese Diaspora in Latin America", in *Asian Americans: Comparative and Global Perspectives*, edited by Shirley Hune et al. Pullman, Washington State University Press, 1991, pp. 5–16; Li Anshan, "Ladin Meizhou Huaqiao Huaren Yanjiu Kaishu" [A Historiographical Survey on the Chinese Immigrants in Latin America], *Yatai Yanjiu Luncun* [*Collected Writings on Asia-Pacific Studies*], vol. 1. Beijing: Beijing University Press, 2004, pp. 236–358.
97. See for example, Liao Chiyang, *Nagasakikasho to higashiajiakouekimounokeisei* [*Chinese Merchants in Nagasaki and the Making of East Asian Trading Networks*]. Tokyo: Kyukosyoin, 2000; Chen Tien-shi, *Kajin diaspora: kashou no network to identity* [*The Networks and Identities of Chinese Entrepreneurs*]. Tokyo: Akashi-shoten, 2001; Zhu Huiling, *Zhongri Guanxi Zhengchanghuay yilaiRriben Huaqiaohuaren Shehui deBbianqian* [*Changes of Overseas Chinese and Chinese Community in Japan since Normalization of Relationship between China and Japan*]. Xiamen: Xiamen University Press, 2003. For some historical studies of the Chinese in Japan, see Noriko Kamachi, "The Chinese in Meiji Japan: Their Interaction with the Japanese before the Sino-Japanese War", in *The Chinese and the Japanese: Essays in Political and Cultural Interactions*, edited by Akira Iriye. Princeton: Princeton University Press, 1980, pp. 58–73.
98. H. Richard Friman, "Evading the Divine Wind Through the Side Door: The Transformation of Chinese Migration to Japan", in *Globalizing Chinese Migration: Trends in Europe and Asia*, edited by Pàl Nyiri and Igor Saveliev. Aldershort: Ashgate, 2002, pp. 9–34.
99. Illegal immigration has constituted a major problem in contemporary Chinese international migration, see for example, Chin Ko-lin, *Smuggled Chinese: Clandestine Immigration to the United States*. Philadelphia: Temple University

Press, 1999; Liang Zai and Wenzhe Ye, "From Fujian to New York: Understanding the New Chinese Immigration", in *Global Human Smuggling: Comparative Perspectives*, edited by David Kyle and Rey Koslowski. Baltimore: Johns Hopkins University Press, 2001, pp. 187–215.

100. Ellen Oxfeld, "Still 'Guest People': The Reproduction of Hakka Identity in Calcutta, India", in *Guest People: Hakka Identity in China and Abroad*, edited by Nicole Constable. Seattle: University of Washington Press, 1996, pp. 149–75.
101. Karen L. Harris, "The Chinese 'South Africans': An Interstitial Community", in *The Chinese Diaspora: Selected Essays*, edited by L. Ling-chi Wang and Wang Gungwu. Singapore: Times Academic Press, 1998, vol. 2, pp. 275–99.
102. For history of the Chinese in South Africa, see Melanie Yap and Dianne Leong Man, *Colour, Confusion and Concessions: The History of the Chinese in South Africa*. Hong Kong: Hong Kong University Press, 1996.
103. See for example, Francis L.K. Hsu, "Influence of South Seas Emigration on Certain Chinese Provinces", *Far East Quarterly* 5 (1945): 47–59. Two recent studies on *qiaoxiang* are Leo Douw, Cen Huang, and Michael Godley, eds., *Qiaoxiang Ties: Interdisciplinary Approaches to 'Cultural Capitalism' in South China*. London: Kegan Paul International, 1999, and Cen Huang, Zhuang Guotu, and Tanaka Kyoko, eds., *New Studies on Chinese Overseas and China*. Leiden: International Institute for Asian Studies, 2000. See also Yuen-fong Woon, "Social Change and Continuity in South China: Overseas Chinese and the Guan Lineage of Kaiping County, 1949–87", *The China Quarterly* 118 (1989), pp. 324–44; and Carolyn L. Cartier, *Globalizing South China*. Malden, MA: Blackwell Publishers, 2001.
104. Ta Chen, "Livelihood", in idem., *Emigrant Communities in South China: A Study of Overseas Migration and Its Influence*. New York: Institute of Pacific Relations, 1940; reprint: New York: AMS Press, 1978, pp. 58–85.
105. Madeline Y. Hsu, "Migration and Native Place: *Qiaokan* and the Imagined Community of Taishan, Guangdong, 1893–1993", *Journal of Asian Studies* 59, no. 2 (2000): 307–31.
106. Li Minghuan, "'To Get Rich Quickly in Europe!' — Reflections on Migration Motivation in Wenzhou", in *Internal and International Migration: Chinese Perspectives*, edited by Frank Pieke and Hein Mallee. Surrey: Curzon Press, 1999, pp. 181–98.
107. While the contribution of the Chinese overseas to China's economic development was mainly through the form of economic capital (foreign direct investment) by the settled generation of the Chinese diaspora in the early stage of China's economic reform and opening-up, the recent years have witnessed the increasing contributions through the form of human capital and knowledge transfer by the new generation of Chinese migrants originated from the mainland. See for example, David Zweig, Chen Changgui and Stanley Rosen, "Globalization and Transnational Human Capital: Overseas Chinese and Returnee Scholars to China", *The China Quarterly* 179 (2004): 735–57.

108. Paul J. Bolt, "Looking to the Diaspora: The Overseas Chinese and China's Economic Development, 1978–1994", *Diaspora: A Journal of Transnational Studies* 5, no. 3 (1996): 467–96.
109. Michael Godley, "The Late Ch'ing Courtship of the Chinese in Southeast Asia", *Journal of Asian Studies* 34, no. 2 (1975): 361–85.
110. Yen Ching-hwang, "Overseas Chinese Nationalism in Singapore and Malaya, 1877–1912", *Modern Asian Studies* 16, no. 3 (1982): 397–425.
111. Wang Gungwu, "Political Chinese: An Aspect of Their Contribution to Modern Southeast Asian History", in *Southeast Asia in Modern World*, edited by Bernard Grossman. Wiesbaden: Otto Harrassowitz, 1972, pp. 115–28.
112. For a more detailed analysis of the pattern of Chinese politics, see Wang Gungwu, "Chinese Politics in Malaya", *The China Quarterly* 43 (1970), pp. 1–30. See also Amy L. Freedman, *Political Participation and Ethnic Minorities: Chinese Overseas in Malaysia, Indonesia, and the United States*. New York: Routledge, 2000; Leo Suryadinata ed., *Ethnic Relations and Nation-Building in Southeast Asia*. Singapore: Institute of Southeast Asian Studies, 2004.
113. Anthony Reid, "Entrepreneurial Minorities, Nationalism, and the State", in *Essential Outsiders: Chinese and Jews in the Modern Transformation of Southeast Asia and Central Europe*, edited by D. Chirot and A. Reid. Seattle: University of Washington Press, 1997, pp. 33–71.
114. William A. Callahan, "Beyond Cosmopolitanism and Nationalism: Diasporic Chinese and Neo-Nationalism in China and Thailand", *International Organization* 57 (Summer 2002): 481–517.
115. Man-houng Lin, "Overseas Chinese Merchants, and Japanese government: Taiwan's Economic Relation with Japan, 1895–1945", *Journal of Asia-Pacific Studies* 4 (2002): 3–20. See also Man-houng Lin, "Decline or Prosperity? Guild Merchants Trading Across the Taiwan Straits, 1820s–1895", in *Commercial Networks in Modern Asia*, edited by S. Sugiyama and Linda Grove. Surrey: Curzon, 2001, pp. 116–39; Man-houng Lin, " Overseas Chinese Merchants and Multiple Nationality: A Means for Reducing Commerical Risk (1895–1935)", *Modern Asian Studies* 35, no. 4 (2001): 985–1009; Michael Hsin-Huang Hsiao, Hong-Zen Wang, I-Chun Kung, eds., *Taiwanese Business in Southeast Asia: Network, Identity and Globalization*. Taipei: Asia-Pacific Research Program, Academia Sinica, 2002 (In Chinese). On the configuration of the Taiwanese in the Chinese diaspora, see Jack Williams, "Who are the Taiwanese? Taiwan in the Chinese Diaspora", in *The Chinese Diaspora*, edited by Ma and Cartier, pp. 163–89.
116. Stephen Fitzgerald, "China and the Overseas Chinese: Perceptions and Policies", *The China Quarterly* 44 (1970): 1–37.
117. See for example, Robert Ross, "China and the Ethnic Chinese: Political Liability/Economic Asset", in *ASEAN and China: An Evolving Relationship*, edited by Joyce K. Kallgren, Noordin Sopiee, and Soedjati Djiwandono. Berkeley: Institute of East Asian Studies, University of California, 1988, pp. 147–73; Ramses

Amer, *The Ethnic Chinese in Vietnam and Sino-Vietnamese Relations* (Kuala Lumpur: Forum, 1991); Melissa Curley and Hong Liu, "Introduction: The Historicity and Multi-dimensionality of Sino-Southeast Asian Socio-Cultural Interactions", in *China and Southeast Asia*, edited by Curley and Liu, pp. 1–10; Ho Khai Leong and Samuel C.Y. Ku, eds., *China and Southeast Asia: Global Changes and Regional Challenges* (Singapore: Institute of Southeast Asian Studies, 2005).

118. Peter H. Koehn and Xiao-huang Yin, eds., *The Expanding Roles of Chinese Americans in U.S.-China Relations: Transnational Networks and Trans-Pacific Interactions*. Armonk, N.Y.: M.E. Sharpe, 2002.
119. Lucie Cheng, "Chinese Americans in the Formation of the Pacific Regional Economy", in *Across the Pacific: Asian Americans and Globalization*, edited by Evelyn Hu-DeHart. New York: Asia Society; Philadelphia: Temple University Press, 1999, pp. 61–78.
120. Hong Liu, "Explaining the Dynamics of Chinese Migration since 1980: A Historical and Demographical Perspective", *Journal of Oriental Studies* 39, no. 1 (2005): 92–110. For an historical perspective on new migrants, see R. Skeldon, "Migration from China", *Journal of International Affairs* 49, no. 2 (1996): 434–55; Wang Gungwu, "New Migrants: How New? Why New?" in *Diasporic Chinese Ventures*, edited by Benton and Liu, pp. 227–38.
121. Mette Thunø, "Reaching Out and Incorporating Chinese Overseas: The Trans-territorial Scope of the PRC by the end of the 20th Century", *The China Quarterly* 168 (2001): 910–29.
122. See also Pàl Nyiri, "Expatriating is Patriotic? The Discourse on 'New Migrants' in the People's Republic of China and Identity Construction among Recent Migrants from the PRC", *Journal of Ethnic and Migration Studies* 27, no. 4 (2001): 635–53.
123. Xiang Biao, "Emigration from China: A Sending Country Perspective", *International Migration Review* 41, no. 3 (2003): 21–46.
124. Hong Liu, "New Migrants and the Revival of Overseas Chinese Nationalism", *Journal of Contemporary China* 14, no. 43 (2005): 291–316.

10

South China Sea Studies in China: A Legal Perspective

Zou Keyuan

PARADIGMS OF THE SOUTH CHINA SEA STUDIES IN CHINA

The South China Sea is categorized as semi-enclosed sea under the general definition set down in the United Nations Convention on the Law of the Sea (the LOS Convention).[1] Article 122 of the convention defines "enclosed or semi-enclosed sea" as "a gulf, basin, or sea surrounded by two or more States and connected to another sea or the ocean by a narrow outlet or consisting entirely or primarily of the territorial seas and exclusive economic zones of two or more coastal States".[2] The South China Sea suits this definition geographically because it is surrounded by six states — China (including Taiwan), Vietnam, Philippines, Brunei, Malaysia and Indonesia.[3] It has an area of 648,000 square nautical miles, twice the area of the Sea of Japan.[4] There are hundreds of small islands in the South China Sea, namely uninhabited islets, shoals, reefs, banks, sands, cays and rocks.[5] According to Workman, they consist mainly of coral reefs.[6] They are widely distributed in the South China Sea in the form of four groups of islands and underwater features, that is, the Pratas Islands (Dongsha Qundao), the Paracel Islands (Xisha Qundao), the Macclesfield Bank (Zhongsha Qundao), and the Spratly Islands (Nansha Qundao). It is interesting to note that in Chinese these groups of small islands have a big name — "*qundao*", or archipelago. Such a nomenclature is questionable in law and/or in geography,[7] particularly for the Macclesfield Bank, which is permanently submerged under water, though it is a common Chinese view to consider the Scarborough Reef as part of the Macclesfield Bank.[8] If such a view could be generally accepted, then the English name should be changed to "the Macclesfield Islands",[9] like those of the other three groups. However, a detailed discussion on it is beyond the scope of the present topic.

The political situation in the South China Sea is complicated, as it contains potential of conflict arising from different national interests. In terms of the island groups, because of their geographical differences, their political situations are accordingly different from one other. The Pratas Islands are under the firm control of the Taiwan Chinese. No competing claims exist there under the current "one China" concept. For the Macclesfield Bank, the only claimant is China including Taiwan.[10] Nevertheless, if the Scarborough Reef is considered part of the Macclesfield, then the Philippines, which recently has also lodged its territorial claim over the Reef, would also have a stake in the Macclesfield Bank. The Paracel Islands are under the control of China, though this is contested by the Vietnamese. Because of the firm control by the Chinese, the political situation around the Paracels is relatively calm and stable in comparison with that around the Spratly Islands. The dispute over the Spratly Islands is the most complicated since it has been lingering on for a long time and involves as many as five states, that is, China including Taiwan, Malaysia, Vietnam, the Philippines, and Brunei. It is not usual in the history of international relations that so many countries make claims over such small islets, in whole or in part, of the Spratly Islands and their surrounding water areas. As many predict, if the issue of the Spratly Islands are not well handled, it could pose a danger or threat to the peace and security in the East Asian region and in the world. In China's view, the issue on disputes over boundaries and sovereignty over areas of the South China Sea is one of the three main factors that might trigger military conflicts in the Asia-Pacific region.[11]

South China Sea studies in China have a relatively long history. In the scientific field, there is a specific research institute called the Institute for the South China Sea directly under the Chinese Academy of Sciences, located in Guangzhou. It is quite understandable that Chinese scientists are interested in conducting research on the South China Sea which is adjacent to China. Scientific results from such research are significant for China's development in science and technology. Although politico-legal studies on the South China Sea also have scientific value in a broader sense, they are related more to China's national interest and rights, that is, to China's soft power. However, it is undeniable that studies on the South China Sea both in natural sciences and social sciences have academic value and have become branches in relevant academic disciplines in China.

In comparison with studies in the field of natural sciences, South China Sea studies in the legal and political fields came about belatedly, but has been greatly reinforced after China occupied six reefs of the Spratly Islands in 1983. Due to its characteristics, South China Sea studies are within the research framework of Southeast Asian Studies on the one hand, and oceanic studies on the other. Since the 1990s, there has been a specific institution for South China Sea studies in China, which will be addressed in the following sections. As the academic interest in the South China Sea in fact spans many disciplines, this chapter will focus mainly on such studies in the legal-political field, particularly in the context of international law.

KEY ISSUES RELATED TO LAW AND POLITICS

The coverage of South China Sea studies in China even within the legal political field is wide. This section selects several recent and current issues discussed and researched within China.

Sovereignty and Jurisdiction

Any territorial and maritime dispute centres on the key question of who owns the disputed land and its surrounding seas. It is no exception in the South China Sea. As observed, the most disputed area in the South China Sea is the Spratly Islands. In this sense, international law is indispensable to adjudicate on a country's sovereignty and jurisdiction over the disputed areas.

Traditional international law allows states to acquire territorial sovereignty through one of the five defined methods, including "accretion", "occupation", "prescription", "conquest", and "cession". However, after the World War II, the United Nations Charter prohibits the illegal use of force, thus forced cession and conquest are no longer valid methods of acquiring territorial sovereignty for a state. Chinese scholars like to cite three important cases concerning territorial acquisition in international law and they are the case of Palmas Island (between the United States and Holland) in 1924; Clipperton Island (between France and Mexico) in 1931; and Eastern Greenland (Denmark *v.* Norway) in 1933.[12] These cases, in the eyes of Chinese scholars, are significant in international law and also meaningful in the context of the territorial sovereignty over the South China Sea islands. As claimed, China discovered the South China Sea islands as early as the Han dynasty. Such discovery is decisive for China to claim sovereignty over them since according to modern international law, only discovery can satisfy the conditions of territorial acquisition.[13]

On the other hand, Chinese scholars realize that it is not enough that the argument for China's sovereignty over the South China Sea islands rests only with China's discovery of these islands, as under modern international law, effective occupation is much more crucial and forceful. Thus attempts have been made to demonstrate the effective occupation of ancient China over the South China Sea islands by listing Chinese activities in the sea, including economic development and operations, such as fishing, planting, house-building, etc.; administrative jurisdiction; navy patrols; and astronomical surveys.[14] However, modern international law tends to recognize more recent effective occupation rather than that of earlier or ancient times.

In addition, a legal argument favoured by Chinese scholars is the concept of inter-temporal law in international law. Inter-temporal law refers to the collective response of international law to temporal disputes. Its rules and principles come from sub-systems of international law, such as the law of treaties and customary international law.[15] In the case of the Palmas Island, Judge Huber considered that "the act creative of a right" has to be judged by the "law in force at the time the right arises".[16] In 1975, the Institut de Droit International adopted a resolution on "the Inter-temporal Problem in Public International Law" which called the states to apply the principle that "the temporal sphere of application of any norm of public international law shall be determined in accordance with the general principle of law by which any fact, action or situation must be assessed in the light of the rules of law that are contemporaneous with it".[17] In the context of the South China Sea islands, any rules in international law applicable to them must be those valid at that time when the rights of a state were created. This argument is favourable for China since it is the earliest country to discover these islands and to conduct relevant human activities in the South China Sea.

Another argument which may not be purely legal concerns Vietnam's early recognition of China's sovereignty over the South China Sea islands. As recorded, in the 1950s and 1960s Vietnam expressedly rendered its recognition to China several times. However, after 1975, Vietnam reversed its position and claimed the Paracel and Spratly Islands. As criticized by the Chinese scholars, such behaviour is in violation of an international law principle called "estoppel" or principle of preclusion. Since Vietnam has already recognized China's sovereignty over these two islands, it should not create disputes with China afterwards.[18]

Legal Status of the U-shaped Line

The U-shaped line is called a Chinese traditional maritime boundary line in China (hereinafter referred to as "the line") and refers to the line with nine segments off the Chinese coast on the South China Sea, as displayed in the Chinese map. People may question the meaning and significance of the line. Does China claim all within the line as its national territory, including the islands, underwater rocks, the seabed as well as the water columns?

The line first appeared in the map in December 1914, which was compiled by Hu Jinjie, a Chinese cartographer, according to some known sources.[19] Maps published during the 1920s and 1930s followed Hu's drawings. [20] The line at that time was characterized as one that only included the Pratas and the Paracels. It began from the Sino-Vietnamese land boundary next to the Gulf of Tonkin, extending southeastwards along the Vietnamese coast, then running eastwards to the west of Luzon Island, then northeastwards along the east side of the Pratas, through the Taiwan Strait, and finally to meet the Chinese boundary line to the East China Sea and the Yellow Sea. The southernmost end of the demarcation was located at about 15° and 16° north latitude.[21] However, no reasons were given why the line should be drawn like this and for what purposes.

The year 1933 seems to be an important time for the modification and emphasis of the line in the Chinese maps. In July that year, France, the then protector of Vietnam, occupied nine small islands of the Spratly Islands. This action was strongly protested by China, and afterwards the line in the maps relating to the South China Sea extended further south to 7°–9° North Latitude.[22] The intention behind was clear, that is, to indicate that the Spratly Islands belonged to China. However, the James Shoal (Zengmu Ansha) was not included. While the line at that time on most of the maps were drawn between 7° and 9° North Latitude, there was at least one atlas collection which included the James Shoal into the line, that is, further extended to 4° North Latitude. This is the *New China's Construction Atlas* edited by Bai Meichu and published in 1936. Actually in 1935, the Committee of Examining the Water and Land Maps of the Republic of China published the names of 132 islets and reefs of the four South China Sea archipelagoes. The publication had an annexed map which marked the James Shoal at the location of about 4° North Latitude, 112° East Longitude, though there was no demarcation of the line on the map. It indicated that the then Chinese Government considered the southernmost territory of China at 4° North Latitude.[23] It is therefore clear that Bai took the above publication to be the basis for the line in his compilation.

It should be noted that all the collections of the above atlases including the line were compiled by individuals. They may, suffice to say, constitute indirect evidence to show the official position of the government. Only until 1947 after World War II, was the line eventually confirmed officially by the Chinese Government. On 1 December 1947, the Chinese Ministry of Interior renamed the islands in the South China Sea and thus formally assigned them under the administration of the Chinese Hainan Special District.[24] Meanwhile, the same ministry prepared a location map of the islands in the South China Sea, which was then first released for internal use. In February 1948, the Atlas of Administrative Areas of the Republic of China was officially published, in which the above map was included. This is the first official map with the line for the South China Sea and it has a significant influence on subsequent maps either published by the mainland or by Taiwan. It has two general characteristics: The southernmost end of the line was set at 4° North Latitude including the James Shoal; and the eleven-segment line was drawn instead of the previous continuous line. According to the then official explanation, the basis for drawing the line was: "[t]he southernmost limit of the South China Sea territory should be at the James Shoal. This limit was followed by our governmental departments, schools and publishers before the anti-Japanese war, and it was also recorded on file in the Ministry of Interior. Accordingly it should remain unchanged."[25] The explanation seems not very clear because one may ask whether the explanation referred to the line or to the southernmost territory of China, and before the Anti-Japanese War, there were a few atlases that marked the line at about 4° North Latitude. A notable compilation was Bai Meichu's edition. It is thus hard to say that the southernmost limit was already consistently followed in practice. The situation remains unclear. On the other hand, the explanation did not give the reasons why the line was drawn this way. Despite all the above doubts, the line on the map has been accepted in Chinese practice ever since.

Chinese scholars face the dilemma of how to define this line in the legal and political context so as to defend China's rights and interests in the South China Sea. The crucial question concerns the legal status of the line: Is it a maritime boundary line like land border lines or a line only indicating that the islands, not the waters, within the line belong to China? This question has been discussed on many academic occasions in China. For example, in 2002, the Hainan Research Institute for the South China Sea (now renamed as National Institute for the South China Sea Studies) held a special conference on the U-shaped line and there was a deep and thorough discussion about it. Though still debated, the majority of Chinese scholars tend to recognize that the line as one which only defines the islands and other territories within the line.[26] After China's publicizing of its baselines encircling the Paracel Islands in 1996 and promulgation of the Law on the Exclusive Economic Zone and the Continental Shelf in 1998, there has been a decrease in the debates arguing that the line is a maritime boundary line between China and its neighbouring countries. On the other hand, the Chinese Government never expressedly stated that this line has been abandoned as it still remains on Chinese maps.

Debate on Historic Rights and Historic Waters

Closely related to the U-shaped line is the debate in China on whether the waters within the line are China's historic waters. The concept of historical waters is not definitive in international law. A scholarly definition was offered by Bouchez: "Historic waters are waters over which the coastal State, contrary to the generally applicable rules of international law, clearly, effectively, continuously, and over a substantial period of time, exercises sovereign rights with the acquiescence of the community of States".[27] It is not formally adopted in the recent LOS Convention. However, a variant term of historic bay and/or historic title is mentioned in the convention, relating to bays, delimitation of the territorial sea between states with opposite or adjacent coasts, and limitations and exceptions in the settlement of disputes.[28] According to the late O'Connell, there are three circumstances under which the waters could be considered as historic waters: (1) bays, claimed by states which are greater in extent, or less in configuration, than standard bays; (2) areas of claimed waters linked to a coast by offshore features but which are not enclosed under the standard rules; and (3) areas of claimed seas which would, but for the claim, be high seas because they are not covered by any rules specially concerned with bays or delimitation of coastal waters (*maria clausa*).[29] Accordingly, the concept is usually applicable to bays and gulfs. Once established as historic waters, then the waters in question are regarded as internal waters. There may be exceptions to this rule, that is, some historic waters claimed by states are not bays or gulfs, but open seas, which therefore could be regarded as internal waters.

The International Law Commission of the United Nations discussed the concept of historic waters and in 1962 its report on the juridical regime of historic waters, including historic bays, was released to the public. The report examined the elements of title to historic waters, the issues of burden of proof, the legal status of waters treated as historic waters, and the settlement of disputes. However, it did not give a conclusive concept of historic waters and the standard according to which this concept could be applied.[30] Thus the theoretical problem in regard to the concept of historic waters has yet to be resolved. Because of the controversy around this concept, the Third UN Conference on the Law of the Sea simply dropped the issue for discussion and only left some wordings in the LOS Convention.[31] Generally there should be three conditions to be fulfilled to sustain a historic waters claim. They are (1) the exercise of the authority over the area; (2) the continuity over time of this exercise of authority; and (3) the attitude of foreign states to the claim.[32]

In state practice, the concept of historic waters has been established as a criterion to determine the jurisdictional waters of a coast state. According to Churchill and Lowe, there are about twenty claims in the world for historic bays.[33] For example, the former Soviet Union claimed the Peter the Great Bay as its "historic bay", and the length of closing line was 108 nautical miles.[34] It was opposed by the Western countries led by the United States. However, China expressedly recognized such a claim.[35] The most controversial example was set by Libya who claimed the Gulf of Sidra in 1974 as its historic bay with 296 nautical miles of closing length. The claim was challenged by the Western countries as well as the former Soviet Union, and later caused a severe conflict between Libya and the United States. Tonga's claim over a rectangle of the water areas in the high seas with several groups of its islands inside as its "historic waters" since 1887, may have some analogous effect upon the line in the South China Sea.[36] It is not clear whether Tonga's claim has ever been challenged since it is located in a relatively unnoticed area.

The issue whether the water areas within the line are Chinese historic waters has been seriously discussed among the scholars in Taiwan. The Taiwan authorities gave the status of historic waters to the water areas within the U-shaped line in 1993 when it issued its South China Sea Policy Guidelines which stated that "the South China Sea area within the historic water limit is the maritime area under the jurisdiction of the Republic of China, in which the Republic of China possesses all rights and interests."[37] However, such a claim could not get a unanimous support — even from Taiwanese scholars. In 1993 a roundtable discussion was held at the National Chengchi University, Taipei. The participants were divided into two groups by their divergent views. One group supported the idea of historic waters and asserted that the water areas within the line were Chinese historic waters. The other group was rather dubious and cautious of the line, taking the view that it was difficult to establish such a claim in international law.[38]

Scholars in mainland China have also expressed their views upon the line. One scholar actively defended this line for his argument of historic waters,[39] and the other advocated claiming the waters in the South China Sea by its name.[40] A recent piece noted that the water within the U-shaped line was China's water of historic title, "China's special EEZ, or historic EEZ", and it should be given the same status as the EEZ prescribed in the LOS Convention.[41] Yet, the author did not explain why the water within the U-shaped line should be China's "historic EEZ". Perhaps he had based his arguments on Article 14 of the EEZ Law.

Generally speaking, whether a certain water area can be established as historic water depends upon whether it can satisfy certain pre-conditions as described above. In the South China Sea, the line provides a basis for a claim of historic waters. However, the exercise of authority in it either by the mainland or Taiwan was weak since the emergence of the line, usually infrequently. Even these occasional exercises focused on the islands within the line rather than on the water areas. The freedom of navigation and freedom of fishery seem to be not affected by these exercises. Thus a question is raised as to whether there is effective control over the area within the line so as to establish it as historic waters. It may be argued that the relative frequency of the exercise of authority should be considered *vis à vis* other claimant countries. Yet there are still doubts as to how China could establish its claim of historic waters in the South China Sea.

As to historic rights, it is generally recognized that there are two types: One is exclusive with full sovereignty, such as historic waters and historic bays; and the other is non-exclusive without full sovereignty, such as historic fishing rights in the high seas. On 26 June 1998, China officially promulgated the Law on the Exclusive Economic Zone and the Continental Shelf in which Article 14 provides that "the provisions of this Law shall not affect the historic rights enjoyed by the People's Republic of China".[42] In this context, this provision seems to help the Chinese scholars end the debate on whether the waters within the U-shaped line are historic waters since China only mentions "historic rights" in its EEZ Law.

Energy Security and Joint Development

Recently, because of China's rapid economic development, the demand for energy has become ever higher. Experts predicted that China would import more than 500 million tonnes of oil and over 100 billion cubic metres of natural gas in 2020 due to its rapid economic growth and demand for energy resources.[43] Energy security in the South China Sea has thus become a critical issue within the South China Sea studies. Oil is an essential factor in the Spratlys dispute. In the Spratly area, there are eight sedimentary basins with an area of 410,000 km^2, and 260,000 km^2 are within China's unilaterally claimed U-shaped line. An incomplete figure from China shows that these eight sedimentary basins contain 34.97 billion tonnes of petroleum reserves, including the discovered 1.182 billion tonnes of oil and 8,000 billion cubic metres of gas. In addition, there is a large quantity of gas hydrate (also known as flammable ice) in the South China Sea.[44] Thus the South China Sea is sometimes called a second "Persian Gulf".

Because of the disputes among the countries concerned, joint development becomes the most feasible option for them to cooperate in the exploration and exploitation of oil and gas in the South China Sea. "Joint development" refers to "an agreement between two States to develop so as to share jointly in agreed proportions by inter-State cooperation and national measures the offshore oil and gas in a designated zone of the seabed and subsoil of the continental shelf to which both or either of the participating States are entitled in international law".[45] It contains several characteristics: (a) It is an arrangement between two countries; (b) it concerns an overlapping boundary maritime area; (c) it is a provisional arrangement pending the settlement of the boundary delimitation disputes between the countries concerned; (d) it is designed to jointly develop the mineral resources in the disputed area. In East Asia, joint development agreements include, *inter alia*, the Japan-South Korean arrangement in the Sea of Japan and the East China Sea in the 1970s, the Malaysia-Thailand joint development area in the Gulf of Thailand and the Australian-Indonesia joint development zone for the Timor Gap.

Encouraged or triggered by all these developments in East Asia, China also put forward the idea of joint development in the disputed sea areas. When Wu Bangguo, Chairman of the National People's Congress, visited the Philippines in August 2003, he proposed to his Philippine counterpart to jointly develop petroleum in the South China Sea.[46] On 11 November 2003, the CNOOC and the Philippine National Oil Company agreed to jointly explore oil and gas in the South China Sea through the signing of a letter of intent between the two sides. A joint committee will be set up to help select exploring areas in the South China Sea. They also agreed to establish a programme to "review, assess and evaluate relevant geographical, geophysical and other technical data available to determine the oil and gas potential in the area".[47] Further developments took place when state-owned oil companies in China, the Philippines and Vietnam signed an unprecedented tripartite agreement on joint seismic surveying activities in the South China Sea on 14 March 2005. The size for cooperation is 143,000 square kilometres.[48] It is perceived that other ASEAN countries may join in this agreement as well.

In November 2004, the National Institute for the South China Sea Studies held a national symposium on "the South China Sea and China's Energy Security" where participants from academic and government departments attended and discussions were focused on three topics: China's energy security; sea lanes security in the South China Sea; and development of oil and gas in the South China Sea.[49] As to joint development, the institute also held a symposium in March 2002 which discussed two specific themes: "Joint development in the South China Sea" and "the legal status of the U-shaped line". It is to be noted that while joint development is an old topic, sea lanes security is a new topic in China's South China Sea studies. This reflects the concerns of the Chinese Government to secure the sea-borne transportation of petroleum resources, particularly from Middle East *via* the Malacca Straits and the South China Sea.

KEY INSTITUTIONS AND PUBLICATIONS

South China Sea studies are certainly within the research interest of all institutions where researchers conduct Southeast Asian Studies. However, South China Sea studies are not regarded as a top priority in institutions which specialize in Southeast Asian Studies. This section will introduce some key institutions in China which have a strong interest in South China Sea studies.

National Institute for the South China Sea Studies

Among all the related institutions which are involved in South China Sea studies, the most important and significant one is the National Institute for South China Sea Studies since it is the only institution in China specializing in South China Sea studies in the social sciences, in particular in the legal and political fields. It is defined as an academic institute attached to Hainan Provincial Government and works under the guidance of the Chinese Foreign Ministry, while receiving professional instructions from the State Oceanic Administration. Its predecessor, the Hainan Research Centre for the South China Sea, was established in 1996 as a research base for South China Sea issues under the approval of Hainan Province and the Foreign Ministry. In July 2004 the State Council approved the upgrade of the centre to be a national level institute renamed as "National Institute for South China Sea Studies".

In terms of the organizational structure of the institute, there are several departments established inside including: (1) The Research Department I, which focuses on history and jurisprudence research on the South China Sea, situation and security of the South China Sea area, politics, economy, diplomacy, military, humanities and history of the neighbouring countries in the South China Sea area; (2) Research Department II, which focuses on the research on the geography, geology, navigation, climate and disaster, environment and resources of the South China Sea, and its impact on economic and social development; (3) Liaison Department, which conducts cooperation and exchanges with domestic and oversea academic institutes, organizing academic conferences, editing and publishing academic findings, as well as managing the library etc; and (4) Secretariat, which is in charge of the administrative work of the institute including personnel, finance, services, etc.[50]

The institute set forth the research framework mainly focusing on the (1) history and geography of the South China Sea; sovereignty of the South China Sea islands; (2) geo-politics of the South China Sea; South China Sea policies of neighbouring countries; (3) applicability of the UN Convention on the Law of the Sea to the South China Sea area; (4) strategic research on peaceful solution of the Spratly dispute; and (5) resource exploitation and environmental protection of the South China Sea.[51] The current on-going research projects of the institute include, *inter alia*, Sino-Vietnam "Two Corridor and One Circle" Economic Cooperation and Economic Development of Hainan (中越"两廊一圈"经济合作规划与海南的经济发展); Security Changes of the South China Sea Area and the Shifts of Foreign Policies of Adjacent Countries (南海地区安全变化与周边国家外交政策调整); Joint Development in the South China Sea and Relevant Maritime Boundary Delimitation (南海共同开发研究有关情况与海域划界); and Interactions between China and the Philippines on the South China Sea (中菲南沙交涉资料).[52] Since 1996, the institute has published quite a number of books, papers, and research reports concerning the South China Sea (see Table 10.2). In late 2005 a quarterly journal — the *South China Sea Studies Quarterly* (南海研究) was launched, a significant academic move in the development of the South China Sea studies in China.

Apart from its regular research work, the institute has established its own independent academic web, and has developed an updated South China Sea Documentation Database. In June 2004 the institute launched a mega-database project, "Digital South China Sea" (数字南海), which refers to a comprehensive information system on islands and ocean spaces of the South China Sea and relevant historical, political and military information about the adjacent countries through VR (Virtual Reality). As planned, it will have been accomplished by December 2007.[53]

Table 10.1
Recent Main Books on the South China Sea in the Legal-Political Context

李金明	南沙争端与国际海洋法，海洋出版社, 2003 中国南海疆域研究, 福建人民出版社, 1999
傅崐成,	南（中国）海法律地位的研究，台北：123资讯, 1995
吴士存,	纵论南沙争端, 海南出版社, 2005 南沙争端的由来与发展, 海洋出版社, 1999
李国强,	南中国海：历史与现状，黑龙江教育出版社出版, 2003
吕一然 (主编),	南海诸岛：历史、地理、主权, 黑龙江教育出版社, 1992
韩振华	林金枝(主编), 我国南海诸岛史料汇编，东方出版社, 1988
韩振华,	南海诸岛史地考证论集, 中华书局, 1981; 西沙群岛和南沙群岛自古以来就是中国的领土, 人民出版社, 1981; 南海诸岛史地研究, 社会科学文献出版社, 1996

Source: Prepared by the author.

The institute has been making extensive domestic and overseas academic exchanges, and organizing academic symposiums on the South China Sea issue every year. In addition to conferences and symposiums within China, the institute formulated in 2001, together with Academia Sinica in Taiwan, the "Cross-Strait South China Sea Forum" under which conferences attended by specialists from both sides have been held alternately in Hainan or Taipei each year, discussing South China Sea issues of common concern and interest.[54] In December 2005, the institute for the first time successfully organized an international conference on "Maritime Security in the South China Sea" in which experts from sixteen countries participated. Through all these constant and earnest efforts, the institute has gained its reputation and status both in China and overseas.

Other Important Institutions

As for other important institutions conducting South China Sea studies, it is worth mentioning another two institutions in China: Xiamen University, and the Institute for Marine Development Strategy.

Xiamen University has a very strong base for Southeast Asian Studies in China and its Centre for Southeast Asian Studies has been designated by the Ministry of Education as a national base in this field. In addition to this centre, there is another important one called Centre for Oceans Policy and Law, which was formally established in November 2003. The Ocean Centre is part of the Xiamen University Law School and the College of Oceanography and Environment. Several experts from departments other than these two schools have also joined the Centre. The Centre's main tasks include (1) research on various marine policies and/or legal issues pertaining to the sea, with emphasis on policy and/or legal issues of marine environment and ocean resources preservation, utilization and management, (2) teaching of marine policies and laws inside or outside Xiamen University, and (3) provision of assistance for governmental agencies, NGOs and other public or private individuals, particularly those in the Asia-Pacific region, to resolve their issues related to marine policies or laws.[55] The South China Sea naturally falls within the research mandate of the centre. In June 2004, it organized a workshop on "Historic Waters and Archipelagic Regimes" specifically designed for the South China Sea studies, and in March 2005, the centre, in cooperation with the Centre of Oceans Law and Policy of Virginia University in the United States, held an international conference on "The Law of the Sea and China" in which there was a panel on "Oil and Gas Development and Environmental Protection in the South China Sea". In addition, the centre launched a journal, *China Oceans Law Review* (中国海洋法学评论) in 2005, which has become the sole journal concerning the law of the sea in China.

The China Institute for Marine Development Strategy, established in November 1987, is a unit under the State Oceanic Administration. It has four research divisions respectively for the law of the sea, marine economy; marine environmental protection and resources; and marine policy and management. Though not a specific institution for South China Sea studies, some of its research projects concern this sea area. For example, it has two on-going research projects concerning the South China Sea: "Maintaining Maritime Rights and Interests in the South China Sea" and "Attitudes of the Adjacent States to the South China Sea towards Joint Development".[56] The advantage this institute has is its location in the capital city and also the fact that it is the secretariat site for the Chinese Society of the Law of the Sea which holds annual conferences on the law of the sea, and issues in the South China Sea have been frequently discussed at this forum.

Related Literature

Publications concerning the South China Sea in the legal and political context are scattered in various journals including those focusing on Southeast

Asian Studies, on law and international law, and on international relations. Some university journals (大学学报) in social sciences also occasionally publish papers addressing South China Sea issues. However, the number of such publications is not large and this may reflect the fact that South China Sea studies are not considered a popular field of study in China and there was no specific academic journal for these studies before the National Institute for the South China Sea Studies launched the *South China Sea Studies Quarterly* in 2005. Books and monographs in this field are even fewer than published papers. Below is a list of the books published after the 1980s concerning the South China Sea in the legal-political context.

It is noted that the National Institute for the South China Sea Studies has published books and collected papers significantly in recent years (see Table 10.2).

Besides printed literature, there are soft copy materials also available in China. The most popular is at <http://www.nansha.org.cn>.[57] However, e-sources regarding the South China Sea in China are not well-developed for various reasons, such as restrictions imposed by the government, or lack of sufficient website technicians and programmers. As for the website of the National Institute for the South China Sea Studies, there have been a lot of complaints about its insufficient information, slow updates and other problems.

Table 10.2
Main Publications of the National Institute for the South China Sea Studies

南海与中国的能源安全研讨会论文集，中国南海研究院, 2005
群岛问题研究，中国南海研究院, 2004
历史性权利与历史性水域研究，中国南海研究院, 2004
有关共同开发的资料选编，中国南海研究院, 2004
南海资源与两岸合作研讨会论文集，中国南海研究院, 2004
南海资料索引, 海南出版社, 1998
南海问题文献汇编，海南出版社, 2001
2004年南海地区形势评估报告, 中国南海研究院, 2005
2003年南海地区形势评估报告, 海南南海研究中心, 2003
2002年南海地区形势评估报告, 海南南海研究中心, 2002
南沙争端的由来与发展, 海洋出版社, 1999
南海问题研讨会论文集2002, 海南南海研究中心
南海问题研讨会论文集2001, 海南南海研究中心
关于南海共同开发的法理与实践, 海南南海研究中心

Source: adapted from http://www.nanhai.org.cn/en/info/aboutus.asp (accessed 14 December 2005).

CONCLUSION

From the above survey, we can see that the South China Sea studies in the legal and political fields have recently been developing and strengthened. The Hainan government has allocated a large piece of land for the National Institute for the South China Sea Studies to build its new headquarters. In this sense, the development in South China Sea studies is remarkable in comparison with other areas of Southeast Asian Studies in China.

Second, South China Sea studies in China mainly provide services for the defence of national interests as well as China's foreign policy. Institutes, whether associated with universities or governments, have a function of providing the government with proposals and suggestions on how to deal with South China Sea issues *vis à vis* other countries adjacent to the South China Sea. For example, the National Institute for the South China Sea Studies regularly provides relevant information as well as its research reports for the Hainan government and the Foreign Ministry.

Thirdly, it is to be noted that South China Sea studies also suffer from various constraints, in particular at the ideological level and in terms of quality. Since the studies are related to China's foreign policy and external relations, they have become a sensitive field. For example, the publication of books relating to the South China Sea is subject to approval by the relevant department of the Ministry of Foreign Affairs. Without such expressed approval, these books can only be published internally (内部发行) since publishers usually take a cautious approach to avoid any potential trouble by publishing these books. On the other hand, no views opposite to the government position are allowed in the South China Sea studies, thus hampering any independent research and scholarship.

As for quality, two dilemmas exist in China's South China Sea studies. With regard to the publications, one may question whether these publications have reach international standards. The other relates to human resources. South China Sea studies, just like other Southeast Asian Studies, are not "hot" areas of research so that not very many young graduates would like to devote themselves to such studies. Thus there is a shortage of sufficient research personnel. The National Institute for the South China Sea Studies also currently faces the problem of recruiting highly qualified scholars who conduct South China Sea studies.

Finally, in comparison with other areas of Southeast Asian Studies in China, South China Sea studies is relatively young but is endeavouring to catch up, particularly in the recent years.

NOTES

1. The LOS Convention was adopted in the Third United Nations Conference on the Law of the Sea on 10 December 1982 and entered into force on 16 November 1994. According to Tommy T.B. Koh, the then President of the Conference, the LOS Convention is "a constitution for the oceans". See United Nations, *The Law of the Sea: Official Text of the United Nations Convention on the Law of the Sea with Annexes and Index*. New York: United Nations, 1983, xxxiv–xxxvii.
2. United Nations, ibid., p. 39.
3. In a broad sense, the Gulf of Thailand is part of the whole South China Sea. However, it is not counted due to its irrelevance to the subject-matter of the present study.
4. J.R.V. Prescott, *The Maritime Political Boundaries of the World*. London: Methuen, 1985, p. 209.
5. According to Hungdah Chiu, there are 127 islands in the South China Sea based upon a survey conducted during 1946–47, sponsored by the then Chinese Ministry of Internal Affairs. Hungdah Chiu, "South China Sea Islands: Implications for Delimiting the Seabed and Future Shipping Routes", *China Quarterly*, no. 72 (1977): 756.
6. See D.R. Workman, "The South China Sea Basin, Its Mineral Resources and Their Exploitation", in *Fishing in Troubled Waters*, edited by R.D. Hill, Norman G. Owen and E.V. Roberts. Proceedings of an Academic Conference on Territorial Claims in the South China Sea. Hong Kong: Centre of Asian Studies, University of Hong Kong, 1991, p. 9.
7. According to Article 46 (b) of the LOS Convention, "archipelago" means a group of islands, including parts of islands, inter-connecting waters and other natural features which are so closely inter-related that such islands, waters and other natural features form an intrinsic geographical, economic and political entity, or which historically have been regarded as such. Clearly, the "*qundao*" in the South China Sea does not fit into this definition.
8. See Jun Jiwu, "Zhongsha Archipelagos in the Middle South China Sea", in *China's South China Sea Islands*, edited by Xin Yejiang. Haiko: Hainan International Information Publishing Centre, 1996 (in Chinese), p. 131.
9. The Chinese name of the Scarborough Reef is Huangyan Dao. It is located 164 miles southeast from the Macclesfield Bank. Such a long distance of separation may defeat the argument that it is part of the Macclesfields in geographical terms.
10. A main reason that there is no other claimant for the Macclesfield Bank is that this bank is permanently submerged under water. Otherwise, Vietnam or the Philippines might have claimed it as well.
11. The other two factors are: Military confrontation in the Korean Peninsula, and the controversial U.S.-Japan military alliance and Taiwan's separatist activities.

See Yan Xuetong, "Cooperation Key to Regional Peace", *China Daily*, 27 March 1998, p. 4.

12. For details, see Wang Liyu, "International Legal Norms Applicable to the Sovereignty Issue of the South China Sea Islands", in *Selected Papers of the Workshop on the South China Sea Islands*, edited by China Institute for Marine Development Strategy (in Chinese), March 1992, pp. 9–12.
13. Ibid., p. 24.
14. Ibid., pp. 24–26.
15. For relevant account, see T.O. Elias "The Doctrine of Intertemporal Law", *American Journal of International Law* 74 (1980): 285–307.
16. Permanent Court of Arbitration. Sole Arbitrator: Huber. 2 R.I.A.A. 829, p. 833.
17. "The Intertemporal Problem in Public International Law", Session of Wiesbaden, 11 August 1975, at <http://www.idi-iil.org/idiE/resolutionsE/1975_wies_01_en.pdf>, accessed 5 January 2006.
18. See Zhao Lihai, *Studies on the Law of the Sea Issues*. Beijing: Peking University Press, 1996 (in Chinese), pp. 14–15.
19. The map was called "the Chinese territorial map before the Qianglong-Jiaqing period" (A.D. 1736–1820) of the Qing dynasty in his compilation, the *New Geographical Atlas of the Republic of China*. See Han Zhenhua, ed., *A Compilation of Historical Materials on China's South China Sea Islands*. Beijing: Oriental Press, 1988 (in Chinese), p. 355.
20. For example, "the Chinese Map of Boundary Changes" in *The New Chinese Situation Atlas*, edited by Tu Shichong, 1927; and "the Chinese Map of Territorial Changes" in *China's Model Atlas*, edited by Chen Duo, 1933. Han, ibid., pp. 355–56.
21. See Zhang Haiwen, *The Legal System Applicable to the Islands in the South China Sea*, Ph.D. dissertation (in Chinese), Peking University, 1995, p. 43 (on file with the author).
22. For example, Chen Duo, ed., *Newly-Made Chinese Atlas* published in August 1934; Tan Lian and Chen Kaoji, eds., *Civilised Geography of China*, 1936; and Ge Shuichen, ed., *Newly-Made Large Hanging Atlas*, 1939. See Han, *supra* note 19, pp. 356–59.
23. See Zhang, *supra* note 21, p. 46.
24. See Ministry of Interior, *An Outline of the Geography of the South China Sea Islands*, National Territory Series, 1947, fig 11, at 861; as cited in J.K.T. Chao, "South China Sea: Boundary Problems Relating to the Nansha and Hsisha Islands", in R.D. Hill et al., eds., *supra* note 6, p. 88.
25. See Han, *supra* note 19, pp. 181–84.
26. For example, see Zhao, *supra* note 18, pp. 37–38.
27. Leo J. Bouchez, *The Regime of Bays in International Law*. Leyden: A.W. Sythoff, 1964, p. 281.
28. Articles 10 (6), 15, and 298 (1)(a)(i) of the LOS Convention.

29. D.P. O'Connell, *The International Law of the Sea*, Vol. 1. Oxford: Clarendon Press, 1982, p. 417.
30. See U.N. Doc. A/CN.4/143, 9 March 1962, entitled "Juridical Regime of Historic Waters, Including Historic Bays", *Yearbook of the International Law Commission*, Vol. 2, 1962, p. 6.
31. Some scholars assume that there are two possible reasons for this. First, the twelve-mile territorial sea had generally been accepted by most coastal states, which made it possible to place the waters concerned under a state's sovereignty and jurisdiction. Second, the development of the legal regimes of the continental shelf, EEZ, and archipelagic waters may bring about a gradual phasing out and eventual elimination of the phenomenon of "historic" claims, See Yann-huei Song and Peter Kien-hong Yu, "China's 'Historic Waters' in the South China Sea: An Analysis from Taiwan, R.O.C.", *The American Asian Review* 12, no. 4 (1994): 91.
32. UN Document, *supra* note 30, p. 13.
33. R.R. Churchill and A.V. Lowe, *The Law of the Sea*. Manchester: Manchester University Press, 1983, p. 37.
34. As a general rule, an accepted length of the closing line is 24 nm (nautical miles).
35. *People's Daily* (in Chinese), 23 September 1957.
36. See O'Cornell, *supra* note 29, p. 418. (He seems to support Tonga's claim by saying that "History might validate the claim to the rectangle, as an exception to the law relating to the high seas, but only as broadening of the area which could be claimed under the standard rules".)
37. See Kuan-Ming Sun, "Policy of the Republic of China towards the South China Sea", 19 *Marine Policy*, 1995, p. 408. Partly due to the differences reflected in the above discussion and partly due to Taiwan's domestic politics, the later developments have indicated that Taiwan has retreated from its 1993 Guidelines position. This can be seen from its 1998 Law on the Territorial Sea and the Contiguous Zone in which an original provision on "historic waters" was dropped before its promulgation.
38. For details, see "Legal Regime of China's Historic Waters in the South China Sea", *Issues and Studies* (Chinese edition) 32, no. 8 (1993): 1–12.
39. Pan Shiying, "South China Sea and the International Practice of the Historic Title", paper presented to the American Enterprise Institute Conference on the South China Sea, Washington, 7–9 September 1994, p. 5.
40. See Wu Fengbing, "Historical Evidence of China's Ownership of the Sovereignty over the Spratly Islands", in *Selected Papers of the Conference on the South China Sea Islands*, edited by China Institute for Marine Development Strategy. Beijing: Ocean Press, 1992 (in Chinese), p. 111.
41. Jiao Yongke, "No Question of Re-demarcation in the South China Sea", *Ocean Development and Management* (in Chinese) 17, no. 2 (2000): 52.
42. See *People's Daily* (in Chinese), 30 June 1998.
43. *CCH Asia China E-News Alert*, no. 43, February 2004.

44. See Wu Shicun and Hong Nong, "The Energy Security of China and the Oil and Gas Exploitation in the Disputed South China Sea Area", in *Recent Developments in the Law of the Sea and China*, edited by Myron H. Nordquist, John Norton Moore and Kuen-chen Fu. Leiden/Boston: Martinus Nijhoff, 2006, p. 148.
45. British Institute of International and Comparative Law, *Joint Development of Offshore Oil and Gas: A Model Agreement for States for Joint Development with Explanatory Commentary*. London: British Institute of International and Comparative Law, 1989, p. 45.
46. "Wu Bangguo proposes a multiple cooperation for oil in the Spratly Islands", *Lianhe Zaobao*, 1 September 2003.
47. "Chinese, Philippine Firms Join Forces to Look for Oil in South China Sea", *Agence France Presse*, 13 November 2003.
48. See "China, Philippines and Vietnam Sign Agreement to Explore Oil in the South China Sea", *Lianhe Zaobao*, 15 March 2005, at <http://www.zaobao.com/gj/yx501_150305.html>, accessed 15 March 2005.
49. The papers presented to the conference were later compiled into a book *Collected Papers of the Symposium on "the South China Sea and China's Energy Security"* published in 2004.
50. See the website of the National Institute for the South China Sea Studies, at <http://www.nanhai.org.cn/en/info/aboutus.asp>, accessed 14 December 2005.
51. Ibid.
52. Ibid.
53. It is acknowledged that the relevant information on "Digital South China Sea" was kindly provided by Ms Hong Nong, Assistant Researcher, National Institute for the South China Sea Studies.
54. For relevant background information, see Yann-huei Song, "Cross-Strait Interactions on the South China Sea Issues: A Need for CBMs", *Marine Policy* 29 (2005): 265–80.
55. It is acknowledged that the relevant information is provided by Professor Kuen-chen Fu, Executive Deputy Director of the Centre for Oceans Policy and Law.
56. See the website of the China Institute for Marine Development Strategy, at <http://www.cima.gov.cn/yanjiuchengguo.htm>, accessed 7 January 2006.
57. This website was closed at the end of 2005 for unknown reasons.

Index

Z